Greenhouse Gardening

Other Publications:

WORLD WAR II

THE GREAT CITIES

HOME REPAIR AND IMPROVEMENT

THE WORLD'S WILD PLACES

THE TIME-LIFE LIBRARY OF BOATING

HUMAN BEHAVIOR

THE ART OF SEWING

THE OLD WEST

THE EMERGENCE OF MAN

THE AMERICAN WILDERNESS

LIFE LIBRARY OF PHOTOGRAPHY

THIS FABULOUS CENTURY

FOODS OF THE WORLD

TIME-LIFE LIBRARY OF AMERICA

TIME-LIFE LIBRARY OF ART

GREAT AGES OF MAN

LIFE SCIENCE LIBRARY

THE LIFE HISTORY OF THE UNITED STATES

TIME READING PROGRAM

LIFE NATURE LIBRARY

LIFE WORLD LIBRARY

FAMILY LIBRARY:
   HOW THINGS WORK IN YOUR HOME
   THE TIME-LIFE BOOK OF THE FAMILY CAR
   THE TIME-LIFE FAMILY LEGAL GUIDE
   THE TIME-LIFE BOOK OF FAMILY FINANCE

Greenhouse Gardening

by
JAMES UNDERWOOD CROCKETT
and
the Editors of TIME-LIFE BOOKS

Mrs Thelma Moody.
March 27, 1978. $8.08

TIME-LIFE BOOKS, ALEXANDRIA, VIRGINIA

THE TIME-LIFE ENCYCLOPEDIA OF GARDENING

EDITORIAL STAFF FOR GREENHOUSE GARDENING:
EDITOR: Robert M. Jones
Assistant Editor: Jeanne LeMonnier
Text Editor: Betsy Frankel
Picture Editors: Jean Tennant, Jane Jordan
Designer: Albert Sherman
Assistant Designer: Andrea Whiting
Staff Writers: Susan Feller, Kathleen Shortall
Researchers: Loretta Britten, Muriel Clarke,
Reese Hassig, Marilyn Murphy, Judith W. Shanks,
Reiko Uyeshima
Editorial Assistant: Kristin Baker

EDITORIAL PRODUCTION
Production Editor: Douglas B. Graham
Operations Manager: Gennaro C. Esposito
Assistant Production Editor: Feliciano Madrid
Quality Control: Robert L. Young (director),
James J. Cox (assistant)
Art Coordinator: Anne B. Landry
Copy Staff: Susan B. Galloway (chief), Kathleen Beakley,
Elizabeth Graham, Florence Keith, Celia Beattie
Picture Department: Dolores A. Littles,
Cathy Doxat-Pratt
Traffic: Barbara Buzan

CORRESPONDENTS: Elisabeth Kraemer (Bonn);
Margot Hapgood, Dorothy Bacon (London);
Susan Jonas, Lucy T. Voulgaris (New York);
Maria Vincenza Aloisi, Josephine du Brusle (Paris);
Ann Natanson (Rome). Valuable assistance was also
provided by Carolyn T. Chubet (New York).

THE AUTHOR: James Underwood Crockett is an eminent horticulturist, writer on gardening subjects and, on television, a teacher of plant care. A graduate of the University of Massachusetts' Stockbridge School of Agriculture, he received an Honorary Doctor of Science degree from the University of Massachusetts at Amherst and has been cited by the American Association of Nurserymen and the American Horticultural Society. He is the author of books on greenhouse, indoor and window-sill gardening, a monthly column for *Horticulture* magazine and a monthly bulletin, "Flowery Talks," for florists. His weekly television program, *Crockett's Victory Garden,* has been broadcast throughout the United States.

GENERAL CONSULTANTS: Dr. T. R. Dudley is Research Botanist at the U.S. National Arboretum; George A. Kalmbacher is Plant Taxonomist at the Brooklyn Botanic Garden; Frank Perlmutter, retired, was a horticulturist for the U.S. Department of Agriculture; Dr. James B. Shanks is Professor of Horticulture at the University of Maryland.

Portions of this book were written by Oliver E. Allen, Angela M. Dews, Harold C. Field, Donna Hilts, Catherine Ireys, Jane Opper, Barbara Ann Peters, Alice Skelsey, Mary Williams and John von Hartz.

Watercolor illustrations for the encyclopedia were provided by Adolph Brotman, Mary Kellner, Rebecca Merrilees, John Murphy, Trudy Nicholson and Eduardo Salgado.

THE COVER: Glowing through greenhouse windows banked in snow are pots of Rieger begonia, poinsettia, geranium, petunia, camellia and columnea. On the December day when this picture was made in Excelsior, Minnesota, the temperature outside was 5° below zero.

CONTENTS

A year-round garden in a house of glass

An orchid, half a hemisphere removed from its birthplace in the Amazon jungle, flourishes in wintry Canada. Roses, larger than any rose has a right to be, blossom in time for Christmas. Fruits and vegetables are ready for the table on a schedule that is set by you, not the planet. Such feats of horticulture become routine once you establish a home greenhouse. You become the absolute ruler of a small and beautiful kingdom. With powers denied monarchs of the past, you can determine the conditions that govern the existence of the inhabitants of that domain. You have the last word on the supply of food, light, heat, air and water—all the requisites of plant life. With light and warmth under your control, soils precisely tailored, nutrients carefully calculated to foster plant health and pruning skillfully executed, you can create almost any plant world you could dream of.

Only recently has such grand command over growing plants been attainable. One of the earliest recorded controlled gardens was made for the Roman emperor Tiberius, who reigned from 14 to 37 A.D. Tiberius had a passion for cucumbers, in or out of season. To satisfy it in that pre-glass era, his gardeners set the plants in beds of dung enclosed in sheets of mica, a mineral that can be split into thin translucent plates, permitting sunlight to penetrate.

Other Roman horticulturists improved this technique. They built *specularia,* sheds with roofs of mica and ducts to carry heated water or air for temperature control. In these buildings grapes, peaches, roses, cucumbers and decorative plants were grown.

But as Rome declined, so did horticulture. Not until the Italian Renaissance were the ancient skills revived, as indicated by accounts of entertainments held in 1295 in the heated garden of Albert Magnus, a celebrated Paduan. By the 17th Century, the growing of orange trees had become the fashion, and structures called orangeries were set up to protect them from frost. In 1619

In a simple pit greenhouse with an A-frame roof a Massachusetts gardener produces an early-spring crop of azaleas, hyacinths and primroses, left; camellias, background and foreground; and primroses in the rear.

Solomon de Caus invented a covering of shutters that was placed over and around 340 orange trees in the municipal garden of Heidelberg each September, then removed at Easter. De Caus's method was improved on by English gardeners at Beddington, where England's first orange trees were grown. John Evelyn, the diarist and amateur horticulturist who is credited with coining the term greenhouse, reported in 1658 that in winter Beddington's orange trees were protected by "a wooden tabernacle and stoves."

But it was at the magnificent palace of Versailles that the orangerie reached its peak. The Versailles building had a solid roof and was heated by the sun's rays streaming through tall windows with southern exposure. The central section of the orangerie was 508 feet long, 42 feet wide and 45 feet high. Eight years after the orangerie was completed, the superintendent of the royal garden designed a hothouse kept warm with stoves.

The fumes from stoves killed plants, so ingenious horticulturists reinvented the Roman method of heating with flues through which hot air flowed. By the time George I became king of England in 1714, the orangerie had become a greenhouse and he, like Tiberius, could indulge a taste for fresh cucumbers at Christmas time. And at St. Petersburg, between 1801 and 1805, Czar Alexander I erected three parallel greenhouses, each 700 feet long, connecting their ends with two more buildings the same length. This enormous structure was heated through Russian winters with wood-burning furnaces.

THE GREENHOUSE BOOM

But it was in 19th Century England that greenhouses became a craze. By now glass was being manufactured in quantity, and a prohibitive tax on it was repealed in 1845. Soon every wealthy family felt it should construct a greenhouse and add a gardener to the household staff. The aristocracy undertook breathtaking ventures, the most notable being the huge glass house built at the Duke of Devonshire's Chatsworth estate. This Great Conservatory, with its soaring, gracefully arched glass walls and roof, was so large that a carriage and pair of horses could be driven through it.

By the middle of the 19th Century all of the techniques needed for successful greenhouse gardening had been developed. But greenhouses, expensive to build and needing full-time gardeners to adjust heat, ventilation and moisture, remained luxuries for the elite. The drawbacks of costly construction and maintenance were not eliminated until after World War II. Then the introduction of mass-produced extruded-aluminum building components reduced the initial investment. And the invention of electrical devices to provide automatic 24-hour climate supervision eliminated the need for full-time gardeners. Today a variety of greenhouses are available, many of them built in modular form to permit easy expansion and designed for do-it-yourself assembly. By the late 1970s, it was possible to build a small one with automatic controls for less than one third the cost of a small car.

It is the automatic controls more than economical structures that have made greenhouse gardening feasible for the part-time gardener. The most important of these automatic assistants are thermostat devices that control heating and ventilation. With their help, a gardener can tend a small greenhouse in as little as 15 minutes a day, plus perhaps one weekend morning a month. Today's challenge, in fact, is of a different dimension. The increasing costs of fuel for heat and light require maximum use of natural illumination and solar warmth. Such considerations as site selection, plant selection, insulation and windbreaks are acquiring an importance unknown until recently.

A number of experimental greenhouses that rely entirely on the sun for warmth have been built at research stations *(pages 34-41)*, and several amateurs have devised their own systems. One gardener in Hyattsville, Maryland, set up a greenhouse with an insulated north wall two feet thick. From the top of the wall a glass roof sloped to the south almost to the ground. It included panels, painted flat black on one side and lined with aluminum foil on the other, that could be tilted to absorb or reflect the sun's rays. Rimming each panel was tubing filled with water that was heated by the sun and piped into barrels under the greenhouse benches. This homemade system maintained a night temperature 30° above the outside temperature without supplemental heat.

The need for energy conservation has also forced a reversal of the conventional advice for beginners. Until recently, the rule was: start with the largest greenhouse you can afford, larger than you think you will ever need. Today the wise course is to start with a small modular greenhouse that can be expanded later, but make the most efficient use possible of every available inch.

A greenhouse can be built to either of two basic designs—attached to a house, generally as a lean-to, or freestanding. The freestanding greenhouse has several advantages. If its long axis is placed in an east-west direction, plants in every corner receive maximum light. Its isolation simplifies pest control, permitting fumigation without danger of toxic fumes leaking into the dwelling. And it may offer a tax economy—in some communities freestanding greenhouses, considered outbuildings, are taxed at a lower rate than attached greenhouses, considered home improvements.

The freestanding prefabricated Victorian greenhouse pictured above was a popular model through the 1880s, ordered by scores of American gardeners. It measured 20 feet wide, 32 feet long and about 15 feet high at the peak and was constructed of steel with wooden supports for the glazing. The kit included a hooded doorway and cast-iron finials and fleurs-de-lys to top off the gambrel roof. In 1880 the price was $2,000 unassembled; today it would cost at least $25,000.

Calculating the costs of heating

The expense of fuel is a major consideration in planning a greenhouse. The map and chart below provide data for calculating the cost of heating the average greenhouse over an average winter. For each of the geographic regions, figures are given for temperatures typical of home greenhouses and the three most commonly used fuels: gas, oil and electricity.

Three steps are involved in the computation. First, locate your home region on the map, which is divided into 12 zones of winter cold. Second, choose the column in the chart that shows the temperature you intend to maintain and the fuel you will use, and from it select the fuel-consumption factor for your zone. This gives fuel consumption per square foot of glass; the third step is to multiply this factor by the area, in square feet, of the total amount of glass in the greenhouse.

The result of your computation will be the season's fuel consumption (in cubic feet of gas, gallons of oil or kilowatt-hours of electricity). Your local fuel supplier or utility company can then tell you how much that quantity of additional fuel will cost.

The figures in the chart are projected for an uninsulated greenhouse on a calm site. A windy site will increase fuel consumption as much as 20 per cent; insulation can lower consumption up to 50 per cent.

FUEL CONSUMPTION PER SQUARE FOOT OF GREENHOUSE GLASS												
Greenhouse temperature		50°			55°			60°			65°		
Fuel		Gas (cu. ft.)	Oil (gal.)	Elec. (KWH)	Gas (cu. ft.)	Oil (gal.)	Elec. (KWH)	Gas (cu. ft.)	Oil (gal.)	Elec. (KWH)	Gas (cu. ft.)	Oil (gal.)	Elec. (KWH)
Zone	A	459	3.7	108	518	4.2	121	599	4.9	140	675	5.5	158
	B	383	3.1	90	427	3.5	100	481	3.9	113	585	4.8	137
	C	293	2.4	69	355	2.9	83	428	3.5	100	495	4.0	116
	D	234	1.9	55	284	2.3	67	343	2.8	80	405	3.3	95
	E	171	1.4	40	220	1.8	52	275	2.2	64	338	2.8	79
	F	152	1.2	36	198	1.6	46	248	2.0	58	292	2.4	69
	G	108	0.9	25	149	1.2	35	194	1.6	45	248	2.0	58
	H	90	0.7	21	112	0.9	26	158	1.3	37	202	1.7	47
	I	54	0.4	13	81	0.7	19	112	0.9	26	158	1.3	37
	J	28	0.2	6	50	0.4	12	76	0.6	18	112	0.9	26
	K	11	0.1	3	22	0.2	5	40	0.3	9	68	0.6	16
	L	1	*	†	5	*	1	9	0.1	2	23	0.2	5

*less than 0.05 gallon   †less than 0.5 kilowatt-hour

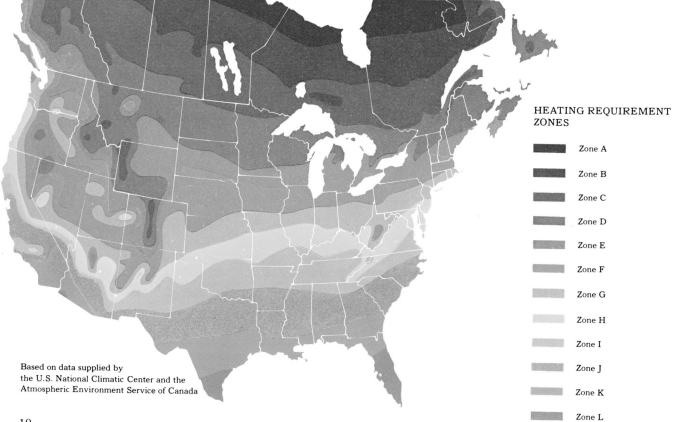

HEATING REQUIREMENT ZONES

- Zone A
- Zone B
- Zone C
- Zone D
- Zone E
- Zone F
- Zone G
- Zone H
- Zone I
- Zone J
- Zone K
- Zone L

Based on data supplied by
the U.S. National Climatic Center and the
Atmospheric Environment Service of Canada

A detached greenhouse, however, is more expensive to erect, to heat and to connect to utility lines than the more popular attached type. The latter saves the cost of one wall, it can be served by heat, water and electricity lines extended from the house, and the house wall not only eliminates heat loss on that side but adds heat from radiation from the house interior.

Ready-to-assemble prefabricated greenhouses of either type are offered with wood or aluminum frames and with glazing of glass, flexible plastic (principally polyethylene) or rigid, corrugated fiberglass. Wood framing is less expensive than aluminum and loses less heat. It needs an annual washing to prevent algae from flourishing in the humid atmosphere, and it must be repainted about every three years with aluminum or white fungus-inhibiting paint. Even with that care, there is still danger of rot. As a result, most people choose aluminum. It never needs painting, and its strength permits framing members to be very thin, admitting maximum light and casting minimum shadows.

Glass is still the most widely used wall and roofing material. It is the least expensive rigid transparent covering, and the most attractive. It is very durable; after 50 years' exposure to the elements, glass transmits almost as much light as it did when it was new. But of course it is breakable.

GLASS OR PLASTIC?

Flexible plastics are transparent or translucent—if floppy and noisy in the wind—and inexpensive, and need only light framing for support, but they have a limited life span. Some must be replaced as often as twice a year because they deteriorate so quickly; other plastics, heavier (and much more expensive), may last up to 10 years.

Rigid fiberglass costs about as much as glass. It is very strong and can be used in large pieces with fewer supporting frames than glass requires. Its resistance to breaking makes it useful in areas where hail is common, or under trees where falling limbs are a hazard. Some gardeners treasure fiberglass for the way it diffuses light, making it possible to grow plants that require sun alongside those needing shade. But fiberglass is translucent rather than transparent, and thus less attractive to many. Its surface eventually crackles, catching dust and reducing light transmission. And it is a fire hazard unless treated with a flame retardant. Many gardeners use a roof of fiberglass, for strength and light diffusion, with walls of glass to let the beauty show through.

Whatever the type of construction, most greenhouses are set on foundations. In a mild climate, it is feasible to set a portable greenhouse on a sill anchored to the ground with tie rods. But in

A greenhouse constructed from a kit

When Russell Morash, an enthusiastic outdoor gardener for more than 20 years, decided to add a greenhouse to his farmhouse in Lexington, Massachusetts, he asked an expert neighbor for advice. Morash was the producer of the television program *Crockett's Victory Garden,* hosted by the author of this book; the neighbor was Jim Crockett. At Crockett's suggestion, he elected to build the largest greenhouse that his house and budget could accommodate. Also, he decided to build it himself, from a prefabricated kit.

The model he chose was 9¾ feet wide and 21 feet long, a glass and aluminum lean-to with a curving eave. He ordered only one extra: motorized vents in the roof for summer cooling. The manufacturer shipped the 50-page instruction manual ahead of the cartons of building materials. "That was fortunate," said Morash; the mason hired to prepare the foundation never appeared. So Morash did the masonry for the project, too.

Although not too sure of himself as a mason, Morash had done a good deal of carpentry, as well as the plumbing, wiring and heating alterations for his renovated farmhouse. When he started the greenhouse project, he considered himself "somewhat skilled." As the weeks passed, however, he began to doubt some of his abilities: Didn't it make more sense to do step 11 after step 29? After he assembled the eight sections of eave glass, only to find they were off by ⅛ inch—too much—Morash swallowed his pride and called in a professional greenhouse builder who in six hours "got me back on the right track." An electrician friend helped with the wiring, a plumber installed the 40 feet of radiant-heating convectors purchased at a scrap yard, and a young neighbor pitched in for three days to help with the actual assembly.

Morash worked 12 weekends in all. His investment in the prefabricated greenhouse, additional materials and outside labor came to less than the price of a small car. He later estimated that heating his greenhouse—the biggest operating expense—would cost him "only about a third of what it would cost to belong to a golf club."

In his greenhouse, Russell Morash waters a calamondin orange. Begonias, geraniums, cyclamen, narcissus and a Boston fern 4 feet wide defy 2½ feet of snow outside.

Assembling a prefab lean-to

Morash lays the first of four courses of concrete blocks to form a foundation 2 feet 8 inches high. The blocks rest on a 3½-foot concrete footing, and enclose a gravel floor 3 inches deep. Excess water drains through gravel into the ground rather than forming puddles on the greenhouse floor. The gravel's surface is 7 inches below the sill of the sliding glass patio doors, to keep soil and water from washing into the adjacent living room.

With seven of the nine rafters in place (two more lie near the doorway), Morash inspects the greenhouse-to-be.

Morash uses a level to check the vertical alignment of each successive course of concrete blocks. He lines up the level with strings stretched between the posts marking the foundation's outer edge.

Sections of aluminum sill to support the framework are joined and laid on top of the foundation. Wooden blocks and wedges level the sill, and remain until the superstructure is assembled. Then the sill is set into mortar.

Using a power saw, Morash cuts a slot 4 inches wide and the height of the greenhouse in the house wall. He will insert a 2-by-4 into the slot and fasten the end rafter to it.

A 2-by-8 is inserted in a slot cut horizontally in the clapboards, just above the greenhouse. It will support a 3-foot-wide plywood deck that will run the length of the greenhouse and will protect the glass from ice that may fall off the roof above.

Morash eases a curved section of the glass roof onto the aluminum rafters. Strips of foam tape placed along the metal ribs cushion the glass.

Using a caulking gun, Morash applies a glazing compound to the edges where glass meets metal, sealing them and anchoring the glass in place.

Metal caps are screwed into place along the exterior of all the rafters to complete securing the glass and waterproofing the structure.

With all the sections in place, Morash again checks the level of the sill before fastening it into its permanent position. The interior of the greenhouse is large enough to hold two plant benches, each 30 inches wide, with more than 30 running feet of growing space. There is also room for a potting bench and two chairs.

Morash screws rust-resistant angles onto a section of the redwood bench that will be set along the outer foundation wall; another bench will be put at the right of the living-room door. By building the benches, he cut the cost in half and got equipment that suited his own needs.

areas where the ground freezes, the foundation footings need to be made of poured concrete extending as far below frost line as the local building code specifies. The foundation wall, generally of concrete block, is best extended aboveground to the height of a greenhouse bench, as a heat-conservation measure. It can be insulated on the inside with sheets of rigid plastic foam set between wood furring strips and covered with gypsum wallboard for fire safety. The top of this wall must be level and the corners square; otherwise the intractable materials of the greenhouse framing will not fit snugly (page 15). Even with a close fit, the joint between greenhouse and foundation must be sealed with a mortar grouting.

The choice of a greenhouse depends partly on where you plan to put it. It ought to have sunlight, of course, a requirement easier to satisfy for the freestanding type than for the attached one, which ideally should nestle against the south side of the house. If such a location is impossible, you can still plant species that manage on little light—many attractive foliage plants need no direct sunlight—and install fluorescent lamps for supplemental illumination. Before settling on the site of either type of greenhouse, however, take a full season to study the changes in the sun's position. You want all the winter light inside your greenhouse that you can get. You will find that some sites are very bright in summer, but at the same time of day in winter are shaded by buildings or trees. For a freestanding greenhouse, the best possible site generally will be in an open area with the long east-west axis tilted perhaps 10° on the compass, northeast to southwest.

CHOOSING A LOCATION

If existing trees cast too much shade, prune them, or if necessary, remove them. But keep in mind that some shade may be desirable in midsummer, depending on what you want to grow, and deciduous trees cast little shade in winter.

On an unobstructed site, winds may make your greenhouse costly to heat; heat loss from a glass greenhouse in a 15-mile-an-hour wind is double that in still air. This problem can be overcome by planting a windbreak (page 19) to create an obstruction that slows the wind's forward velocity, deflecting as much as half of the air stream up and over the greenhouse. For the best windbreak, use evergreens as tall as the greenhouse, with branches to the ground, planted in a staggered row 15 to 25 feet from the greenhouse and located so that it will block the prevailing winter wind. If the property is not large enough to permit such a living windbreak, build a fence instead; commercial snow fence works well.

When you have decided what kind of greenhouse you will build and where you will put it, you can turn your thoughts to the fixtures that will control its climate. The four factors that make up the greenhouse climate—heat, air, water and light—will determine what you can grow there. Horticulturists divide greenhouse plants into three groups according to the night temperatures they require —cool (45° to 50°), intermediate (50° to 60°) and warm (60° to 70°). For economical operation, most home greenhouses are set up for cool-temperature plants. But because the temperature is seldom entirely uniform you can generally find some zones near the ceiling or house wall of a cool greenhouse to support a few warm- and intermediate-greenhouse plants.

SYSTEMS FOR HEATING

The simplest and least expensive way to heat an attached greenhouse is to extend pipes, ducts or wiring from your home heating system; most homes have unused capacity. However, adding a special thermostat to control the greenhouse zone separately from the house may prove complicated. For this reason you may need an independent thermostatically controlled heater, which will be required in any case if your home system does not have sufficient capacity or if you are building a freestanding greenhouse some distance away. Which system—gas, oil or electricity—to install will depend mainly on the availability of fuel and its relative cost *(page 10),* but simple electric heaters are generally suited to small attached greenhouses.

Ventilators are as important as the heating system to cool the greenhouse and supply the plants with fresh air. Movable panels have been used to provide ventilation just about as long as there have been greenhouses. In the past, however, these panels, installed at the highest point in the greenhouse walls, were opened and closed by hand. This required the nearly constant presence of someone to adjust the ventilators. In a modern system, a thermostatic control operates motors to open and close the ventilators as the inside temperature rises and falls. Both the ventilator thermostat and the heater thermostat should be installed at bench level, where most of the plants will grow, rather than at more convenient eye level. In another automatic ventilator system, a fan moves air in at a low level and out near the roof as needed to keep the inside temperature the same as it is outdoors.

THE EMERGENCY ALARM

Because automatic devices sometimes fail (and power blackouts occur), you need a temperature alarm to warn you against fatal temperature plunges in winter or soaring heat, equally disastrous, in summer. This warning device is called a maximum-minimum alarm. Independently powered by batteries, it rings a bell in the house when the greenhouse temperature is too low or too high, summoning you to save your plants.

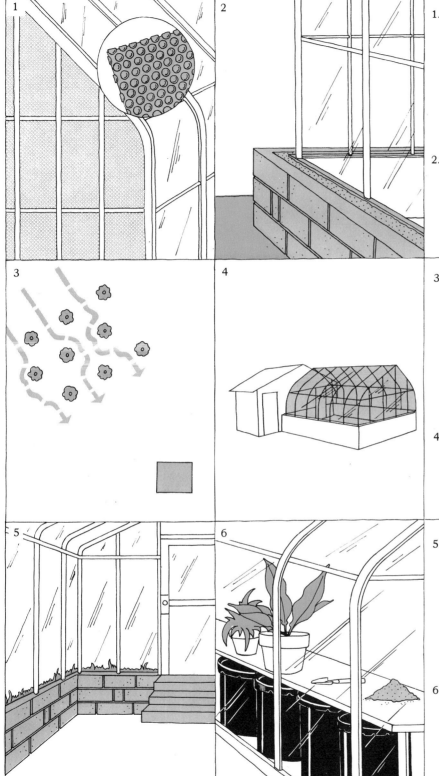

SIX WAYS TO SAVE HEAT

1. *The best way to prevent heat loss through the glass of greenhouse walls is with an insulating layer of air. This can be provided by applying a sheet of bubble plastic (detail) to the inside of the glass. Wet the smooth side and press it to the glass; it will stick by itself. Alternatively, tape a sheet of plastic film to the interior frame.*

2. *To prevent heat loss through an aboveground foundation, build a wall of masonry block outside the foundation and fill the space between the two with dirt—or better yet, with foamed plastic insulating boards.*

3. *A windbreak of trees helps to protect the greenhouse from blasts of cold air. The ideal shield is staggered rows of low-branching evergreens as high as the greenhouse, planted 15 to 25 feet away in the path of the prevailing winter winds. The windbreak should be wide enough to deflect turbulent winds from the greenhouse ends.*

4. *Place a potting shed at the north end of the greenhouse, which gets the least sun, creating in effect a vestibule to cut down heat loss. Paint the interior shed wall white to reflect light into the greenhouse.*

5. *Instead of setting the greenhouse glass atop an exposed foundation wall, sink the foundation below ground, making a partially sunken structure with less outside exposure. You can also line the foundation with rigid foam insulation attached with mastic and covered with gypsum wallboard (the foam is otherwise a fire risk).*

6. *Add free heat to the greenhouse for winter nights with homemade solar energy collectors. Fill black metal 5-gallon paint cans with water and place them under the planting benches along a south wall; the water will store heat during the day and release it at night.*

1	2	3

For a basic bench frame, construct two leg sections from eight 1-by-4s, cut to the length and width desired. Nail them together with rust-proof galvanized nails, and join the leg sections with two horizontal 2-by-2s.

Using the frame, make a bench for potted plants by laying 1-by-4s across the top, spacing them about ½-inch apart to permit drainage. Two 1-by-6s, added below, make a shelf for plants that need shade.

Convert a slatted bench into a planting bed for cut flowers by fitting it with side boards 6 to 8 inches high. Cover the slats with a layer of chopped straw or a piece of burlap; then fill the bench with potting soil.

Automatic equipment controls watering in commercial greenhouses, but most home gardeners, growing a few examples of many kinds of plants, each with its own moisture requirement, perform this chore manually. You do need water outlets, both hot and cold, with a mixing faucet threaded for a garden hose. Mixing provides the tepid water valuable in winter, when cold water can harm plants. Also useful is a water breaker, a device that lets you control the force of the stream from a hose.

BENCHES AND WALKWAYS

A few other simple pieces of equipment complete the greenhouse. Benches (*above*), to support pots of plants at a comfortable working height, or to be filled with soil like oversized garden flats, are traditionally built of wood that is rot and moisture resistant, such as redwood, cypress or cedar, but they can be built less expensively of pine treated with a wood preservative such as copper naphthenate that does not harm plants. Their support surfaces are slats, cement-asbestos panels (which are impervious to rot), or the wire mesh called hardware cloth, which is especially suited to orchid growing because it allows easy circulation of air and water vapor. Since greenhouse floors are almost constantly damp, they need walkways made of wooden slats or of brick or flagstone laid in sand over an earthen floor.

One of the most essential elements in a greenhouse—and one

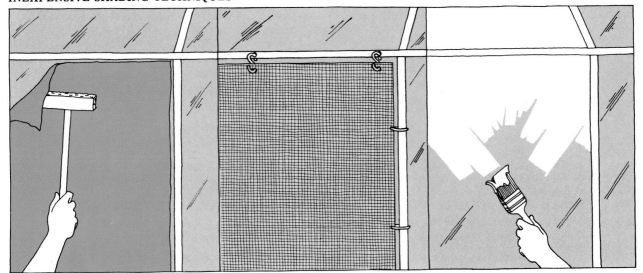

To reduce the amount of light entering a greenhouse, cut colored plastic film to fit each pane. Wet the glass and smooth the plastic against it with a squeegee. The depth of color in the plastic determines the light reduction.

Hang woven shade cloth, available at greenhouse supply centers, on hooks mounted on the rafters. The closeness of the mesh determines the density of the shade, usually 45 to 65 per cent light reduction.

To shade the greenhouse in summer, paint the outside with a shading compound, sold at garden centers. Rain will slowly wear it away so that by fall most of it will be gone, admitting more light when the plants need it.

of the oddest, considering that a greenhouse is designed mainly to provide maximum light—is some form of shade. In summer overly bright illumination may burn leaves and dry out plants. Flexible shade can be provided by a roller blind installed on top of the glass so it can be rolled up and down with a cord and pulley, or by a kind of venetian blind of aluminum strips held in slotted tracks. For temporary shade in a small area, you can tape muslin to the greenhouse rafters over the plants that need protection. Another method of shading is to apply green plastic sheets to the inside of each pane; these can be peeled off as the days grow short and saved for the following year. Or, for special flair, you can hang old, framed stained-glass windows strategically to filter the sun's rays. But the easiest way to dim sunlight is to coat the glass panes with any of several commercial compounds made for the purpose. One such compound is cleverly formulated to be opaque on sunny days, translucent when the sky is cloudy.

One greenhouse gardener who had difficulty shading the top panes of his roof made his own shading compound of hydrated lime, applied with a sponge to the inside of the glass. At summer's end he simply washed it off with a hose. His formula: 5 pounds of hydrated lime, 8 ounces of green poster paint and just enough water to make a thick, no-drip green whitewash.

A choice of plants, methods and temperature 2

The conventional impression of a greenhouse is of a warm, moist place redolent of the tropics. The air is gentle and fragrant. In your mind's ear you can hear the screeching of jungle birds and the roar of a waterfall. It can be a surprise, then, to visit a friend's greenhouse in midwinter and, upon being ushered into the glassed-in plant area, to discover that the humidity is quite comfortable and the temperature is markedly lower than you expected—you need a sweater. There is nothing tropical about the place. The feeling is more that of a cool mountainside.

There are two kinds of greenhouses. Which of these, cool or warm, you prefer depends on several considerations. The decision rests partly on economics—a warm greenhouse obviously uses more fuel and thus costs more to operate (Chapter 1). Also involved is the amount of work you are willing to do—pests multiply more rapidly in a warm greenhouse—and your choice of what you want to grow. The conditions beneficial to carnations, an import from southern Europe, differ from those that please begonias, which come from Central and South American jungles. Orchids, favored by countless greenhouse gardeners, come from all over the world, and while many are tropical or subtropical, there are many from dry cliffsides in the temperate zones and a few from the far north.

Although the temperatures are different and the plants that will grow are different, the two kinds of greenhouse gardening are otherwise much alike. The basic techniques differ from those for growing things outdoors or in the house on a window sill, but they apply across the board in the greenhouse. The care needed in plant selection is the same, regardless of temperature. Soil mixtures are similar, since they depend on the type of plant, not on temperature itself. And the general rules for fertilizing, watering and pest control, while specific for careful greenhouse gardening, must be followed in both warm and cool types.

Even the relatively chilly air of the cool greenhouse can provide superb blossoms in midwinter; the hyacinths, anemones, kalanchoes, geraniums and cyclamens at left thrive in night temperatures of 45°.

The cool greenhouse will be no warmer than 55° or 60° during winter days and at night will have a minimum reading of 50° or even 45°. The warm greenhouse, on the other hand, is one in which the daytime temperature will be in the seventies or eighties, and the night reading will not be allowed to drop below 60°. In both cases the critical figure is the night minimum. Although most plants will tolerate abnormal heat for a short period provided they do not lack moisture, they can be severely hurt if subjected to greater cold than is proper for them, even without being brought down to freezing. Some tropical plants, for example, will turn yellow at 50°. Other plants can endure a wide range but need a particular level to do their best; they just stop growing if the temperature is too low.

COST OF HIGH TEMPERATURE

High fuel costs have made a warm greenhouse seem a luxury. But some gardeners are willing to sacrifice to grow flowers they treasure. One couple that long favored tropical orchids altered their living habits to suit their plants. Their house is small, heavily insulated and kept at 55° at night and during the day while they are at work. Evenings and weekends the thermostat is set at 60°. By contrast, their attached greenhouse has a night temperature of 60° and a day temperature in the seventies.

"We can put on sweaters; our plants can't," they explained. "We cut down on energy everywhere else and our bills are no higher than our neighbors' with this size house. Our greenhouse is a big part of our lives; we would cut almost everywhere else before we would let it go."

A neighboring greenhouse owner did not agree. "With heating bills what they are now," he said, "our greenhouse is only for plants that can take cool temperatures. We don't heat it above 50° at night, but we are not lacking for plants."

In his greenhouse, foliage plants were everywhere—ferns, edible figs, Norfolk Island pines, cacti, as well as such flowers as camellias, geraniums, even jasmine.

"I had given up on the jasmine, and even put it under the bench. And there it is, growing up around the side and in bloom. The African violets are another matter; it is too cold for them out here, but they do well in the kitchen."

PART OF BOTH WORLDS

Between these two extremes of choice, fortunately, is a middle ground that enables you to grow—economically—some tropical plants along with others suited to a cool greenhouse. For example, one compromise is the intermediate greenhouse, which has a daytime temperature of 65° to 75° and a nighttime minimum of 55° or 50°. It provides a home for the less demanding tropicals on the one hand and for some of the more resilient cool-greenhouse plants on the other. Many greenhouse owners, reluctant to pay the cost of supporting a truly warm greenhouse but wanting to experiment with some of the plants needing higher temperatures, maintain an intermediate greenhouse and bring one section of it up to a warmer level. You can do this by partitioning off that section with a glass or plastic wall-and-door unit, sold by many greenhouse manufacturers, or by finding out what part of your greenhouse is naturally warmer and building up the heat in that area.

Almost all greenhouses have some warm spots and some colder ones. To identify them, use a maximum-minimum thermometer, which has a U-shaped column of mercury, one side recording the day's high temperature and the other the day's low. Keep track of temperature extremes over 24-hour periods at various locations and under various weather conditions. Check the temperature at various times of the day, too—at one moment you might find that it is 60° next to the glass on the shady side near the house, while in a sunny place the reading is over 70°. A warm area can be made still warmer with auxiliary heat or with heavy insulation (page 19).

To add warmth to one part of the greenhouse, use a special kerosene heater designed for greenhouse use and vented outside, or simply plug in a portable electric heater. More efficient spot control over temperature is possible with thermostatically regulated soil-heating cables or mats, available at garden centers or from greenhouse supply firms. They warm the soil in benches or pots, supplying what is called bottom heat because it originates below the plants. Such a cable is looped back and forth beneath the soil to warm plants in a bench; for plants in pots it is looped in the gravel drainage bed. This bottom heat is surprisingly effective. Cuttings warmed to 70° will root in one third the usual time, and four to five times as many seeds will germinate in a seed bed that is heated, as will in an unheated bed.

Whatever kind of greenhouse you decide to have, you will find a wide choice of plants that are able to flourish in that environment. The encyclopedia listing of Chapter 5 classifies them as warm-greenhouse, intermediate-greenhouse or cool-greenhouse plants and specifies special temperature requirements within these broad groupings.

In the equatorial world of the warm greenhouse, the opportunities are almost unlimited. You can grow bougainvillea, gardenias, hibiscus and gesneriads—not only African violets but also gloxinias, the Javanese lipstick plant, cape primrose and many others—as well as bizarre bromeliads like earth stars or pineapples, a wide variety of tropical ferns, such aroids as dieffenbachia and calla

FINDING MICROCLIMATES

COLOR FROM THE TROPICS

lilies, and the magnificent orchids of Central America and the South Pacific. Other orchids are suited to the intermediate greenhouse, where nighttime temperatures are kept above 50°—the cattleyas so popular for corsages, the dancing lady orchids whose blossoms flutter in a slight breeze, and a multitude of remarkable hybrids whose flowers are unlike anything found growing naturally.

Many plants from these same families can be grown in the cool greenhouse if the genera are chosen for their tolerance of lower temperatures. Orchids such as lady's-slippers, cymbidiums and dendrobiums are popular choices. Other suitable plants include cacti, many ferns, tulips, hyacinths, small citrus trees and an assortment of spectacular pot plants—pocketbook flowers, camellias and fuchsias. But many owners of cool greenhouses use much of their space to raise flowers for cutting and arranging—calendulas, carnations, chrysanthemums and marigolds grow under glass to a size and perfection unattainable outdoors or on a window sill.

In any greenhouse you can grow the same varieties that you set outdoors or cultivate indoors as house plants, but in doing so you may miss much of the enjoyment. Better results are attainable with varieties that flourish only in the carefully controlled environment that a greenhouse makes possible—with greenhouse varieties of snapdragons, for example, you will get plants larger than the varieties that grow outdoors in the garden, with more spectacular blooms, and with blossoms at specially desirable times. These types of plants have long been used by professional florists and nurserymen; many of them are identified as such in catalogs, and some special greenhouse catalogs, once circulated only among commercial buyers, are now also offered to amateurs in advertisements in gardening magazines.

VARIETIES FOR BOUQUETS

For cut flowers particularly, the greenhouse varieties enable you to produce very large blossoms at specific dates—for example, rooted cuttings for the winter-blooming carnations known as perpetual-flowering or florists' carnations are available in some 25 different colors. In some cases, specialized breeding has produced so many varieties that they are classified according to characteristics of particular interest, such as color, size or blooming period. For three popular cut flowers—chrysanthemums, gladioluses and snapdragons—numbered classification systems have been established, and some catalogues list seeds or corms by the numbers.

Seeds for cultivating snapdragons in a greenhouse are divided into four groups identified by Roman numerals according to the season in which they bloom. In Group I are the white Sierra, pink Spanish Lady, lavender Señorita and other varieties that bloom

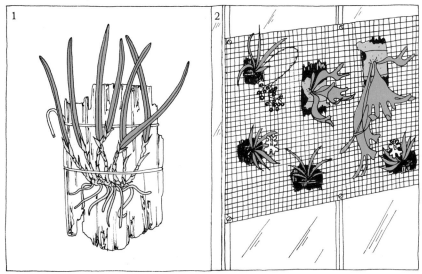

A plant that takes its nourishment from the air may be mounted on a slab of tree fern bark. Use wire (any kind but copper, which is injurious to plants) to attach the plant to the bark until the roots are established.

To display several bark-mounted air plants, cut hardware cloth, a wire mesh, to the size you want. Fasten it to the wall where it will block the least light from other plants, and wire the bark-mounted plants onto the mesh.

under glass in early winter in the North, that is, north of the 38th parallel, which runs near San Francisco, Wichita and Richmond. (The latitude makes a difference because it determines the day length, which governs blooming.) If Group I seeds are planted around August 16, the snapdragons flower between December 16 and January 1; planted about August 28 they flower between January 20 and February 10. Varieties in Group II—Treasure Chest or Debutante, for example—blossom in late fall or early spring north of the 38th parallel and in winter south of that line, the exact dates again depending on planting time. In a similar way, Group III snapdragons bloom in spring and fall in the North, in late fall or spring in the South; Group IV snapdragons bloom in summer in the North, summer or early fall in the South. Data specified in the seed catalogues for each group enable you to have snapdragon flowers at almost any time you like.

A different scheme applies to chrysanthemums. Their rooted cuttings are classified in two ways in some catalogs. First, a variety may carry a numeral between 7 and 15, indicating the number of weeks that generally elapses between the start of 14-hour nights and bloom. Those in the 7-and-8-week group are garden varieties that ordinarily bloom outdoors in the fall; but the 10-or-11-week

SCHEDULING MUMS

kinds bloom in the greenhouse in November, and the 12-to-15-week kinds bloom under glass in December.

In a further refinement, catalogs relate certain mum varieties to the latitude that influences time of bloom. If you want pompom mums in spring, for example, you can plant a 10-to-11-week variety (the white Polaris, the pink Dark Delight, the bronze Tuneful or the yellow Iceberg, for example) in Chicago or Boston, but you would use a 9-to-10-week variety (the white Icecap, the pink Delmonico) in Dallas, Atlanta or Fort Myers, Florida. Similar lists of choices related to geography are given for other kinds of mums.

Still a different system classifies the hybrid gladioluses. They are grown from bulblike corms classified in five series: the 100s, with flowers less than 2 inches wide; the 200s, with small flowers about 2 inches wide; the 300s, with medium flowers about 3 inches wide; the 400s, with large flowers about 4 inches wide; and the 500s, with giant flowers more than 5 inches wide. In addition to the series number, the catalog may code the variety's color by number, following a system devised by the North American Gladiolus Council for classifying exhibition blooms. For example, in the number 500 the 5 indicates that it is of the giant series, but the 00 means that it is pure white; the same huge white gladiolus with a color

EASY-TO-BUILD VINE SUPPORTS

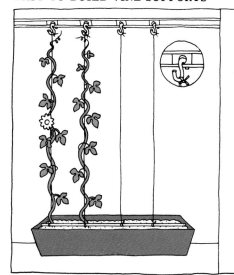

For a row of vines, drop lengths of cord from hooks inserted in holes in the rafters. Fasten the bottom of each string to a dowel wedged in the planting box and anchored with U-shaped lengths of coat-hanger wire.

For a cylindrical support, cut a piece of plastic-coated-wire garden fencing with a 1-by-2-inch mesh. Its width will be the cylinder's height. Shape the fencing to fit inside the pot and twist the cut ends together.

For a conical support, space stakes three feet long at equal intervals around the inside rim of a flowerpot. Brace the stakes against the side of the pot and join them at the top with wire or twine to form a tripod.

spot would be numbered 501. A 410 is a large (4) yellow (10) glad; 414 is the same size but light yellow; 416 is medium yellow, 418 is dark yellow, 422 is light orange, 426 is deep orange. The entire system covers 28 basic colors, but so many distinct shades are included that the classification numbers begin with 00 (white) and run through 96 and 97 (tan and brown).

Each of these plants, as well as many others popular among greenhouse gardeners, calls for its own cultivation methods (*Chapter 5*), and the controlled conditions of the greenhouse make it easy to adjust cultivation to specific needs. These adjustments, however, are mostly minor modifications to the standard conditions that suit a great many greenhouse plants. In general, most of them have similar basic requirements for soil, fertilizer and maintenance.

Although no soil at all is needed for some greenhouse favorites—the epiphytic orchids draw their nourishment from moisture in the air and from pieces of fern fiber or fir bark—proper soil is essential to most to serve as a reservoir of water and nutrients, and as a place suitable for roots to grow and function. Each plant has only a limited amount of soil, and frequent waterings tend to compact it and leach out the nutrients. Most greenhouse plants do well in a soil that contains a good proportion of both organic material, for nourishment and moisture retention, and inorganic material such as sand, for good drainage. Many commercial growers mix their own soil of one part garden loam, one part peat moss and one part sand. But homemade soil mix is almost certain to contain insects, insect eggs, infectious organisms and weed seeds, and it must be sterilized, a troublesome process. A better choice is one of the ready-made potting soils available at garden centers; it should be sterile and contain the necessary ingredients in proper proportion. An alternative is the so-called soilless mix—peat moss, ground bark, sawdust and perlite or vermiculite enriched with chemical nutrients. Although such mixes require more maintenance than potting soils—the nutrients must be replenished more frequently, and they are more difficult to moisten if they get dry— they are light in weight, and uniform bag to bag.

For plants in pots, replenish the soil only as needed when you repot. But if you raise cut flowers in soil-filled benches rather than in pots, replace the soil completely at least every other year, and preferably once a year; otherwise, fertilizer residues may build up or fungus diseases may develop.

Close control over soil conditions is necessary if you want to get the most from your special greenhouse plants, and the problem is complicated by the fact that the plants are in small amounts of

A STANDARD SOIL MIX

soil in pots or benches isolated from the balancing effects of natural conditions outdoors. For routine feeding, liquid house-plant fertilizer is recommended in most cases, the dilution depending on the plant *(Chapter 5)*. However, some gardeners favor capsules of slow-release fertilizers, which automatically spread the application over a long period of time, perhaps even the entire life of a greenhouse plant. Their long-lasting effect also may be a disadvantage—the capsules may still be stimulating growth at a time when the plant is ready for a period of dormancy. For plants that require such a period, you must choose a slow-release fertilizer that will last just long enough to match the active growing period—some are compounded to last two months, others as long as 18 months.

CUSTOM-TAILORED NUTRITION

Such mixes, liquid or solid, contain standardized proportions of the three most important nutrient elements—nitrogen, which makes foliage lush and green; phosphorus, which stimulates root growth and flowering; and potassium (usually called potash), which helps a plant to resist disease. The percentage of each is indicated by a sequence of numbers: a common liquid fertilizer is labeled 10-15-10, meaning that, undiluted, it contains 10 per cent nitrogen compounds, 15 per cent phosphorus and 10 per cent potash. For most greenhouse plants, a mixture containing the three elements in the ratio of 1-2-1—it may be labeled 5-10-5 or 10-20-10—is suitable when diluted as explained in the encyclopedia section of this volume; if other proportions are required for a particular plant, that fact is noted in its encyclopedia entry.

While regular application of a fertilizer mix suffices as a routine, it does not provide the subtle variations in conditions, attainable only in a greenhouse, that make the difference between ordinary plants and spectacular ones. For precise control over nutrient levels—and also of soil acidity—you should test the soil to learn how much of each essential element is present, and then, if the proportions are out of balance, redress the balance.

A number of easy-to-use testing kits are on the market. Some measure acidity only, while others also indicate the levels of the three nutrient elements. The simple kits consist of glass vials in which you mix soil samples with one after the other of several liquids; the mixture turns color, and you match the color to a chart to find the content of the element being tested.

To check for nitrogen with a typical kit, you fill the miniature test tube one-quarter full of soil, add the solution marked "Nitrogen" until the tube is half full, shake, then let the soil settle. If the liquid turns a reddish brown, reference to the kit's color chart indicates that a low-nitrogen fertilizer, one containing only 2 per cent nitrogen compounds, is called for. At the other end of the scale, a lime green color would call for more nitrogen, supplied by a mix containing 8 per cent nitrogen compounds. In a similar way, the needs for phosphorus and potash can be measured.

The simplest way to redress the chemical balance of the soil is to select a fertilizer mix that is suitably proportioned; a wide variety, high in one element and low in others, is available. But specific inadequacies can be more precisely remedied by supplying each element separately in exactly the quantity needed, retesting after each application until a satisfactory reading is achieved. Various compounds for this purpose are sold in gardening stores; they must be mixed with soil to provide the strength desired. To add nitrogen, use sodium nitrate or ammonium sulfate; for phosphorus, use superphosphate; for potash, use potassium sulfate (potash of sulfate) or potassium chloride.

Much the same technique determines the acidity of the soil on the pH scale of 1 (acid) to 14 (alkaline), with 7.0 as neutral. Most greenhouse plants do best in neutral or slightly acid soil, pH 6.0 to 7.0, but some, such as camellias and gardenias, require greater acidity, while cacti generally are adapted to greater alkalinity. The pH is adjusted toward alkalinity with ground limestone, toward acidity with peat moss, ground sulfur or iron sulfate. You can simply sprinkle the chemical on the soil surface and then water, but it is better to mix the additive thoroughly into the soil. How much to use to cause a desired pH change is specified in the test kits.

The beginning period, when soil and plants are new, is the time to start guarding against pests and diseases. Because the greenhouse is a closed environment with a mild climate, trouble can spread fast. But because it is closed, ailments spotted early can be contained. If you see signs of an outbreak, spray immediately.

Many of the strictures that limit the use of chemical sprays on outdoor gardens or house plants do not apply so strongly in the greenhouse. Its environment is so circumscribed that ecological damage is remote. The chemicals cannot harm birds or beneficial insects, nor are they likely to be a residual hazard to pets or children. For this reason, general-purpose sprays, effective against an entire spectrum of pests, can be used regularly in the greenhouse although they ought to be avoided elsewhere. Of course, the chemicals are still dangerous to the user while they are being applied, and normal precautions must be observed; read the labels.

An efficient and safe all-purpose spray that will guard most greenhouse plants against both insects and diseases can be made by adding 1½ teaspoons of malathion (50 per cent emulsifiable con-

SPACING HANGING PLANTS

An easy way to space hanging plants as they grow larger and bushier is to slide them along a ceiling-mounted metal rod. The inch-thick rod is cradled on metal shower-curtain hooks inserted into holes drilled in the greenhouse rafters. Place the hooks about 2 feet apart, depending on the length of the rod and the number and weight of the baskets that are to be suspended from it.

AN ALL-PURPOSE SPRAY

HYDROPONICS IN A DISHPAN

If you are curious about hydroponics, try this homemade rig, using a plastic dishpan half full of gravel. Cut a $\frac{5}{8}$-inch hole in the dishpan and insert a 1-foot length of $\frac{5}{8}$-inch plastic tubing, fastening it with epoxy cement. Rest the dishpan on two supports and slide a clean 1-gallon gas can underneath. Fit a gasket with a $\frac{5}{8}$-inch hole into the can's pouring spout and insert the other end of the tubing. Connect an electric timer to an aquarium aerator and insert its tube into the can's air hole. Fill the can with a standard solution of house-plant fertilizer and pump it through the dishpan twice a day for 20 or 30 minutes. Replace the solution weekly.

centrate), 1 teaspoon of dicofol (18.5 per cent emulsifiable concentrate), 2 tablespoons of captan (50 per cent wettable powder) and a quarter of a teaspoon of household detergent to a gallon of water. Apply this mixture every two weeks in spring, summer and fall, and every three weeks in winter, avoiding plants that are in flower. Be sure the spray reaches the undersides of the leaves.

Read the labels on the chemical bottles carefully to find out whether any of the plants you are growing should not be sprayed, since no all-purpose spray is truly all-purpose. The one just described would be toxic to many ferns, for example.

Once the greenhouse is insect-free, it will stay that way if openings are screened and if you are reasonably careful to spray all new plants before you add them to your collection. Be particularly vigilant in the fall, when you are bringing plants into the greenhouse after they have spent the summer outdoors; all sorts of bugs will be hitching a ride into your pleasant winter resort. Inspect the plants carefully and hose them off thoroughly but gently, then spray them with the all-purpose spray. If despite these measures you detect signs of trouble, move the infected plants back out of the greenhouse at once, and treat them specifically as indicated in the chart on page 148.

With these precautions, you will be able to grow a great assortment of healthy plants. Just how great an assortment is up to you to decide, but start on a limited scale; as your skill increases, so will your desire for a greater variety of plants.

With new plants acquired and set out, and with a good fertilizing and spraying program planned, your principal day-to-day concern will be watering. Use water that is roughly the same temperature as the air—every greenhouse needs a hot- and cold-water supply with a mixing faucet. And check the pH of the water with your soil-testing kit. The water from many city supplies is alkaline, and therefore harmful to the majority of greenhouse plants, which require an acid or neutral growing medium. If the pH reading is over 8.0, water your plants every two weeks with a solution of 1 ounce of iron sulfate to 2 gallons of water. Do not use softened water; softeners introduce chemicals that can harm plants.

Water only when the soil has started to become dry, then water until the soil is saturated—but be sure that all excess water can quickly drain away. There are several ways to find out whether a plant needs water. First, inspect both plant and soil. Do they look or feel dry? Is the soil light when it normally darkens when moist? Tap the pot if it is clay; if the sound is dull the soil will be wet, but if you get a ringing sound the plant needs water. Benches can be tested by plunging a trowel into the soil and digging some up to see if it is dry beneath the surface. Plastic pots can be tested by lifting them; those that need watering will be noticeably lighter than those that are moist. (Plants in clay pots require watering perhaps three times as often as the same plants in plastic pots.)

Plants need more water when they are in active growth or are flowering, much less when they are dormant. Large plants require more water than small ones. During hot, sunny weather, greenhouse plants need more frequent watering; on cloudy, mild days less is needed, often none at all. Any unusual air movement may dry plants, as does continuous heater operation in cold weather.

High humidity is important to most plants, especially orchids. Plants enhance their own atmosphere by transpiration, whereby they release moisture, but often this is insufficient. One way to raise the greenhouse humidity is to wet the floor and bench areas at least once a day during hot, dry weather. To maintain a constantly high moisture level automatically, you may need a humidifier. But do not buy one until you have operated your greenhouse for some time; most greenhouse gardeners find that normal watering routines provide adequate humidity.

Such attention to details pays off. Carefully regulating the amount and kind of moisture, adjusting temperatures, providing adequate light, choosing the right kind of soil, watching out for pests, and all the many other steps of patient, vigilant care make the difference between success and failure in greenhouse gardening. By following them with common-sense attention you can make plants grow the way you want them to, when you want them to.

JUDGING WATER NEEDS

The shapes of greenhouses to come

Some three billion years ago, when the earth was young, the very first plants that came into being lived in shallow pools of water warmed by the rays of the sun; later they grew not in water but in soil. For millions of years after that nothing much changed. Then in modern times man developed the greenhouse, which added artificial heat to the equation.

Today a curious turnabout is occurring. Shortages of fertile acreage outdoors have rekindled interest in water as a growing medium for plants. And increasing shortages of fuels have made greenhouse gardeners turn back to the sun not only for growth-assisting radiation but for heat. In the process, the greenhouse has become a hotbed of technological activity that is changing both its appearance and its role.

The plants in the greenhouse at right, for example, are growing hydroponically, entirely without soil. They are anchored in gravel, which contains no nutrients, and regularly flooded with water to which have been added all the substances they need for ideal growth. The results, reports the greenhouse owner, William Hazelett, are harvests of astonishing quality and quantity; they supply the Hazelett household with tomatoes, lettuce, cucumbers, zucchini, chard and Persian melon during all the months when field-grown produce is out-of-season.

Hazelett's soilless greenhouse gets the supplementary heat it needs from electric heaters. But at research stations around the country, greenhouses are being developed that rely entirely on radiation from the sun and dispense with energy from conventional sources *(pages 38-39)*. All have devices for trapping and storing solar heat in air or water, then for releasing the warmth to nurture the plants. Most of these experiments were undertaken in attempts to reduce the operating costs of commercial growers. But the devices and techniques they are perfecting foreshadow those that amateur gardeners may have to adopt in a time when scarcities of the world's fuel resources make conservation essential.

Hydroponically grown tomato plants 8 feet tall (left) and cucumber vines 25 feet long (right) rise from gravel-filled beds in William Hazelett's greenhouse.

A kitchen garden in wet gravel

In an 8-by-12-foot prefabricated fiberglass greenhouse behind his Arizona home, William Hazelett reaps a six-month bounty of vegetables from two strips of gravel on the greenhouse floor. Automatic controls flood the beds with a nutrient solution three times a day. The solution remains around the roots of the plants for 18 minutes, then drains back into the nutrient tank, which is under the center walkway. According to Hazelett, the plants start growing upward earlier, grow taller and bear fruit sooner than they would in soil.

Every two weeks during the growing season, Hazelett empties the 50-gallon tank and refills it with fresh water and nutrients. He shuts down the greenhouse for two months each summer and sterilizes the gravel with chlorine bleach.

Tomato plants, visible through the open door of the soilless greenhouse, reach almost to the roof. In front of them in a hanging basket is a conventionally grown begonia.

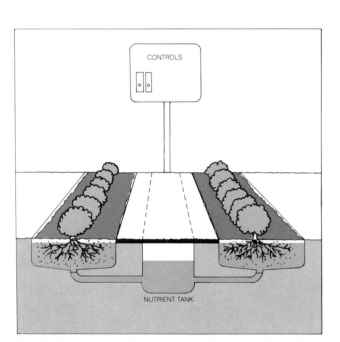

In a hydroponic greenhouse, a pump drives water from the holding tank, set below the level of the planting beds, into the beds themselves. When the water level reaches the top of the bed, the pump cuts off, gravity takes over and the water gradually recedes back into the tank. Some beds are slanted slightly to facilitate drainage.

William Hazelett admires a pair of hydroponically grown cucumbers, two of 90 produced in two months by just three plants.

Ripe and ripening tomatoes flourish on one of 10 hydroponic plants, which yield steadily from December through June.

Schemes for trapping the sun

Designed for a fuel-scarce world, the experimental solar heating systems shown here in schematic drawings were built at three research centers with the aid of government grants in a federally sponsored program that began in 1975. Each system uses a solar collector separate from the greenhouse itself, in order to interfere as little as possible with the internal space of the greenhouse and its natural light. Each uses water as the heat-collecting medium. In the one below, the collector is a salt-water pool; in the one opposite it is a heat-absorbing black plastic panel over which water trickles; in a third it is a three-dimensional aluminum panel with a core of tubing filled with water. All three were intended to be used with heavily insulated greenhouses.

At the Agricultural Research and Development Center in Wooster, Ohio, two identical greenhouses are built side by side for comparison. One is heated by the solar pond at right, the other by natural gas.

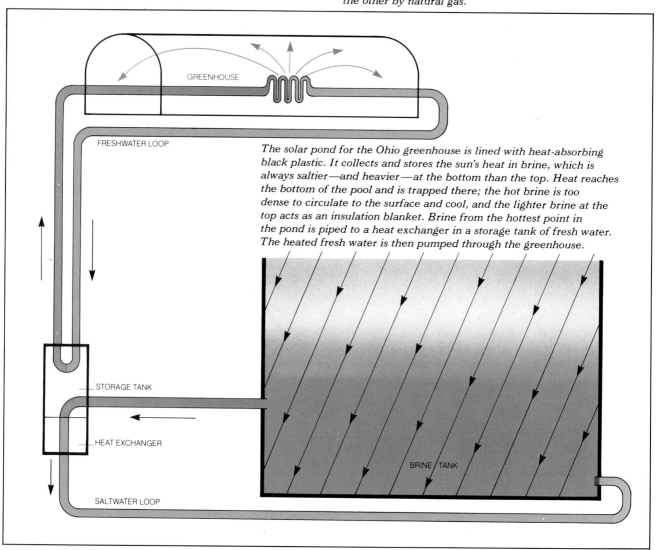

The solar pond for the Ohio greenhouse is lined with heat-absorbing black plastic. It collects and stores the sun's heat in brine, which is always saltier—and heavier—at the bottom than the top. Heat reaches the bottom of the pool and is trapped there; the hot brine is too dense to circulate to the surface and cool, and the lighter brine at the top acts as an insulation blanket. Brine from the hottest point in the pond is piped to a heat exchanger in a storage tank of fresh water. The heated fresh water is then pumped through the greenhouse.

GREENHOUSE

FRESHWATER LOOP

STORAGE TANK

HEAT EXCHANGER

BRINE TANK

SALTWATER LOOP

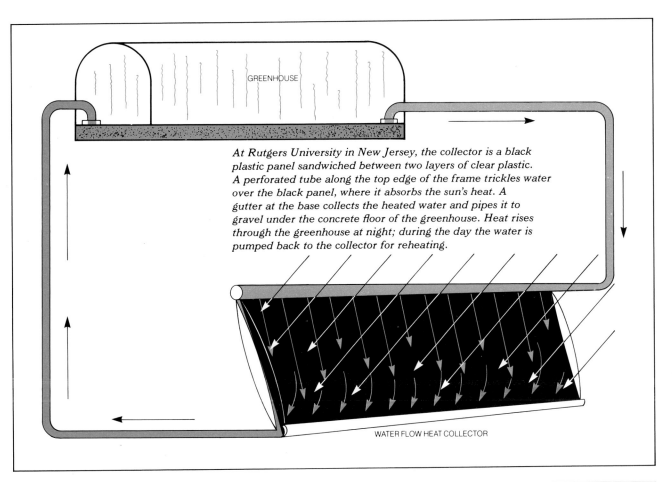

At Rutgers University in New Jersey, the collector is a black plastic panel sandwiched between two layers of clear plastic. A perforated tube along the top edge of the frame trickles water over the black panel, where it absorbs the sun's heat. A gutter at the base collects the heated water and pipes it to gravel under the concrete floor of the greenhouse. Heat rises through the greenhouse at night; during the day the water is pumped back to the collector for reheating.

GREENHOUSE

WATER FLOW HEAT COLLECTOR

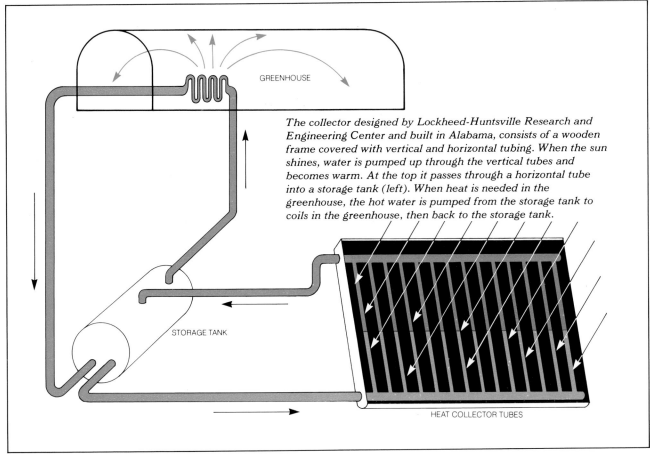

The collector designed by Lockheed-Huntsville Research and Engineering Center and built in Alabama, consists of a wooden frame covered with vertical and horizontal tubing. When the sun shines, water is pumped up through the vertical tubes and becomes warm. At the top it passes through a horizontal tube into a storage tank (left). When heat is needed in the greenhouse, the hot water is pumped from the storage tank to coils in the greenhouse, then back to the storage tank.

GREENHOUSE

STORAGE TANK

HEAT COLLECTOR TUBES

A window wall to harness heat

The research greenhouse built by the University of Arizona uses an ingeniously designed double glass wall to collect heat. Black-painted venetian blinds, sandwiched between glass, heat trapped air, which is then blown underground for storage (*diagrams, below*). At night, a pump sprays fire-extinguisher foam into the air space between the two layers of the inflated plastic roof, blocking heat loss. During the day, when the pump is off, the foam liquefies and drains out, and the sun's heat rays can get in.

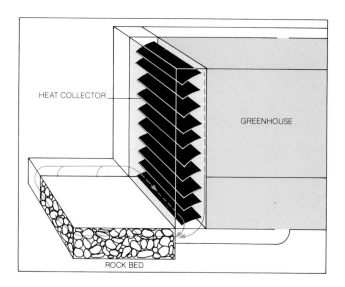

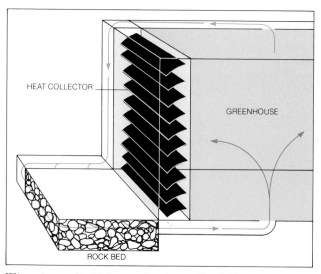

When the sun is shining on the glass walls of this greenhouse, a stream of hot air is generated by the black-painted venetian-blind heat collector. The air travels through ducts and warms a subterranean bed of rocks (top). At night and on cloudy days, the air inside the greenhouse is blown across the hot rocks, picks up heat and is circulated through the greenhouse (bottom).

Tomatoes, peppers, cucumbers, lettuce, eggplants and herbs grow in pots, beds and hanging baskets in the Arizona greenhouse.

Getting flowers the size you want when you want

3

It is December, and the azaleas you selected for forcing in late summer are in full flower, vibrant against snow outdoors. Or it is a special anniversary, and the roses you programed weeks ago are blooming on schedule, ready for cutting as a gift. Or at any time of year, the fat yellow football mums you have coaxed along, one to a plant, are the biggest, most beautiful you have ever seen.

Such triumphs—the flower out of season, the spectacular blossom, the bloom timed for a special event—are the rewards awaiting the greenhouse gardener. Some people think that the greenhouse itself brings this magic capacity to control bloom. To a certain extent it does, for its light and warmth will influence the size and timing of blossoms. But for precise control—making flowers appear on a specific date, big or little, singly or in multiples—a number of different techniques must be employed to induce a plant to do what it would not do naturally. Variations in temperature—not just extra warmth, but periods of cold as well—have an effect. Certain chemicals or the regulation of nutrients can stimulate or inhibit blossoming. Artificial light or dark can reset a plant's calendar to make it bloom out of season. And pinching—removing parts of a plant by squeezing them off between your thumb and forefinger—can delay bloom, increase or decrease flower size, and change plant shape.

Some of these techniques are so old they were presumably employed by the men who tended the Hanging Gardens of Babylon. Others are the result of 20th Century research that is painstakingly unraveling the mysteries of plant growth.

Most involve only relatively simple adjustments to ordinary practice. The simplest, perhaps, depends on the choice of a variety and the time to start it.

Much of a plant's performance—its size, shape and time of bloom—depends on its heritage. Therefore, one of the most important things a greenhouse gardener can do in his quest for perfect

A greenhouse is brightened in midwinter by pots of calceolaria, the pocketbook flower. Normally April-to-May-flowering, it was brought into bloom out of its normal season with a 50° night temperature.

THE NEED FOR COOL NIGHTS

blooms at the right time is to know the capabilities of his plants. If a rose grower seeks to produce long-stemmed roses under glass, he should seek out a hybrid tea variety such as Cara Mia or Carina that will give him that characteristic under greenhouse conditions. For more flowers on a small bush, he might choose a modern floribunda like Mary De Vor with its profuse tea-rose-shaped flowers blooming continuously as an evergreen bush.

The choice of a variety influences not only the shape of the plant and the size of its blossoms but also the date you can expect flowers. There are Carefree Bright Pink geraniums that blossom 19 weeks after their seeds are planted, and Sprinter Salmon geraniums that blossom after 15 weeks. This variation occurs outdoors as well as under glass, of course, but there the season determines planting time. Inside the greenhouse you have another option—you can, in many cases, choose your planting time. If you want snapdragons for Christmas, plant the seeds in August; if you want them for St. Valentine's Day, plant them in September.

Once you have chosen the plants and they are growing, your ability to exercise close control over the general conditions in the greenhouse enables you to speed up or slow down the normal pattern of their growth. Adjustments in moisture and nutrients are fairly simple. So are variations in temperature—you simply regulate artificial heat or move the plant to a part of the greenhouse that is warmer or cooler than average.

In general, growth speeds up when plants are given warmer temperatures than they naturally require, and slows down at cooler temperatures. You can gauge how much extra warmth to provide by knowing the climate in which the plant originated. Accelerated growth can be used to advantage in hastening a bud into bloom, but it can be a disadvantage if it stimulates a plant to grow rapidly but produce weak stems and unattractive flowers. Once the plant blooms, high temperature will shorten the duration of bloom; a tulip that might last two weeks at 55° will quickly fade at 85°.

People unfamiliar with the process of making plants flower out of season may think a greenhouse is used to provide a warm place for plants in winter, not just above freezing but really warm. For many plants, warm temperatures do more harm than good. Plants manufacture most of their food with the help of sunlight during the day, but they do most of their growing at night. That makes night temperature critical, which is fortunate, since night temperature is more readily controlled than day temperature. In winter, when days are short and the sun's rays are weak, plants do not produce as much food as in summer. If they are exposed to summer-like night temperatures, which push the plant to grow, they are forced to draw on food reserves. The result can be weak, spindly plants and, during flowering, blooms that deteriorate rapidly. Cool night temperatures, under 50°, are a way to hold many plants in good condition in the greenhouse, to delay bloom and to prolong bloom.

Not just cool temperatures but actual cold is necessary to reschedule flowering in some cases. Many plants require a dormant period at temperatures below 45° (but above freezing) before they blossom once more. If you want to get them to bloom out of season, you must give them the cold dormancy out of season, then bring them into the artificial warmth of the greenhouse. To the plants, winter has come and gone and spring has arrived.

Bulbs are often coaxed into flower by such chilling and warming. Flowering hyacinths, daffodils, tulips, crocuses and other hardy bulbs are splendid additions to a winter greenhouse. They can create spring while it is still January outside. To prepare such a treat, plant the bulbs in the fall in commercial potting soil, water thoroughly, then place them in a cold frame for 12 to 15 weeks. During this time, roots will be forming. The temperature should be kept as close to 40° as possible; it should not drop below freezing. For the most robust blooms, be patient and wait for a strong root system to develop before you move the bulbs into the greenhouse. Then place the pots in a part of the greenhouse where the temperature can be kept between 50° and 55°. Shade the plants from direct sunlight for about a week while they become acclimated to the new location. When plants are 4 to 6 inches tall, move the pots into the sunlight, but when the flower buds show color, move them back into indirect sunlight to make the blossoms last.

In the North, a nearby cold frame is the most convenient place to tuck hardy bulbs for chilling before they are forced into bloom, but any place where they can be exposed to temperatures below 45 degrees but not below freezing will do. Many people use the kitchen refrigerator. One gardener plants the bulbs in small flower pots to keep them upright on the refrigerator shelves, and sets the temperature at 45°. As for giving up the refrigerator space to the bulbs, she says, "I would no more think of facing winter without flowers than I would without food. I always plan to have at least two dozen hyacinths and crocuses in bloom to feast my eyes on in January." At a few nurseries you can buy bulbs that have already been given a cold treatment, but they must be planted immediately after purchase or the effect is lost.

There are any number of other plants that are easy to force into bloom out of season if they are kept in low temperature—35

FORCING BY CHILLING

REFRIGERATING BULBS

to 45 degrees—at night. Azaleas, for example, can be kept out of doors in summer, placed in a cold frame, then moved into the greenhouse at intervals from November on to provide a succession of bloom through the winter.

Nutrition of a plant has varied effects. If you are very generous with fertilizer and moisture, you will get big, bushy plants with heavy foliage, but you may delay flowering or, in some plants, hide the flowers with leaves. Other plants, roses and chrysanthemums among them, respond by producing larger flowers if they are fed the maximum amount recommended on the label of a standard house-plant fertilizer.

EFFECT OF LIGHT AND DARK

Nutrition, temperature and plant selection generally cause only slight modification in flowering times. A much more powerful tool in getting certain plants to blossom exactly when you want them to is light. Its importance to plants is obvious, yet only about a half century has passed since scientists discovered that many plants respond precisely to the number of hours of light and dark that they receive each day—and then the researchers initially drew the wrong conclusion.

When this phenomenon, now called photoperiodism, was first discovered, scientists believed that the length of the daylight period was responsible for flowering, so a number of different plants were studied under controlled conditions and were placed in the following general categories:

● Short-day plants, which bloom when daylight lasts 10 to 12 hours, but will not bloom with longer periods of light.
● Long-day plants, which bloom when daylight lasts 14 hours or more, but will not bloom with shorter periods of light.
● Intermediate plants, which bloom somewhere between the extremes, with 12 to 14 hours of light, but will not bloom with either shorter or longer periods of light.
● Day-neutral plants, which obligingly bloom during short, intermediate or long days.

These findings were of enormous value to commercial growers, who used them to produce flowers for all seasons and at specific times—poinsettias for Christmas, cut flowers all through the year. Then the nurserymen began to report that plant responses to the length of the day were not always as predicted. More research demonstrated that the classification by day length was a mistake. It was not the hours of daylight but the hours of darkness—the length of the night—that governed flowering. Adding light in the middle of the night could keep a plant from blooming, but adding darkness during the day had no effect on it.

MAKING AN ORCHID BENCH

1. *A stepped bench, which displays many plants in a compact space and allows the constant air circulation needed by orchids, is easily built of 1-by-12 shelving and 1-by-2 strips. To make a three-step bench, first cut 8-inch notches into one long edge of each of two 1-by-12 boards 3 feet long.*

2. *To the inside of each stepped board, nail a 1-by-2 leg. Then join the two stepped pieces with a 1-by-2 strip, 3 feet long, across the top so that the assembled framework will stand upright.*

3. *Nail 1-by-2 strips across the tops of the sidepiece notches to frame the long edges of each shelf. Staple galvanized hardware cloth to the framing strips or, instead of hardware cloth, fit a third 1-by-2 between the edge strips to make a slatted shelf.*

4. *Each shelf of the stepped bench will hold up to a dozen 4-inch pots or eight 6-inch pots, with all plants well ventilated through the wire mesh. The wood parts, especially the cut edges with exposed end grain, should be protected from rot with brushed-on copper naphthenate.*

That distinction resolved several mysteries. Why, for example, were poinsettias, so-called short-day plants, failing to flower in time for Christmas? Perhaps a watchman was routinely checking the greenhouse at night, sweeping a flashlight beam ahead of him. In the process he was halting the blooms. Or perhaps a small light used to illuminate a thermometer cast a faint glow. Perhaps a distant street lamp, or a light on a neighbor's porch, could be seen from the greenhouse. In each case there were no blooms, and the explanation was the same: The poinsettias were being disturbed in the middle of the night. The plants, in effect given short nights, were simply waiting for longer uninterrupted darkness.

Greenhouse gardeners now know that short-day, long-night plants such as poinsettias must be shielded from any night light if

Orchestrating a floral display

In a greenhouse many plants can produce flowers at a specific time, depending on when they are started, when the tips or buds are pinched, or when temperature or light are modified. The plants listed here respond particularly well to such treatment. The effect of these manipulations, however, cannot be predicted exactly, since no two greenhouses are exactly alike, and nature can throw off schedules with cloudy days or unseasonable temperatures.

The left-hand column of the chart gives normal blooming time with no special manipulation beyond the selection of a starting time; many of the plants listed bloom at any desired time if they are started sufficiently in advance. For closer control, the right-hand column describes special treatments to force blossoming out of season, delay it, or in a few cases, advance it. With most plants, the easiest way to advance blossoming is to start them earlier.

NORMAL BLOOMING TIME IN A GREENHOUSE	MANIPULATION TO RESCHEDULE BLOOM
ANTIRRHINUM MAJUS SNAPDRAGON Any season, 16 to 20 weeks after seeding	To delay bloom four weeks, pinch the tip when the plant is 8 inches tall.
BEGONIA ELATIOR RIEGER BEGONIA Fall or winter, 14 to 16 weeks after cuttings are started	For blooms out of season, illuminate to provide five weeks of 14-hour days, followed by nine to 11 weeks of 11-hour days. To delay bloom, extend the period of 14-hour days to as much as eight to 10 weeks.
CALCEOLARIA HERBEOHYBRIDA POCKETBOOK FLOWER Spring, 29 to 32 weeks after seeding	For winter blooms, sow seeds in summer, and after 23 weeks keep night temperatures between 45° and 50°. Plants will bloom six to 10 weeks after cooler temperatures are provided.
CHRYSANTHEMUM MORIFOLIUM FLORISTS' CHRYSANTHEMUM Fall, 14 to 16 weeks after cuttings are started	For blooms out of season, illuminate cuttings to provide five weeks of 15-hour days, pinch the tips, then shade to provide seven weeks of 12-hour nights; they will bloom two to four weeks later. To delay bloom, extend the period of 15-hour days and pinch the tips of side branches when 4 inches long.
CROCUS HYBRIDS CROCUS Early spring, four to six weeks after potted bulbs are moved from the outdoor cold frame into the greenhouse	For blooms out of season, chill potted bulbs 10 to 14 weeks in the refrigerator at 40° to 48°, then move them to the greenhouse and keep the night temperature at 45° to 50° until blooms appear. To delay blooms, extend chilling period as long as 10 additional weeks at 35°.
DIANTHUS CARYOPHYLLUS CARNATION Continuous, beginning 11 to 14 weeks after cuttings are started	To delay bloom, pinch tips. Plants pinched until early summer bloom 11 to 14 weeks after the last pinch; those pinched until midsummer bloom in 20 to 22 weeks; those pinched until early fall bloom in six months. To reduce the time between the last pinch and blossoming by four to six weeks, illuminate for 20-hour days for four weeks starting when plants are 2 to 4 inches tall.
EUPHORBIA FULGENS SCARLET PLUME *EUPHORBIA PULCHERRIMA* POINSETTIA Winter	To advance bloom, shade for nine to 11 weeks of 14-hour nights. To delay bloom, illuminate for 14-hour days until nine to 11 weeks before flowers are desired.
GODETIA HYBRIDS SATINFLOWER Any season, 17 to 19 weeks after seeding	To delay bloom four weeks, pinch tips when the plant is 4 to 5 inches tall.

NORMAL BLOOMING TIME IN A GREENHOUSE	MANIPULATION TO RESCHEDULE BLOOM
HYACINTHUS ORIENTALIS LARGE-FLOWERED HYACINTH Early winter, two to four weeks after potted bulbs are moved from the outdoor cold frame into the greenhouse	For blooms out of season, chill potted bulbs for 12 weeks in a refrigerator at 40° to 48°, then move them into the greenhouse and maintain a night temperature of 40° to 50°; they will blossom two to four weeks later. To delay bloom, extend the chilling period to as much as 24 weeks at 35°.
IMPATIENS WALLERANA, I. NEW GUINEA HYBRIDS PATIENT LUCY Any season, 14 to 16 weeks after seeds are sown or cuttings are started	To delay bloom four weeks, pinch off flower buds as they appear.
KALANCHOE HYBRIDS KALANCHOE Midwinter, 26 to 30 weeks after seeding	To advance bloom, illuminate for six weeks of 14-hour nights; plants will blossom six to eight weeks later.
LILIUM LONGIFLORUM VARIETIES EASTER LILY Spring, 17 to 19 weeks after potted bulbs are moved from the outdoor cold frame into the greenhouse	For blooms out of season, store potted bulbs for six weeks in a refrigerator at 40° to 48°, then move them into the greenhouse and keep the night temperature between 40° and 50°; they will blossom 17 to 19 weeks later. To delay bloom, extend the chilling period to as much as 26 weeks at 35°; for further delay after moving to the greenhouse, maintain a temperature of 50°. To advance bloom after moving to the greenhouse, increase the temperature to 72° to 78° for eight to 10 weeks before bloom is desired, and illuminate plants from midnight to dawn for three weeks when the plants are 4 inches tall.
MATHIOLA INCANA COMMON STOCK Winter and spring, 22 to 24 weeks after seeding	To advance bloom, grow plants 16 to 20 weeks at night temperatures between 45° and 50°. To delay bloom, keep night temperatures above 60° for four weeks after seedlings are established.
NARCISSUS HYBRIDS TRUMPET DAFFODIL, HARDY TAZETTA NARCISSUS Spring, two to three weeks after potted bulbs are moved from the outdoor cold frame into the greenhouse	For blooms out of season, store potted bulbs for 15 weeks in a refrigerator at 40° to 48°, then move them into the greenhouse and keep the night temperature at 50° to 55°; they will blossom two to four weeks later. To delay bloom, extend the chilling period to as much as 23 weeks at 35°.
PELARGONIUM HORTORUM ZONAL GERANIUM **PELARGONIUM PELTATUM** IVY GERANIUM Any season, 13 to 15 weeks after cuttings are started	To delay bloom four weeks, pinch tips when the plant is 6 to 8 inches tall. To delay four more weeks, pinch side branches.
RHODODENDRON (AZALEA) HYBRIDS AZALEA Spring, five to seven weeks after potted plants are moved into the greenhouse from outdoors	To advance bloom, chill plants six weeks outdoors (or in a refrigerator if possible) at 35° to 45°, then move them into the greenhouse and maintain a night temperature of 40° to 55°; they will blossom five to seven weeks later. To delay bloom, extend the chilling period to as much as 18 weeks.
ROSA HYBRIDS ROSE Any season, six to eight weeks after the start of new growth	To delay bloom, pinch tips of new growth six to eight weeks before flowers are desired.
TAGETES ERECTA AFRICAN MARIGOLD Any season, 10 to 12 weeks after seeding	To delay bloom four weeks, pinch the tip when the plant is 4 to 6 inches tall. To delay four more weeks, pinch the side branches.
TULIPA HYBRIDS TULIP Spring, three to four weeks after potted bulbs are moved from the outdoor cold frame into the greenhouse	For blooms out of season, chill potted bulbs 14 weeks in the refrigerator at 40° to 48°, then move them into the greenhouse and maintain a night temperature of 40° to 45°; they will blossom three to four weeks later. To delay bloom, extend the chilling period to as much as 27 weeks at 35°.

flowers are to be assured. By the same token these short-day plants—chrysanthemums, for example—can be deliberately lighted during the night to delay their blooms until they are wanted.

If you would like to use light and dark to schedule the blooming times of certain plants, select a place in the greenhouse where you can provide total darkness for short-day plants and extra light for long-day plants. You can use the darkest corner of your greenhouse, since you will be creating an artificial environment.

In allotting this space, keep in mind that it will be off limits for other plants that might be affected in some unpredictable fashion by the abnormal day length you are creating. If you are lighting China asters at night to bring them into bloom in winter, for example, do not let that light spill onto other plants.

A TENT TO BLOCK LIGHT

To shield plants from light, you will need an opaque material. Professionals use a heavy grade of black cotton sateen. Do not use what greenhouse suppliers call shade cloth; the latter is of varying density, blocking only part of the light, and is meant to protect plants from the burning rays of the sun. It admits far too much light to be effective in controlling a plant's photoperiodic response.

You will need to support the opaque cloth in such a way that it can be lifted from the top and pulled back from the sides to admit sunlight and let air circulate during the day. And you will need to

CONTROLLING THE SIZE AND SHAPE OF ROSES

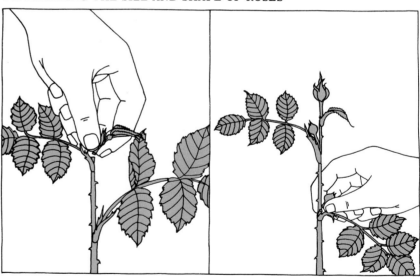

To make a hybrid tea rose produce a blossom atop a long, straight stem, pinch off the top bud when it is about ⅛ inch across. If the timing is just right this increases the stem's length and delays the bloom about eight weeks.

If you want an extra-large single rose, use the technique called disbudding. When the top bud is about ¼ inch across, rub off the buds growing at the bases of leaves on that cane, forcing the plant's energy into the single flower.

rig the cloth to suit the plants being sheltered. You can, for example, suspend the side curtains on wires supported by pipes or posts at the corners of a greenhouse bench. The curtains can be tied to these supports at night to exclude all light, and be pulled into the corners when not in use. A separate piece of cloth can be placed over the top of the frame so it laps down over the side curtains. This is simply removed each morning and put back each evening while the plants are getting short days and long nights.

Some plants, including poinsettias, have such an extreme sensitivity to light that they can sense the approach of light before dawn and retain their reaction to light as dusk deepens into dark. If you wish to delay the bloom of such a short-day plant by interrupting the dark period rather than extending the day length, the interruption must occur when it is truly dark, that is, in the middle of the night, between 10 p.m. and 2 a.m.

Arranging a greenhouse so you can provide special light or dark treatments for your plants takes careful planning. Until you gain experience, it is better to start with one or the other. Either cover some short-day plants periodically to make them bloom, or supplement the sun in such a way that you delay bloom on short-day plants or stimulate bloom on long-day plants.

To add sufficient light to lengthen the day, use ordinary 60-watt incandescent bulbs in reflectors available at photo supply stores. Place the units at 4-foot intervals along the plant bench, hanging each lamp about 2 feet above the top of the bench in such a way that it can be raised as the plants grow. Some greenhouse gardeners prefer to use brighter bulbs—from 75 to 100 watts—hung 4 feet above the tops of the plants. This arrangement eliminates the need for having to raise the lights but it adds heat to a crowded area—and temperature alters the influence of the light.

A difference of only 5 to 10 degrees in the night temperature can affect a poinsettia, for example. With a 60° temperature at night, the plant will flower as if it were getting 12 hours of uninterrupted darkness. If the temperature is 70° or higher, however, the plant will require a longer period of darkness to bring it into bloom.

To add to the complexity of manipulating light, the number of nights of shade or added light required to induce flowering will differ even among varieties of one species. Chrysanthemums, for example, may take from seven to 15 weeks of short days to flower, depending on the variety. Once started, the routine of lights on, lights off, cloth on, cloth off must be faithfully followed, and you must maintain careful records.

The final touch in controlling plant growth, and in many ways

MULTIPLYING BLOOM

Snapdragons are among the many greenhouse plants that can be made to produce abundant flowers through pinching. When the plant is about 4 inches tall, snip off the soft stem tip with your fingers, removing it above a pair of leaves near the top. This surgery stimulates lower buds to start growing. When the branches that result are about 4 inches long, you can pinch off the tip of each one to produce still more branches. Repeated pinching makes the plant short and bushy, bearing many flower clusters instead of one.

the most direct influence, is literally a final touch: pinching. Pinching is a kind of pruning. Instead of clipping through a stem, you remove either the growing tip of the stem or a bud, the fresh, soft bump that forms on a stem to produce a side branch or develop into a flower. You can use clippers if you like, but most gardeners pinch with their fingers, snipping off fresh growth by squeezing it between the nail of the thumb and the tip of the forefinger or rolling a bud off with the side of the thumb. Depending on what is snipped at what time, pinching can delay flowering, make flowers bigger or smaller, limit or multiply the number of flowers, and make the plant low and bushy or tall and slender.

A bud—occasionally more than one—appears at each joint where a leaf is attached to the main stem or branch. On some plants these buds can easily be seen, on others they cannot. But the buds are always there, awaiting a signal to grow into side branches, leaves or flowers. So long as the main stem keeps growing and forming new leaves at the top, the buds in the leaf joints below remain just buds waiting their turn to grow—they are restrained by a growth-inhibiting hormone released by the developing tissue at the stem tip. This hormone shuts off, permitting side branches to develop, when the stem tip stops growing and forms a flower. Pinching prematurely stops the hormone flow to control the way the stem, branches and flowers grow.

PINCHING TO SLOW FLOWERS

If you want to delay flowering, pinch off the top of the main stem before a flower bud starts there. By removing the developing tissue at the tip, you cut off the supply of growth inhibitor so that the side branches can sprout. The plant's energy will go into the development of leaves and branches at the sides—mainly from buds immediately below the pinch—so that the plant fills out into a bushy shape and does not grow tall. The tip of the stem will not flower, but many flower buds will appear on the new side branches. The result is a large number of moderate-sized blossoms, produced later than the single blossom that would have appeared at the stem tip if it had not been pinched.

The new side branches can in turn be pinched to induce further branching and even more flowers. A pompon chrysanthemum, for example, may bear up to a dozen flowers on a single stem. But if you pinch its main stem tip when it is about 4 inches tall and its side branch tips three to four weeks later, that same plant might produce 100 flowers on 15 or 16 stems.

Eventually, it becomes too late to pinch. Once a plant starts to form flower buds—signaled to do so by its age, the length of the day, the temperature, its general health, crowded roots or some other indication that its time has come—the crucial growth hormone disappears; further pinching is not likely to induce attractive branching and instead only sacrifices flowers.

Tip pinching encourages the leaf-joint buds to grow. Doing it the other way round—letting the tips grow and pinching the leaf-joint buds, a technique called disbudding—has the opposite effect. If you let the tip of a stem (or side branch) grow, it will eventually start to produce a flower bud and stop producing growth inhibitor. If there are no leaf-joint buds to respond to the absence of inhibitor—because you have removed them—the plant's energy will be shunted into enlarging the flower developing at the stem tip.

Disbudding is the technique to use for growing a large bloom on a tall stem for display in a vase. Leave the main stem tip unpinched, but remove all leaf-joint buds. The result will be one long, straight stem bearing one huge, perfect blossom.

By combining disbudding with tip pinching, you can make many kinds of plants arrange their branches and flowers to suit your taste at a time you choose. For a gardener new to the greenhouse and eager to see it glowing, consider what pinching and disbudding can do for the African marigold. Sow the seed in September so that flowers can be expected in midwinter. Begin pinch-

SUPPORTS FOR TALL FLOWERS

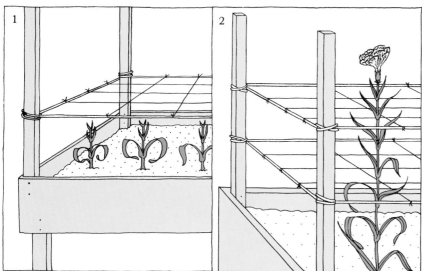

To keep long-stemmed flowers upright, nail four stakes, each 2½ feet tall, to the corners of the planting bench. Fasten wire around them, about 6 inches above the soil, and tie strings in both directions, spaced 6 inches apart.

When the plants are 9 inches tall, run a second level of string supports 6 inches above the first in the same pattern. These supports give each plant its own growing area and protect it from being crowded by wayward neighbors.

ing the stem to encourage branching after two pairs of leaves are formed. As the plant grows, continue pinching to encourage more branching; remove any unwanted branches to improve future flower placement, and pinch off all but wanted flower buds to direct energy into producing larger flowers in the most effective places.

When you disbud, try to catch the flower buds early enough so they can be rolled off with the side of the thumb, leaving no trace behind. The earlier you disbud, the smoother the flower stem will be. Since the top flower bud is formed first, its appearance is your signal to watch for more buds lower down on the stem. In December and January you will be rewarded when your plant turns into what seems to be a hemispherical surface covered with blossoms. One greenhouse gardener claims that her pots of African marigolds can pass for majolica, the richly enameled Italian pottery, because the plants are so uniformly compact and the blooms so brilliant. If you practice your prowess at pinching and disbudding on a follow-up planting of marigolds in January, you can have equally spectacular blooms in April and May.

SCHEDULING CARNATIONS

The interdependence of flower timing and flower size is illustrated by the effects of these techniques on the greenhouse carnation. Cuttings rooted in January, if left unpinched, will produce conventional flowers in April and May. If you remove all flower buds on each stem except the main one, each stem will bloom on its normal schedule but will produce a single, large, perfect bloom. In contrast, if you pinch the center stem before it begins forming a flower, you delay flowering for several weeks and at the same time stimulate the branching of perhaps half-a-dozen new stems. In order to achieve maximum flower production, commercial carnation growers continue to pinch off potential flower stalks until midsummer; by that time the original single stem will have multiplied to a dozen or more. Due to the increased size of the plant and its abundant foliage, it will produce a great number of large flowers during the following fall, winter and spring. So you have the option of growing one great exhibition bloom early or abundant flowers for cutting later on, depending on the way you pinch.

Pinching and disbudding achieve their maximum effect in the "standard"—a tall, slender plant with a single straight stem topped by a large cloud of foliage and flowers, or even just a huge solitary blossom. To create a standard, remove all leaf-joint buds, allowing only the main stem tip and the leaves growing from the main stem to remain. When the stem reaches the desired height, pinch it off.

One gardener, who each year produces a pair of bright, salmon-colored geranium standards (often called tree geraniums) on schedule for Easter, insists that "one standard is useless; you must have pairs." If you position one standard on either side of an object of interest, from a doorway to a fireplace to a bench, that focal point acquires an élan that it could take on in no other way.

You can start a pair of geranium standards any time of the year in a greenhouse. If your target is a special occasion, begin 12 to 15 months in advance. Select small, healthy plants with sturdy, straight stems, and start at least four standards so you have some leeway in selecting the two that look most like identical twins.

Leave the tip of the main stem intact until it reaches the desired height, perhaps 3 or 4 feet, tying it loosely with soft cord to a stake of bamboo or reed an inch or so away from the stem.

When the plant has reached the desired height, pinch the tip. The new shoots that result are in turn pinched to encourage further branching until the long main stem has acquired a shapely crown. Then wait for the flowers to develop. The leaves that grow along the stem will fall off naturally with age, or they can be removed as top foliage develops. In time, the long stem may become stiff enough so the stake can be removed.

Fuchsia, heliotrope and lantana can also be pinched to produce standards. It takes them about two years to develop good top growth. Standards will live many years if they are fertilized monthly and moved to larger pots before their roots become crowded.

Precision pinching becomes an art with the hybrid tea rose; producing a single beautiful bloom atop a long stem is a traditional challenge for greenhouse gardeners. One enthusiast, who each January presents his daughter with blooms of the Tropicana rose to mark her wedding anniversary, is coping with the challenge of making the right pinch at the right time to attain the longest possible stem. It is, as he puts it, precisely a matter of "a pinch in time." The pinch must be made at the time a flower bud about 1/8 inch long has formed on an upright branch. At this stage the branch is immature enough so the new growth thus stimulated will merge into it and add to the final stem length. If the pinch is made too early, when the flower bud is smaller, or too late, when the flower bud is larger, the resulting growth will not blend into the stem but will take off in a new direction, and the long-stemmed bud being sought will be lost.

This rose gardener, after years of experimentation, has created long-stemmed beauties that would delight many greenhouse owners—but none satisfy him. The challenge of the ideal blossom at the ideal time still has to be met. It is just this challenge that makes the greenhouse a special world of gardening adventure.

THE LONG-STEMMED ROSE

The amateur's exotic favorite —orchids

The most glamorous of all greenhouse plants, and the one that is most particular in its demands, is undoubtedly the orchid. Although some species grow on window sills like ordinary house plants, most are very special plants with unusual habits and requirements. Some require cold and can be found only in such unlikely places as Alaska and the Himalayas; some need the steamy heat of the Brazilian jungle. There are orchids that live quite literally in the air, suspended from trees, with free-ranging roots that take their nourishment from the surrounding atmosphere. Others live more conventionally on the ground, but even these barely make contact with the soil; their roots move just beneath the fallen leaves and feed on decayed vegetable matter.

Subtle combinations of humidity, light, temperature and moving air may be required to support growth. In the tropics, the natural homeland of the popular greenhouse orchids, some species thrive on the sultry air of the lowlands, while others need the cooler mountainsides. Most, in addition, are accustomed to being washed regularly by tropical rains and stirred by warm breezes. Little wonder that for years orchid culture was the hobby of people who could afford conservatories and full-time gardeners to tend them.

But the modern greenhouse with its semiautomatic environmental controls has brought orchid growing within the reach of amateurs like Henry Rothman and Ann and H. Phillips Jesup, whose greenhouses are pictured here and on the pages that follow. Rothman specializes in orchids with spectacular flowers, the Jesups in miniature orchids. Their greenhouses, marvels of automation, include such devices as separate thermostats to regulate day and night temperatures, humidistats that activate misting jets when the moisture falls below a certain level, and fans that keep the air in continuous motion 24 hours a day. In Henry Rothman's lean-to, attached to one wall of his home, fluorescent lights on the dark side of the greenhouse are triggered by an electric eye that monitors the natural light—in effect duplicating the rising and setting of the sun.

Blooming orchids in Henry Rothman's greenhouse are massed on a platform against a fiberglass sculpture, visible from the dining room through sliding glass doors.

Awash in splendid hybrids

Henry Rothman began growing orchids in 1967 with two familiar types—*Phalaenopsis* and *Paphiopedilum*—in a glass-enclosed indoor planter. Six years later he was filling up a greenhouse that measured 16 by 31 feet; two years after that, 1,300 plants were providing a succession of the world's most beautiful, delicate flowers. The greenhouse largely takes care of itself—Rothman needs to water only once a week.

Surrounded by orchids of at least a dozen different kinds, Rothman and his wife examine a hybrid variety named after her, Paphiopedilum Fran Rothman. Because many of Rothman's orchids are air plants, they take up relatively little room—and most of that is air space. The pots and teak baskets they grow in simply supply support; the roots themselves live outside, gathering airborne nutrients.

Rothman's award-winning orchid hybrid, Laeliocattleya Dorset Gold Orchidhurst (right), has double blooms each measuring 6 inches across.

A hybrid of the Vanda and Ascocentrum orchids, this 16-inch specimen of Ascocenda Lady Boonkua blooms twice a year in the Rothman greenhouse.

Brassavola nodosa clings to tree-fern bark, as it does in its native Honduras. The flowers, 2½ to 3 inches wide, are fragrant at night, inspiring the name lady-of-the-night.

Delicate flowers spring from a spray of the hybrid aerial orchid Dendrobium phalaenopsis Dale Takiguchi.

A Lilliputian collection

Ann and H. Phillips Jesup, who have been growing orchids ever since 1953, have one of the most unusual orchid collections in the country: they have 5,000 miniature plants, with flowers so small that they are measured in millimeters. The entire collection fits into a greenhouse 18 feet wide and 30 feet long, and the standard clay pots for their plants are only 1 inch across. Ann Jesup, an amateur potter, often buys clay and makes her own.

Ann Jesup removes a spent bloom as her husband waters. Although the Jesups group their orchids according to the plants' cultural requirements, there are so many shadings of difference in the requirements of the tiny plants that each orchid must be watered individually, on a daily basis.

Oncidium pusillum blooms in a snail shell less than 2 inches across. The flower measures 20 millimeters across (about ¾ inch).

A single plant of the O'Brieniana variety of Masdevallia simula is shown actual size at left; the pot is 1 inch in diameter. Although the flower (below) is only ¾ inch across, it resembles a standard orchid.

Growing in a pot made by Ann Jesup is a Lepanthes woodiana, shown in actual size. The flower (below) is only ⅛ inch wide.

The shimmering flowers of Lepanthes, pictured at left in one of the Jesups' miniature pots, are each only ¼ inch long (below).

Standing on 8-inch bricks, these 21 miniature orchids from the collection of Ann and Phillips Jesup range from 1 to 10 inches high. In addition to being small, some are so rare that they cannot be bought commercially. The Jesups brought back many of them from visits to the West Indies, and some were brought back from South America by traveling friends.

The orchids in the photograph at left are keyed to the drawing below.

1. Sophronitis cernua
2. Brassotonia John M. Miller
3. Masdevallia wageneriana
4. Polystachya fallax
5. Masdevallia simula O'Brieniana
6. Lepanthes woodiana
7. Dendrobium coerulescens
8. Pleurothallis phalangifera
9. Barbosella species
10. Pleurothallis lanceola
11. Ascocenda Little Leo
12. Masdevallia species
13. Polystachya aconitiflora
14. Dipteranthus species
15. Lepanthes species
16. Oncidium pusillum
17. Pleurothallis sibatensis
18. Sophronitis coccinea
19. Leptotes unicolor
20. Restrepia species
21. Sophronitis rosea

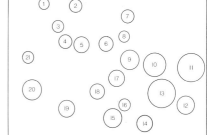

The fine art of creating new plants

A greenhouse is a place of magic. Out of its gentle climate come plants never before known in the history of the world. Sweet Sue, the impatiens shown with its parents on the opposite page, is such a one. Its color is dazzling, its variegated foliage is handsome, it duplicates itself from seeds, and in a warm, humid greenhouse it flowers all year long without pause.

Sweet Sue is a new flower in the giant family of impatiens, which grow wild in scattered parts of Asia, Africa, North and Central America and the South Pacific. It is the swan offspring of ugly duckling parentage. On one side was a species introduced from the Celebes Island east of Borneo. From it botanists developed a variety called Tangerine, with vivid blossoms but unfortunately awkward, spindly stems. The possibility of breeding out Tangerine's deficiencies arose in 1970, when American plant hunters returned from New Guinea with new stock, 25 impatiens of divergent colors, shapes and growing habits. Toru Arisumi, a botanist at the U.S. Department of Agriculture's florist and nursery crop laboratory at Beltsville, Maryland, promptly set about making crosses between them. After about six months, the offspring were ready for recrossing. With every generation the number of Arisumi's plants increased, spilling over from one greenhouse to a second, while he scrutinized each new plant for its vigor, compactness, foliage pattern, petal texture, and form and color of blossom. After five years he found one that seemed worthy to mate with Tangerine.

The odds that two plant parents will pass along only their virtues are so small as to defy calculation. Yet Arisumi succeeded on the first try. The result was Sweet Sue. It was a sensation among fellow scientists but, like many crosses between species, completely sterile. Arisumi might have stopped there, since sterile plants can be propagated by cuttings. But he wanted a flower that any greenhouse owner could grow from seed. To restore the plant's

The glowing 2- to 2½-inch flowers and variegated foliage of greenhouse-hybridized impatiens Sweet Sue are the product of a cross between the straggly Tangerine, rear, and the compact New Guinea hybrid, left.

fertility, he treated it with the drug colchicine, which also made the flowers even bigger and more vivid. Finally, to ensure that the seeds of each Sweet Sue plant would produce seedlings true to their parent, he fertilized it with its own pollen (a process called selfing) until his final selections bred true and uniform.

For all his years of effort, Arisumi's excitement when he later spoke of the hybrid still broke through his veil of scientific detachment. "I won't pretend I'm not pleased," he said. Arisumi's modesty is typical. The French hybridizer, Francis Meilland, creator of the famous Peace rose, wanted something even better. "It is all right," he said, "but a little stingy in the bloom."

An achievement like Peace or Sweet Sue is a triumph of highly trained botanists, often working with sophisticated laboratory equipment, chemicals and techniques beyond those available to the amateur. And yet every greenhouse owner can share in that excitement. In the controlled climate of a greenhouse you can grow practically anything in existence—by controlling the light, heat and humidity of this indoor world. You can start such gems as edelweiss from seed. You can grow many glamorous exotics from cuttings. You can graft lilacs onto young ash trees or privets. If you see an outstanding camellia or fuchsia, you need only make a few stem cuttings for rooting. For propagating the rare and unusual plant the greenhouse greatly increases the chance of success.

Many greenhouse owners go beyond cultivation of the exotic to challenge the professionals at plant breeding. In America there are thousands of such hybridizers, producing every year an uncountable assortment of new irises, lilies, gloxinias, African violets, orchids, calceolarias and many others. Nearly a thousand new day lilies alone are introduced each year, and there are more than 15,000 officially named varieties.

The special reward of hybridizing is the privilege of naming the variety. Louise Koehler, a farm woman of Bixby, Minnesota, looked for a fresh interest after her children were grown. She had long admired the wild *michiganense* lilies that bloomed in the waste areas around her farm. With plants from a nearby lily grower, she started making crosses, and in 1968 produced a winner: a vigorous, gracefully arching plant with a profusion of white blossoms, each petal delicately recurved. Friends insisted that she call it Louise, and it was introduced to the market where it met with acclaim.

Successful hybridization calls for more than tinkering. You must keep careful records, logging in every cross as well as labeling seeds and the resulting seedlings. Only that way can you establish a plant's ancestry and note promising (or unpromising) directions for

SHAKING MUMS TO SIZE

Greenhouse gardeners who want to keep their plants compact can profit from recent experiments at Purdue University. Horticulturists there found a novel way to stunt the growth of plants such as chrysanthemums, and force them into attractive bushy shapes. By shaking the top of a chrysanthemum stem sideways 30 seconds a day for eight weeks they reduced its height by 25 per cent; marigolds were 30 per cent shorter, tomatoes 50 per cent. Soybeans responded simply to touch: a finger placed on top of the soybean's stem twice a day for 30 seconds stunted its height in one week by 61.6 per cent.

A NEED FOR PATIENCE

future work. You need patience. Orchid hybridizers may wait for six years or more for a cross to bloom. Daffodil breeders have a seven-year wait. Rose breeders must wait three years and longer, since roses do not produce their true blossoms during the first year. And you must keep abreast of what other hybridizers have done, so you do not duplicate an existing plant.

One amateur hybridizer of gloxinias began after seeing them at a flower show. "I had never seen *Sinningia* before," she reported, "and I bought one of each kind they had—a total of two. When I put them in my greenhouse, it seemed only natural to wonder what it would be like to cross them." The cross was made, between *S. pusilla* and *S. canescens*. The flower that resulted was splendid. But investigation revealed it was Pink Imp, a cross made earlier, registered, and well known to gloxinia growers.

"I was chagrined, to say the least," the hybridizer said. "I didn't even know that plant stud books existed; I had never thought of a plant as a stud before. The successful cross was pleasing, of course, but it is more fun to be first with a new plant. Now I study the stud book." Plant societies can direct you to libraries where such stud books can be found. You also need to know the basic laws of genetics and something of the ancestry of the plants you are working with. If the parents used in a cross are each inbred—that is, not themselves hybrids—every seedling resulting from that cross will be identical. These are known as F1 hybrids, the "F" for filial, the "1" for first generation. Such plants are often more vigorous in growth, size of flower, productiveness and other characteristics than either of their parents, especially if the parents were quite unlike each other. This is the hybrid vigor that seed catalogues extol.

However, if these F1 hybrids are then crossed for a second generation, F2, their characteristics recombine and the resulting seedlings will differ wildly. For this reason the F2 generation is often called the segregating generation. All of the characteristics of the grandparents have separated and recombined in a great reshuffling of the plants' ancestry. New features show up that were not at all apparent in the F1 generation, much as an aunt's red hair might turn up in one of her niece's children although none of her nieces or nephews had red hair. This will be true whether the parents are a single variety that is self-pollinated, or "selfed"; a parent mated with its own offspring (back-crossed); or two offspring from the previous cross that are "sibling-crossed," or "sibbed."

Since the first cross produces a fine new plant only in such exceptional cases as Sweet Sue, hybridizers depend largely on the segregating generation to lead them to the desired prize. Here

RESULTS OF A SECOND CROSS

numbers become important. The more seedlings you grow from the F2 generation, the more combinations of characteristics you will see, and the more chance you have to find the unusual feature for future breeding. Many of these plants will be inferior to those of the F1 generation, but you may find a truly superior plant. The segregating generation is a roll of genetic dice on a grand scale.

Because space is so precious in a greenhouse, hybridizers begin to "rogue out" inferior plants as soon as possible, eliminating those with misshapen leaves, weak growth or muddy flower colors.

The danger of mix-ups is great. You must immediately tag every plant used with the name of the male and female parents and the date of the cross, marking wooden sticks with an indelible pencil. Add a number for cross reference to your notebook. Under the same number, record the rest of the parent plants' heritage as you know it, plus other relevant information.

To keep things straight, one hybridizer writes the identities and numbers on seedling stakes before she begins. She places each of these underneath the container she is working with.

HOW TO CROSS PLANTS

The mechanics of hybridizing are simple. Remove the petals and the stamens, the slender pollen-bearing male organs, from the female parent. Then use a small, soft artist's brush to dab pollen from the male parent—picking it up from the anthers at the top of the stamens—onto the sticky stigma at the top of the central pistil of the female plant. Finally, if there is any chance that other pollen might reach that stigma, cover it with a bag. Be sure to label both parents. When the seeds have ripened, collect them for planting.

If you are crossing two varieties of one species, your chance of success is high. When two species within one genus are crossed, you have a smaller but still reasonable chance of producing a hybrid. A successful cross between two genera is rare.

Day lilies respond well to such crossing, and are popular among amateur breeders. The procedure starts in an outdoor bed of day lilies. Early on a summer morning, strip off the anthers of a flower of the plant you choose to be the female or pod parent. Then, using an anther from the selected male parent, rub pollen onto the stigma of the female. Label a tag with the pod parent listed first and the pollen parent second, add the date, and attach it to the stalk. Record the same information in your notebook.

In 42 days the pod will ripen and, if it is average, will contain 10 seeds. Remove the seeds from the pod, wet them in a glass of water containing a fungicide, place them in a small plastic bag containing moist peat moss or vermiculite, and store them in a refrigerator (but not in the freezing compartment). After six weeks of this cold storage, the seeds will germinate as rapidly as if they had spent all winter in the ground outside; one hybridizer reported 80 per cent germination within two days after planting.

Miniature gloxinias are another good choice for hybridizing in a home greenhouse. They do not take up much space, and, like other gesneriads, they are susceptible to some crossing at the genus and species level as well as between varieties, increasing beyond count the possible combinations waiting.

To cross miniature gloxinias, select two desirable plants. Just before a flower of one of them opens, use a needle to make a vertical slit down the side of the bud. Gently peel away the petals without disturbing the pistil inside or the tiny pollen-bearing stamens that surround its base. Use manicure scissors to clip off the stamens and their anthers, so the plant cannot self-pollinate; the stamens are smaller than an eyelash but easy to see. What remains is the stigma; when it becomes sticky, it is ready for pollination. From the other parent, pick a flower, fold back the petals, and dab the anthers onto the exposed stigma. The dustlike pollen will cling.

After the seed pods form and ripen—they will be about the size of peas and will turn from light green to soft brown—harvest the hybrid seed. Slip a small envelope over the pod and snip the stem, letting the pod drop into the envelope. While the pod is still in the envelope, gently rub it to free the seeds; you may get 100 or more from one pod. Plant them in moist, sterile starting mix. Not all of the seeds will germinate, perhaps only a few, but from those that do you will have blossoms in six to seven months.

GLOXINIA EXPERIMENTING

MAKING AN OUTSIZED TUB

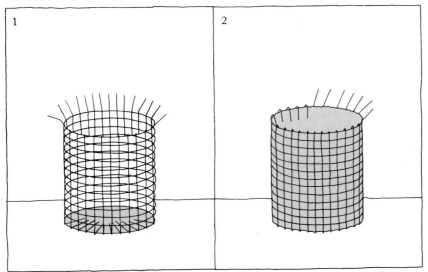

1. *To make an inexpensive substitute for a tub, use plastic-coated garden fencing with a 1-by-2-inch mesh, cutting it and curling it to the diameter you need. Wire the edges together. Bend the cut edges at the bottom inward.*

2. *Cut a circular bottom for the cylinder from hardware cloth, a wire mesh fine enough to hold soil but open enough to permit drainage. Line the sides of the cylinder with black roofing paper. With pliers, bend down the cut edges at the top of the cylinder to secure the paper. Fill the tub with potting soil; set in the plant as you do so. Be sure the heavy tub is placed where it is to remain.*

Hybridizers quickly learn to take every precaution in propagating the progeny of their controlled matings. Hybrid seeds are no harder to start than any other, but the more that sprout the greater the choice in selecting new plants. The techniques used to start precious hybrid seeds are equally useful when the object is not the breeding of new kinds of flowers but simply propagating plants.

HELPING SEEDS GERMINATE

To begin, make sure container and soil are sterile. Scrub the container with laundry bleach, one part liquid bleach to nine parts water. To make a starting soil mixture that will retain moisture without becoming waterlogged, mix equal parts of commercial potting soil and builder's sand. Firm this mix in the container, then sprinkle the seed on top. Unless the seeds are very tiny, cover them to a depth of once or twice their diameter with starting mix. If possible, set the container in a pan of tepid water until the surface of the soil is moist. If that is not possible, make sure the starting mix is evenly moist before you plant the seed.

Some seeds need light to speed germination, others need to be shielded from the light, so it is important to follow the instructions on the seed packet carefully. In both instances germination can be speeded with bottom heat, provided with a heating cable set at about 70° under the containers or in the soil *(page 26)*. (Once the seeds have germinated, the heat should be turned off.)

The secret of achieving a high level of germination is to keep the seed bed continuously moist. During the critical germination period this can be done by covering the container with plastic film or sliding it into a plastic bag, then setting it in the shade. In effect you are creating a moist, humid greenhouse within your greenhouse. Be sure to remove the plastic the day that seedlings emerge; plants left under plastic grow spindly and soft.

Keep the tender seedlings in the warmest part of your greenhouse, well shielded from drafts and abrupt temperature changes. To shelter them from the sun, suspend muslin over them to provide partial shade. When the second pair of true leaves emerges—leaves identifiable as those of the species—the seedlings are ready to be transplanted into individual containers.

HOW TO ROOT CUTTINGS

Greenhouse conditions are as helpful in other methods of propagation as they are in seed germination. The rooting medium in each case can be builder's sand, peat moss, sphagnum moss, vermiculite, perlite, or a mixture of these; the goal is to combine water-holding capacity with good drainage and an open structure that lets air enter. Again, the rooting medium must be sterile.

Perhaps the simplest kind of propagation is by leaf cuttings, the way African violets are started. Cleanliness is vital. Sever the

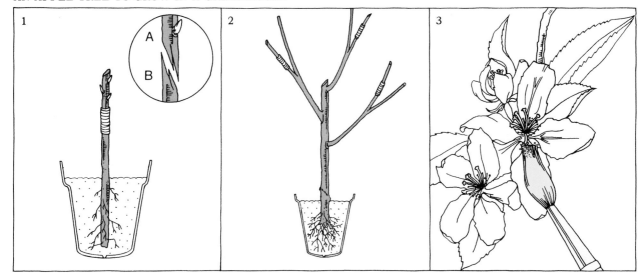

In early spring, plant in a pot a "dwarfing rootstock" for grafting from an apple-tree nursery. Cut a young branch from a tree of a desired apple variety. Slice matching clefts (inset), bind them and seal with wax.

In the early spring of the second year graft several branches of a different variety onto the first to provide the different blooms needed for fruiting. The next winter, keep the tree between 20° and 40° for four months.

In the third spring, use an artist's brush to transfer pollen from blossoms of one variety to the stigmas of another variety. Apples will be ready to pick in four months. Chill every winter thereafter and pollinate each spring.

leaf, retaining an inch or so of the leafstalk to give it firm support, dip the cut end in hormone rooting powder, punch a hole in the rooting medium, insert half an inch of the leafstalk and firm the rooting medium around it. Leaf cuttings succeed almost as well with gloxinias, rex begonias, hoya, peperomias and many succulents. Keep the humidity high and shield the leaf from direct sunlight until roots form, which may take three or four weeks.

The giant leaves of the rex begonia can be induced to bring forth new leaves with a touch of surgery. Lay a leaf on the rooting medium and make two or three cuts across its main veins. Secure it to the soil with toothpicks or hairpins, or weight it down with pebbles. In a few weeks, new plants will emerge from these cuts.

Small pieces of a plant's roots can also be propagated, though the time required is longer. Woody vines like wisteria and bittersweet respond well, as do perennials like bleeding heart, babies'-breath and phlox. Dig a vigorous root in the late summer, cut it into 2- or 3-inch lengths with a sharp knife, and plant the cuttings horizontally, ½ to 1 inch deep, in rooting medium. Keep the medium moist, and by spring you will have new plants.

The commonest method of vegetative propagation is by stem cuttings. With little effort, you can multiply any favorite variety or a new hybrid of such plants as geraniums, gardenias, wax begonias

PROPAGATING WITH GRAFTS

or fuchsias until they flood your greenhouse. Take cuttings of new growth 3 or 4 inches long in spring or summer, severing them just below leaf nodes with a sharp knife. Dip the cut ends into rooting powder and insert in the rooting medium. Remove only those leaves that would otherwise be buried and rot. Keep moist, humid and shielded from the sun until the roots form.

A technique called misting has all but revolutionized the propagation of stem cuttings that once were very difficult to root, including azaleas, camellias, jasmine, roses, holly, and even spruces and pine. All you need is a misting nozzle and timer, available at horticultural supply houses. With this equipment you can keep cuttings constantly moist by spraying them intermittently according to a preset schedule: for example, 10 seconds on and 90 seconds off through the daylight hours. A 24-hour timer, to turn the device on in the morning and off at night, is convenient but not essential.

Misting speeds rooting because the cooled cuttings can be kept in direct sunlight without either cooking or drying out, while the leaves continue to manufacture a maximum amount of food. Secure the spray head two or three feet above the cuttings and provide a drain for runoff. To keep the rest of the greenhouse from getting too humid, some gardeners enclose the misting operation in a hut framed with wood and covered with plastic film.

There is still another way to propagate: by grafting, that is, affixing plants onto host plants. Grafting is the only way that many desirable plants—including many special forms of evergreens like blue spruces and weeping hemlocks—can be propagated. Plants to be grafted should be related—a graft of one variety onto another is usually successful; almost all grafting of species will also work; graftings at the genus level work less often but are not rare.

In grafting, the plant that is the host to the graft and supplies the root system is called the understock; the desired variety to be grafted on is the scion. Union between the two is accomplished by cutting and binding them to bring into close contact their cambium layers—the living growth tissue between the bark and the wood. Successful grafting requires clean cuts with a very sharp knife, careful matching of cambium layers, snug fastening and protection with grafting wax to prevent the tissues from drying out.

Most fine new roses are propagated by a special grafting technique known as budding. Take a dormant stalk in winter from the rose you want to duplicate; that is the scion. As the host, or understock, use a strong rose growing vigorously in your greenhouse. With a sterile, sharp knife, make a T-shaped incision in the bark of the host just above ground level. Next, slice a single dormant bud from the scion, with half an inch of bark attached above and below it, cutting deeply enough to include a sliver of wood. Open the incision with the knife and insert the bud under the flaps, cut side inward. Close the flaps and wrap the incision with rubber bands, leaving only the bud exposed. After a week in the warmth of the greenhouse, the previously dormant bud should swell, indicating that all is well with the graft. If the binding does not disintegrate shortly, cut it loose.

When growth from the bud is well under way, prune the new growing stalk as necessary to force branching. Then cut away all stems of the host. Soon you will have a new rose, with roots of one kind and flower-bearing canes of another.

Should you be anxious to achieve early flowering of seedling roses you can do so with another type of grafting particularly suited to greenhouse work, known as approach grafting. In this case both plants remain attached to their roots, usually in separate pots, while the graft is made. About an inch of bark is sliced from a cane of the seedling rose and the same amount from a vigorously growing rose, then the cuts are bound together so the cambium layers match. When the union is accomplished, the seedling is severed just below the joint, leaving its cane growing on the older rose.

Cacti are among the most popular plants for greenhouse grafting because several different-looking types can be joined to create unusual effects. The ones that have colorful globular tops are all the result of grafts; these tops lack chlorophyll and could not survive on their own roots. Usually they are grafted onto an understock of columnar *Trichocereus*. To make such a graft, slice off the top of the understock, then cut a shallow V across the top just deep enough to accommodate the matching wedge-shaped base of the scion, then bind with thread or plant ties.

INVENTING A CACTUS

Such legerdemain makes greenhouse gardening an opportunity for adventure. Some amateur breeders try to produce day lily blossoms that will last more than the one day that gives the flower its name. Others seek natural mutations—the chance appearance of a new type—that they can nourish and propagate. And in the professionals' laboratories, experiments are leading to new ways to produce better plants—drugs and radiation treatments that force growth or stimulate genetic changes, even methods of fusing cells to generate combination plants previously undreamed of. It is conceivable, said one scientist, that cell fusion might create an eggplant potato. "We might well add to that mix tomatoes and peppers," he added. "They are all in the same family, you know." The result, presumably, would be a one-plant source of vegetable stew.

Oases of green designed to be lived in

The imaginative gardeners pictured on the following pages use their greenhouses not just as plant laboratories but also as living spaces in which to read, eat, paint, swim, watch television, entertain or even, as young Michael Scherer demonstrates in the photograph opposite, bathe. The Scherer greenhouse flows from the bathroom proper through sliding glass doors into a rectangle measuring 8 by 12 feet that was formerly a second-floor deck. Never remaining the same for very long, its horticultural contents rotate between greenhouse and house because the Scherers like to decorate their home with living plants. When the plants need perking up, they are returned to the greenhouse, which functions rather like a plant hospital for its physician-owner.

Dr. Martin Scherer can devote to his greenhouse an average of 10 to 12 hours a week, mostly at night, and he designed it for minimal upkeep. An insulated floor and double-glazed roof and walls enable him to keep daytime temperatures at a constant 70° with only a single electric floor heater. Because his home is in a woodland setting, vulnerable to damage from falling tree limbs, the roof and walls of his greenhouse are made of the high-impact plastic that is used for airplane windshields.

Owners of other live-in greenhouses, faced with the problem of maintaining temperatures that are suitable to humans as well as plants, have resorted to a variety of solutions—depending upon the site, the climate and the cost of heating fuel. The Massachusetts gardeners shown on pages 76-77 conserve heat in their greenhouse with a roof made of two layers of plastic. On pages 80-81, the owner of a greenhouse with a swimming pool uses supplementary heat from the water in the pool, which is kept between 70° and 80°, and from a freestanding fireplace. And in Minnesota, where winter temperatures frequently plummet far below zero, the owners of a greenhouse that doubles as an artist's studio depend on a southern exposure coupled with three gas-fired heaters to keep their oasis green and comfortable.

Young Michael Scherer bathes in privacy,
thanks to his father's greenhouse. Even
when the trees are bare, the many plants hide
the bathroom from the neighbor's view.

Moving in with the plants

What had been an open porch and grassy patio in a Boston suburb was enclosed in order to create this spectacular greenhouse, 40 feet long by 24 feet wide, where plants grow directly in the ground around a flagstoned seating area. With a small pool and waterfall, a fireplace (built into the house wall) and television, the greenhouse provides a garden that is a comfortable year-round living room; its owners, the Winthrop Bakers, are "always out there."

Winthrop Baker reads as his wife Priscilla tends the greenhouse constructed from a porch to her specifications. Baker, a professional builder, installed a heating duct along a section of the former porch roof (top left). Louvers in the duct are adjustable and can be slanted to direct the heat as needed.

Art amid the greenery

When the temperature in Minnesota dips as low as -30°, Carol Ann Mackay's lean-to greenhouse remains a comfortable 70°, warm enough for Mrs. Mackay, a professional artist, to use as a studio. It offers space not only for her work but, on benches of two depths, room to grow vegetables, to force chrysanthemums from her garden into an extra flowering cycle, and to raise both annuals and perennials for winter cut flowers, "my greatest luxury."

Framed by the arching fronds of a butterfly palm, a model poses for a brush-and-ink nude in the Mackay greenhouse. At night the temperature may drop to 50°; many of the plants grown here are species requiring warm days and cool nights.

A tropical paradise

A heated swimming pool helps to keep this 50-year-old greenhouse humid for its tropical foliage plants. Transplanted from an estate to suburban New York City by its present owner, interior landscape designer Roger Wohrle, the freestanding glass-and-steel structure measures 35 by 93 feet; its peak is high enough to accommodate trees 15 feet tall. The owner, who frequently entertains in his greenhouse, claims that "40 people can easily get lost in it."

Seated near a conical fireplace, Wohrle entertains in a tropical paradise of vines, trees, ferns and orchids. To make the setting seem more natural, heating pipes are concealed beneath the greenhouse benches or screened by banks of plants— among which hop live crickets, frogs and tree toads.

An encyclopedia of plants for the greenhouse 5

Though the plants that grow in a greenhouse are often the same species that grow outdoors, they are subjected to an assortment of special treatments—pinching, pruning, disbudding, chilling and longer or shorter hours of daylight than normal—in order to make them grow larger or smaller, flower more luxuriantly, and produce flowers earlier, later or longer than they normally do. The plants in this encyclopedia were specifically chosen for their ability to respond to these ministrations. They are divided into three temperature categories: some are for cool greenhouses, with night temperatures of 45° to 50°, others are for warm greenhouses, with a 60° to 70° minimum at night, and some are for intermediate greenhouses, 50° to 60° at night.

In most cases a commercial potting mixture is recommended because it is free of weed seeds, pests or diseases. As an added precaution many gardeners routinely spray their greenhouses with an all-purpose insecticide/fungicide/miticide. For control of specific pests and diseases, see the chart on pages 148 through 151. Also important to the health of greenhouse plants is good ventilation and a regular program of feeding. Unless otherwise indicated, all these plants thrive on a standard house-plant fertilizer containing a balanced mixture of nitrogen, phosphorus and potash; powdered forms can be used, but a liquid form is easier to dilute.

The plants are listed alphabetically by their Latin botanical names, followed by their common names. Each botanical name gives the genus first, followed by the species and then, in many cases, by the name of a particular variety. Many of the varietal names are set off by single quotation marks, indicating that the plant is a cultivated variety, usually named by the originator. These varieties often cannot be reproduced from seed; they can only be propagated vegetatively. Varieties selected for this book are especially attractive for greenhouse culture.

A sampling of plants for the greenhouse includes cyclamen, statice, nasturtium and snapdragon, at top; shrimp plant and gloxinera, at right; clerodendrum and iris, at left; and at the bottom a trio of orchids.

A

ABUTILON

A. hybridum 'Golden Fleece'; *A. megapotamicum variegatum; A. striatum thompsonii* (all called flowering maple)

Flowering maples are tropical shrubs, mostly native to South America. In the greenhouse they are grown as pot plants and are suited to intermediate temperatures, between warm and cool. They are named for their maple-shaped, often downy leaves, 2 to 3 inches long. The hanging bell-like flowers, 2 to 3 inches across, bloom almost continuously throughout the year in various shades of white, orange or yellow, salmon or purple. Golden Fleece, a bushy variety, blooms prolifically and may grow to a height of about 3 feet but can be kept much smaller by pruning. *A. megapotamicum variegatum,* a species from Brazil, has trailing stems up to 5 feet long and is ideal for hanging baskets. Its red-and-yellow flowers droop from short flower stalks; beneath each bloom hangs a cluster of dark brown anthers that look like the clapper of a bell. The narrow, mottled leaves are 1½ to 3 inches long. *A. striatum thompsonii* is a bushy variant of a Guatemalan species that is grown primarily for its striated, smooth yellow-and-green leaves, although it also produces decorative orange flowers with red veins. This variety, like Golden Fleece, can be pruned back to 2 feet or less.

HOW TO GROW. Large specimens of flowering maple are sometimes grown in 10-inch pots or small tubs if the greenhouse has sufficient room, but plants often begin to blossom when they are less than 1 foot tall, so they may also be grown in small flowerpots. They do best with night temperatures of 50° to 55°, day temperatures of about 68° to 72°, and at least four hours of direct sunlight except in the summer, when they should be lightly shaded from intense sunlight. They grow well in commerical potting soil; the soil must be kept moist, but water must not stand around the roots.

You can buy plants of named varieties or species. You can also grow them from seeds, although seeds yield variable results. Sow seeds in the spring; bottom heat of 60° to 65° will speed germination. Plants started from seed often will not flower until nearly a year after sowing. Fertilize mature plants each month with a liquid fertilizer diluted to the strength recommended on the label. Pinch off new growth at any time to encourage branching, thus increasing the number of flowers. Large old plants should be cut back and repotted, yielding handsome specimens three or four months later. Propagate flowering maples, especially the named varieties, from stem cuttings taken during the spring. Root the cuttings in coarse sand, vermiculite, perlite or a mixture of equal parts coarse sand and peat moss, with heat applied from the bottom. Plant the rooted cuttings first in 3-inch pots; then, as they increase in size, transfer them to larger pots.

ACACIA

A. armata (acacia, kangaroo thorn); *A.drummondii* (Drummond's acacia); *A. pubescens* (hairy wattle)

The fluffy yellow flowers of the acacias, blooming in northern greenhouses in the early spring, announce winter's end. Florists often sell them as cut flowers under the misnomer mimosa. These delicate-looking shrubs and dwarf trees with graceful compound leaves are native to Australia. Like their edible relatives in the pea family, they produce seed-filled pods. They are grown in cool greenhouses, in large pots and small tubs that can be placed outside during the summer. Kangaroo thorn is a bristly shrub which grows, unpruned, up to 10 feet tall and 20 feet wide in its native land. Its solitary or paired fragrant flowers, about ¼ inch across, grow on short stems at the base of the leaves and look like puff balls.

FLOWERING MAPLE
Abutilon hybridum 'Golden Fleece'

Drummond's acacia, a smaller species 4 to 6 feet high, bears its flowers in tassels 1 to 1½ inches long. The hairy wattle ranges from 3 to 5 feet tall and has a drooping habit of growth and feathery foliage. Its dense flower heads are often cut for bouquets and will remain fresh for several days.

HOW TO GROW. Acacias do best in a cool, airy sunny greenhouse with night temperatures of 40° to 55°. They need a soil that is moist but not soggy, and should be watered generously during the summer. Plant them in 6- to 10-inch pots, using a commercial potting soil. Mist the plants frequently—they thrive on humidity—and feed them every other week from spring to midsummer with a liquid fertilizer diluted to half the strength recommended on the label. In the late spring, after the plants have flowered, prune back new growth to keep the plants fuller and more shapely. Acacias benefit by being set outdoors in the summer, but they must be returned to the greenhouse before the first frost. They grow rapidly and need to be repotted every two or three years. Propagate new plants in the early summer or late fall from stem cuttings taken from young but firm new growth. Root them in moist sand or a mixture of peat moss and sand, heated from the bottom to 60° to 70°. Keep humidity high by covering the container with a plastic bag. Shade the cuttings lightly until rooted; transplant before the new roots exceed 1 inch as they are very brittle. Transfer plants to larger containers as they grow.

Acacias can also be propagated from seed, but they will take two or three years to flower. Sow seeds at any time, allowing from two to six weeks for them to germinate. To hasten germination, pour boiling water over the seeds and soak them for 12 to 48 hours; sow them while they are wet.

ACHIMENES
A. hybrids (all called magic flower, nut orchid, widow's-tear)

From late spring until fall, the velvety-flowered achimenes burst forth in a rainbow of colors ranging from pale pink and blue to brilliant red, yellow and purple. They are tropical plants, members of the gesneriad family, and require the moist environment of a warm greenhouse. Bushy in habit, with spreading branches, they are seldom more than 12 inches tall and are grown in either hanging baskets or shallow azalea pots. The leaves are 1½ to 3 inches long and the flowers are 1 to 2½ inches across, depending on the variety; the achimenes have been hybridized extensively. After the plants have flowered, they become dormant and their cone-like roots, or rhizomes, must be allowed to dry out until the following year.

HOW TO GROW. Achimenes need night temperatures of 65° to 70°, day temperatures of 75° to 80° and a relative humidity of 50 to 60 per cent. For a continuous display of flowers from late spring through fall, plant rhizomes from the early spring to summer. Blossoms will appear eight to 10 weeks after planting. Plant rhizomes in shallow bulb pans, or put them in hanging baskets lined with sphagnum moss. Use a commercial potting soil recommended for African violets. Keep the soil barely moist until the shoots appear, then water frequently enough so that the soil never becomes dry. Place them in a bright part of the greenhouse in the spring but give them light shade during the summer. Feed the plants monthly with a liquid fertilizer diluted to half the strength recommended on the label. Nip off the growing tips when they are about 6 inches long to encourage branching. When blossoms appear, a slightly lower temperature will help them to last longer. After flowering, gradually reduce watering and allow the foliage to die back. Store the pots on their sides in a dark, dry place or, if space is limited, dig up

DRUMMOND'S ACACIA
Acacia drummondii

MAGIC FLOWER
Achimenes 'Sassy Pink'

LIPSTICK PLANT
Aeschynanthus pulcher

HENDERSON ALLAMANDA
Allamanda cathartica 'Hendersonii'

the rhizomes and store them in a plastic bag filled with dry peat moss, vermiculite or perlite. Propagate additional plants by root division or from leaf or stem cuttings rooted in a mixture of peat moss and sand. Achimenes can also be propagated from seeds, but seed-grown offspring seldom run true and give rise to many variations.

AESCHYNANTHUS, also called TRICHOSPORUM
A. parvifolius, also called *A. lobbianus; A. pulcher; A. speciosus* (all called lipstick plant and basketvine)

The tubular red-orange flowers of these trailing gesneriads resemble tiny lipsticks, hence their common name. All three species are native to the rain forests of Southeast Asia and are ideal plants for the warm, moist greenhouse. They have willowy stems, 2 to 3 feet long, covered with pairs of dark waxy leaves about 1½ inches long. Their glossy blossoms, 2 to 4 inches long, grow at intervals all along the stem, and usually bloom in the winter, spring and summer, although some hybrids, like Black Pagoda, blossom continuously. *A. parvifolius* and *A. pulcher* both have yellow-throated red flowers, but the outer petals, or calyxes, of *A. parvifolius* are purple, while those of *A. pulcher* are green. *A. speciosus* has bright orange blossoms with red tips. All three species are most suitable for hanging baskets, but they can also be grown in azalea pots.

HOW TO GROW. Lipstick plants do best in night temperatures of 65° to 70°, day temperatures of 75° to 80° and a relative humidity of 50 to 60 per cent. Plant them in commercial potting soil recommended for African violets. Give them bright sun in the winter and filtered sun or light shade the rest of the year. During the growing season keep the soil constantly moist and feed the plants every two weeks with liquid fertilizer diluted to half the strength recommended on the label. In the winter, when the plants enter their period of rest, keep the soil almost dry and stop fertilizing. In their first year, the stem tips of lipstick plants should be pinched back whenever new growth is 3 or 4 inches long, to encourage bushier plants, and thus more flowers the following year. After the first year, cut back the stems to about 6 inches long after they have flowered, to stimulate more branching. To propagate additional plants, take stem cuttings at any time and root them in a mixture of peat moss and sand heated from below to 70° to 80°. Transfer the rooted cuttings to hanging baskets or azalea pots, setting four or five plants in an 8-inch basket or pot.

AFRICAN MARIGOLD See *Tagetes*
AFRICAN VIOLET See *Saintpaulia*
ALGERIAN STATICE See *Limonium*

ALLAMANDA
A. cathartica hendersonii (Henderson allamanda); *A. cathartica williamsii* (Williams allamanda); *A. violacea* (violet allamanda)

The evergreen allamandas bloom all year but put on the most spectacular display of their 3- to 5-inch trumpet-shaped blossoms from late spring until fall. These tropical South American plants with their large, 4- to 6-inch long waxy leaves are climbing vines in their native habitat, reaching as high as 30 feet. In the warm greenhouse, they can be trained to climb trellises to the greenhouse roof or pruned back to make 2- to 4-foot shrubs. Henderson allamanda, a robust, fast-growing species from Guiana, bears yellow flowers that are streaked with white. Williams allamanda, from Brazil, another vigorous climber, has golden-yellow flowers with red-brown centers. The less sturdy Brazilian species, violet allamanda, produces distinctive purple-red blossoms with deep maroon centers. This weaker plant does best if it is grafted onto the roots of one of the *cathartica* species. The allamandas can be grown in large pots or tubs, and flower most profusely when they are slightly root bound.

HOW TO GROW. The allamandas thrive in night temperatures of 60° to 65° and day temperatures of 70° or higher. Grow them in commercial potting soil. Place them in the sunniest part of the greenhouse but shade them lightly during the summer when the sun is most intense. Keep the soil moist during their active growing season and feed them every other week using a liquid fertilizer diluted to the strength recommended on the label. During the winter, when they are resting, do not feed them, and keep the soil almost dry. They can, if desired, be forced to continue blooming by eliminating this rest period, but this will lessen the number of blossoms they produce the following spring and summer. Prune the plants in January, just before new growth appears, to keep them bushy. If a plant is being trained to a trellis, arrange the new shoots around the base each spring, otherwise the bottom of the plant will rapidly become bare and blooms will appear only on the upper section. Propagate additional allamandas from 3-inch stem cuttings taken in the spring. Root them in sand or vermiculite, and apply bottom heat of 75° to 80°. When roots have formed, plant the cuttings in 3- or 4-inch pots; then transfer them to 6-inch pots. Repot them to slightly larger containers early each spring, when the new growth is less than 6 inches long, until the plants reach the desired size.

AMARYLLIS See *Hippeastrum*

ANEMONE
A. coronaria (poppy-flowered anemone)

Throughout the winter and spring, the poppy-flowered anemone, a native of southern Europe, decorates the cool greenhouse with a profusion of gaily colored flowers 3 inches wide in shades of pink, white, red, purple and blue. The solitary blossoms grow on smooth stalks, 12 to 18 inches tall, that rise from mounds of finely divided deep green leaves. The flowers are good for cutting and come in single, double and semidouble forms; the varieties St. Brigid, de Caen and Creagh Castle are particularly popular. The plants grow from tuberous roots and are suitable for planting in benches, flats or bulb pans.

HOW TO GROW. Poppy-flowered anemones need full sun and do best in night temperatures of 45° to 50°. Plant them in commercial potting soil mixed with equal parts of sand. For winter and spring flowers, plant the tuberous roots in the early fall; flowers will begin to bloom about three months later. Or sow seeds in the early spring to produce flowering-size plants by midfall that will continue to bloom until late spring. Seed-grown plants are more satisfactory than those grown from tubers because they are more apt to be free of disease. Space bench-grown plants 4 inches apart in rows 10 inches apart. If grown in bulb pans, put one plant in each 6- to 8-inch pan. Place a ½-inch layer of gravel or pot shards at the bottom to provide proper drainage and fill with soil to approximately 1 inch from the top. Place the plant or tuber so that its crown is level with the soil surface. Keep cool and water lightly until leaves begin to show; the soil should be barely damp at this stage or the tubers will rot. When the plants have finished blooming, allow them to die back. Dig up the tubers and store them in dry peat moss, perlite or vermiculite in a cool, dark place until early fall, when they should be replanted in fresh soil.

POPPY-FLOWERED ANEMONE
Anemone coronaria 'St. Brigid'

ANTHURIUM

A. andreanum (tailflower); *A. scherzerianum* (flamingo flower, pigtail plant)

The exotic anthuriums from tropical South America grow all year round in a warm greenhouse and produce a steady succession of blooms. The waxy, heart-shaped flower is not truly a flower but a leaflike structure called a spathe. This spathe comes in orange, pink, red or white, and from it protrudes the columnar structure known as a spadix, which bears the true flowers. The tailflower, a Colombian species, grows 2 to 3 feet tall and has bracts 4 to 6 inches across; the leaves are about 12 inches long and 6 inches wide. The smaller flamingo flower, from Costa Rica, is only 12 inches high and has bracts 2 to 3 inches long in scarlet, yellow, pink or white. Its leaves are 6 to 8 inches long. Both plants can be grown in either large pots or benches. The bracts, if they are not cut, may last a month; as cut flowers they are also long lasting, remaining beautiful for two or three weeks.

HOW TO GROW. The anthuriums do best in a greenhouse with night temperatures between 60° and 65°, day temperatures of 68° or higher, and a relative humidity of 45 to 60 per cent. Place them in a bright part of the greenhouse, but shield them from the direct sun. Plant them in a mixture of 2 parts fir bark to 1 part coarse peat moss; like orchids, the spongy-rooted anthuriums will rot if planted in ordinary soil. Wrap the stems in damp sphagnum moss before planting to moisten them and speed growth. Place the pot in a humidifying tray—a bed of pebbles surrounded by water—keeping the planting medium moist at all times. Feed plants every other week with a high-nitrogen fertilizer such as one labeled 20-10-10 diluted to half the strength recommended on the label. As the roots push through the top of the planting medium, cover them with moist sphagnum moss. Repot to larger containers in the spring every two or three years, keeping the top of the roots above the surface of the soil, but covered with moss. Propagate additional plants by removing offshoots, with their aerial roots, from the main stem. Plant them in 3- or 4-inch pots filled with a mixture of 2 parts fir bark to 1 part coarse peat moss. Anthuriums can also be propagated from seeds sown in the spring in a pan filled with a mixture of sand and sphagnum moss. Apply bottom heat of 75° to 80°, and do not allow the planting medium to dry out. Seed-grown plants will flower in about three years.

ANTIRRHINUM

A. majus (snapdragon)

Snapdragons, beloved by children for their snap-open blossoms, are popular bench-grown plants for the cool greenhouse, useful for both display and cutting because their erect flower spikes open in stages from the bottom to the top and thus are in bloom for a long time. Modern varieties of these native Mediterranean plants come with both single and double blossoms and in three sizes. Dwarf varieties range from 6 to 9 inches tall; intermediates from 18 to 24 inches; and tall types as high as 3 or 4 feet. It is the tall-growing types that are suited to greenhouse culture during the winter months. The flowers come in yellow, pink, red, lavender, orange, white and bronze. Although some gardeners allow snapdragons to grow naturally, producing single flower spikes, most pinch off the tips of seedlings, causing each to branch out into four to six somewhat smaller flower spikes. Snapdragons are bred for various seasons of flowering, so they can be grown in the greenhouse throughout the year if varieties are chosen for specific flowering dates.

HOW TO GROW. Snapdragons do well in a cool greenhouse with night temperatures between 45° and 50°, and in a

TAILFLOWER
Anthurium andreanum

commercial potting soil with a pH of 6.0 to 6.5. All single snapdragons are raised from seeds; most winter-flowering varieties are propagated from stem cuttings, but summer-blooming double-flowering types are seed-grown. Be sure to choose seeds of greenhouse rather than garden varieties, and choose the varieties bred for the desired season of flowering. For example, only winter-flowering varieties will bloom satisfactorily during the winter months. Sow winter-flowering seeds in the late summer to early fall, spring-flowering seeds in the fall or winter, checking seed packages for precise planting times. Sow seeds in a container of potting soil covered with a ⅛-inch layer of milled sphagnum moss or vermiculite, sprinkling them lightly over the surface. Mist the surface until barely moist, and place the container in a dark place with a temperature of 68° until the seeds germinate. Move the seedlings into the light until they are sturdy enough to be handled. Transplant them into 2½-inch pots and, when they are 4 to 6 inches high, into benches, spacing them 7 to 8 inches apart if they are to be grown with multiple stems, or 4 inches apart if they are to be grown with single stems. An alternate method is to transplant the young seedlings directly from the seedbed into the benches. Keep night temperatures above 55° while plants are less than 6 inches tall, then lower the night temperatures to 50°. For multiple-stemmed plants, pinch off the tops to encourage branching when the plants are approximately 8 inches tall, leaving three or four sets of leaves. Keep the soil moist but not soggy. Keep the leaves dry at all times, as wet plants may develop rust. Fertilize with a liquid fertilizer diluted to half the strength recommended on the label at approximately two-week intervals during the flowering period. After flowering, cut the stems to 6 inches and they will flower again, but they probably will have smaller flower spikes. Stake taller varieties with wire bench frames or use temporary canes tied with string. Single-stemmed flowers are not pinched but they likewise will flower again if the old flowers are removed.

AZALEA See *Rhododendron*
AZTEC MARIGOLD See *Tagetes*

B

BABIES'-BREATH, ANNUAL See *Gypsophila*
BACHELOR'S BUTTON See *Centaurea*
BANANA PLANT See *Musa*
BARBERTON DAISY See *Gerbera*
BASKETVINE See *Aeschynanthus*

BEGONIA

B. rex (rex begonia, fancy-leaf begonia); *B. elatior* (Rieger begonia); *B. semperflorens* (wax begonia); *B. tuberhybrida* (tuberous-rooted begonia)

The begonias are an extraordinarily large and varied genus of plants known to almost every greenhouse gardener for their remarkable flowers and attractive foliage. Although the species differ considerably—depending on whether they are grown from fibrous roots, tubers or rhizomes—all do best in an intermediate or warm greenhouse. The rex begonia, one of many rhizomatous species, was discovered in the humid rain forests of Assam. Several types are grown mainly for their large, sometimes hairy, iridescent leaves, 8 to 12 inches long, which are shaped like elephant ears and patterned like tapestry in hues of red, bronze, silver, pink and green. However, they do produce modest pink or white flowers, 1 to 2 inches wide, in the late winter or early spring. Rieger begonias, which are tuberous-rooted man-made hybrids of complex ancestry, are available in many colors and growth hab-

SNAPDRAGON
Antirrhinum majus 'Bright Butterflies'

its. The hybrid Aphrodite Pink, a popular trailing variety, bears a profusion of large double flowers, up to 4 inches across, in seven distinct shades of pink. Other Rieger hybrids have blossoms in shades of white, pink, yellow, orange and red. These relatively small plants, which grow 12 to 18 inches high, have glossy, asymmetrical leaves in various shades of green and many of them can be forced to bloom again and again between appropriate rest periods.

The satiny pink, red or white single or double blossoms of the wax begonia, usually less than an inch wide, bloom abundantly throughout the year, making this native Brazilian plant a favorite greenhouse species. It has fibrous roots and waxy-looking green or red-tinted leaves, up to 4 inches long, growing from stems 6 to 14 inches high. In the sun the color of both the leaves and flowers deepens.

The tuberous-rooted begonias produce spectacular 3- to 8-inch-wide single or double blossoms in many colors and configurations; some have ruffled or frilled petals and resemble roses, camellias or carnations. Upright tuberous-rooted begonias grow 18 to 24 inches tall and make beautiful pot plants, while the trailing varieties, with stems 4 to 5 feet long, make splendid displays in hanging baskets.

HOW TO GROW. Begonias do best in night temperatures between 55° and 60° and day temperatures between 68° and 72°. Wax and Rieger begonias require at least four hours of direct sunlight daily during the winter and filtered sunlight the rest of the year. Rex begonias need partial shade all year round. Tuberous-rooted begonias require partial shade in the summer, their period of flowering. Plant all begonias in commercial potting soil. Keep the soil of rex begonias barely moist at all times; allow the soil of tuberous-rooted, Reiger and wax begonias to dry slightly between waterings. Feed wax, rex and tuberous-rooted begonias every two weeks during the growing season; feed Rieger begonias only once a month. In all cases, use a liquid fertilizer diluted to the strength recommended on the label. Pinch off dead blossoms of wax begonias and Rieger begonias to encourage more flowers. To produce larger flowers on tuberous-rooted begonias, pinch off all the first buds and, when the second set of buds appears, pinch off all but the central bud on each stem. In the fall, after tuberous-rooted begonias have bloomed, allow the plants to die back. Dig up the tuberous roots and store them in a cool dry place, at 40° to 50°; replant them in the early spring. Wax begonias flower most freely when the plants are young; propagate new plants each year. Tuberous-rooted begonias, however, increase in size with each growing season and can be kept for an indefinite number of years.

All of these begonias except the Rieger species can be grown from seed. The seeds are minute, but the germination rate is very high and great numbers of plants can be grown rather quickly. The seedbed, a mixture of peat moss and sand, must be kept constantly moist during germination. The degree of moisture is critical. If the seedbed is too wet, the seedlings will be subject to the disease called damping-off. Germination takes two or three weeks, and during that period the seedbed must have light during the day and a night temperature of 65° to 70°.

Begonias can also be propagated in a number of other ways. Named varieties of rex begonias are propagated from rhizome division and from leaf cuttings. Wax begonias are propagated from easily rooted stem cuttings or by division of root clumps. Tuberous-rooted begonias are propagated by stem cuttings or by division of tubers. Rieger begonias are propagated by stem or leaf-bud cuttings; seeds for them are not available because they are complex hybrids and therefore often sterile.

RIEGER BEGONIA
Begonia elatior 'Aphrodite Pink'

Take cuttings from most begonias at any time and root them in sand heated from the bottom to 68° to 70°. Take cuttings from tuberous-rooted begonias in the spring or early summer; such cutting-grown plants will make tubers during the summer that can be stored for later use. Divide the rhizomes of rex begonia in the spring or fall, the fibrous roots of wax begonia at any time, and the tubers of tuberous-rooted begonias in the late winter, just as the plants are ending their period of dormancy and the first buds appear. Repot rex and wax begonias in pots suitable to the size of the root clump. Place root sections of tuberous-rooted begonias in shallow pans and cover them with a mixture of peat moss and sand; keep the mixture moist but not soggy, and place the pans in a spot where night temperatures are between 60° and 65°. When shoots appear, in about four or five weeks, transfer the tubers to 4-, 5- or 6-inch azalea pots, depending on the tuber's size.

To force Rieger begonias into bloom as often as three times a year, prune them back to half their size after each blooming period and subject them to a cycle of alternately long and short days, giving them the equivalent of 14-hour days for about a month followed by 11-hour days for about 10 weeks. Depending upon the time of year, the long-day treatment may require the use of artificial light for up to four hours a day, and the short-day treatment may require the use of artificial shading with an opaque cloth. The long days promote vegetative growth, and the short days encourage bud formation and flowering.

BELLFLOWER See *Campanula*

BELOPERONE, also called JUSTICIA
B. guttata, also called *J. brandegeana; B. comosa*, also called *J. fulvieomo* (both called shrimp plant)
The exotic Mexican shrimp plant decorates the intermediate greenhouse throughout the year with its curling, overlapping bracts, 3 to 4 inches long, shaped like shrimp tails. Depending on the species, the bracts come in color combinations of bronze, red and yellow, and yellow-green; each bract surrounds a tiny white true flower, less than 1 inch long. The soft, hairy, oval leaves are often as long as the overlapping bracts and also vary in color. *B. comosa* has green foliage edged with red, while the leaves of *B. guttata* are pea green; this species also has less colorful bracts. In their native environment, these evergreen shrubs grow 3 to 8 feet tall, but as greenhouse plants they are usually kept trimmed to a height of 12 to 18 inches. They can be planted in standard pots or hanging baskets and will grow in either a warm or intermediate greenhouse.

HOW TO GROW. Shrimp plants do best in night temperatures of 50° to 55° and day temperatures of 68° to 72°. Place them in the sunniest part of the greenhouse. Plant in 5- or 6-inch pots in commercial potting soil. Water only when the soil becomes almost dry, but then water thoroughly. Feed every other week using a liquid fertilizer diluted to the strength recommended on the label. Pinch off tips at any time to keep the plants from becoming spindly, or cut them back to half their height after flowering. Propagate additional plants from stem cuttings taken at any time, or from the pinched-off tips, rooting them in moist sand, perlite or vermiculite, warmed from below to a temperature of 70°.

BIRD-OF-PARADISE FLOWER See *Strelitzia*
BLUEBOTTLE See *Centaurea*
BLUE LACE FLOWER See *Trachymene*
BOSTON DAISY See *Chrysanthemum*

SHRIMP PLANT
Beloperone guttata

BRASSAVOLA

B. cordata; B. digbyana, also called *Laelia digbyana; B. nodosa* (all brassavola orchids; *B. nodosa* is also called lady-of-the-night)

The brassavola orchids, natives of tropical America, are prized in the warm greenhouse for their sweet smell as well as their green-tinged white flowers. In the wild these orchids attach themselves to tree bark, living off the organic food collected by their aerial roots; they are epiphytic orchids. Like other orchids of this type, brassavolas have swollen bulblike storage stems called pseudobulbs. *B. digbyana* is the most distinguished member of this genus, valued as a breeding orchid for many hybrid variants. Its huge, solitary blossom, 4 to 5 inches wide, has a wide, deeply fringed lip so distinctive that orchid breeders refer to its appearance in other flowers as the "brasso lip." Originally from Honduras, it grows about 8 inches tall and bears flowers in the late summer. A smaller Jamaican member of the species, *B. cordata,* is only 3 to 5 inches tall and has a flower 1½ inches across, with a heart-shaped lip marked with purple. This orchid blooms only in the fall. *B. nodosa,* a species from Central America, is known as lady-of-the-night because its spidery, fragrant, white flowers open only from dusk until midnight. Its long-lasting 3- to 4-inch flowers are tinged with yellow as well as pale green, and have round, flared lips. Lady-of-the-night blooms profusely all year and may produce as many as 50 blossoms on a plant 6 to 9 inches tall.

HOW TO GROW. Brassavolas require night temperatures of about 60° to 65° and day temperatures of about 68°, or approximately 10° higher. They need bright indirect sunlight in the winter and light shade during the summer. Grow them on a slab of tree fern or in pots, in a mixture of 2 parts fir bark to 1 part coarse peat moss. Place pots in a humidifying tray and water sparingly until the plants are established, keeping the growing medium slightly on the dry side for the first few weeks. Then water once or twice a week, just enough to keep the growing medium moist to the touch. Feed monthly with a high-nitrogen fertilizer, such as one labeled 20-10-10, diluted ¼ teaspoon to a quart of water. After flowering, allow plants to rest by watering less often, but never allow the growing medium to dry out completely. Repot brassavolas whenever the roots grow over the edge of the pot, usually every two or three years. To repot, divide the pseudobulbs into groups of three or four, never less than that; repot after flowering, when the plant is resting.

BRAZILIAN EDELWEISS See *Rechsteineria*
BROOM, YELLOW See *Cytisus*
BUSY LIZZIE See *Impatiens*
BUTTERCUP See *Ranunculus*
BUTTERFLY FLOWER See *Schizanthus*

C

CALANTHE

C. vestita (calanthe orchid)

Calanthe orchids are terrestrial, or earth-bound, plants, living and growing in soil rather than on the bark of trees, and many of them, like *C. vestita,* are deciduous. This native of Burma and Malaysia blooms in the winter and is a candidate for the warm, moist greenhouse. It bears sprays of six to 10 white flowers, 2 to 3 inches wide, on stems as much as 2½ feet long, and is a popular flower for winter corsages. When the flowers fade, broad leaves as much as 2 feet long rise from the plant's swollen stem, or pseudobulb. Eventually the leaves turn yellow and fall off, and the pseudobulb is lifted and stored for the next growing season. *C. vestita*

LADY-OF-THE-NIGHT ORCHID
Brassavola nodosa

comes in many hybridized varieties; some begin to bloom as early as October and others continue to bloom as late as March. Their white blossoms may be shaded or striped with rose, blotched with yellow, or have crimson or purple eyes.

HOW TO GROW. Calanthe orchids do best in night temperatures of 55° to 65° and day temperatures about 10° higher. They need light but should be protected from the sun's most intense rays. Grow them in 5- to 7-inch pots in a mixture of 1 part peat moss, 1 part sand, and 2 parts potting soil, covering the pseudobulbs with ¼ inch of this growing medium. Water sparingly at first, just enough to keep the growing medium barely damp. When growth starts, increase the watering so that the growing medium is moist but not soggy, and feed the plants every two weeks with a liquid fertilizer diluted to half the strength recommended on the label. When foliage begins to die, omit feedings and decrease the amount of water until soil becomes dry. Remove the pseudobulbs from the pots and store them in a sand-filled tray at a temperature of 60°. They should rest for about four to six weeks before repotting. For additional plants, divide the new pseudobulbs from the old stock, and repot them separately.

CALCEOLARIA
C. herbeohybrida (pocketbook flower, slipperwort, lady's pocketbook)

The pocketbook flower is named for the unusual shape of its swollen, pouchlike, two-lipped blossoms whose lower lips are from ½ to 2 inches wide. Natives of the cool South American Andes, these striking flowers come in rich hues of yellow, orange, red, pink, bronze and maroon, often spotted with brown or purple specks. Pocketbook flowers bloom profusely during the spring in a cool greenhouse. The blossoms often cover the entire plant and may almost obscure the large, downy 6-inch leaves. The plants range in size from 6 to 12 inches high, and when they are mature they will fill 5- to 6-inch azalea pots. Most of them die after they have produced flowers and seeds.

HOW TO GROW. Pocketbook flowers do best in temperatures of less than 60°, ideally with night temperatures between 40° and 50° and day temperatures between 55° and 60°. Unlike many flowers, the cooler the temperatures, the more abundantly they bloom. They need some filtered sunlight in the winter and partial shade the rest of the year; too much shade causes weak stems, and direct sunlight burns their fragile leaves. Sow the tiny seeds of pocketbook flower in flat bulb pans filled with potting soil topped with a ¼-inch layer of damp vermiculite or milled sphagnum moss. Keep the germinating seeds very cool, and transplant the seedlings first into 2½-inch pots, then into successively larger azalea pots; 6-inch pots are suitable for mature plants. Use a commercial potting soil, and water it lightly—by evening, soil watered in the morning should have dried out completely. Be careful not to wet the leaves, or they may rot. Be sure to give the plants plenty of room so there is good air circulation among them. Feed the young plants once a month until flower buds form with a liquid fertilizer diluted to one quarter the strength recommended on the label; do not feed the plants after they are in bloom. Seeds sown in August or September will produce flowering plants the following spring from March to May.

CALENDULA
C. officinalis (calendula, pot marigold)

The multipetaled blossoms of the calendula, a Mediterranean annual, bloom from winter to spring in a cool greenhouse, providing cut flowers for bouquets in colors ranging

CALANTHE ORCHID
Calanthe vestita

POCKETBOOK FLOWER
Calceolaria herbeohybrida 'Multiflora Mixed'

CALENDULA
Calendula officinalis 'Pacific Beauty'

from creamy white and pale yellow to bright orange and rust red. The flowers are 2 to 4 inches across; the stems 18 to 24 inches high; and the thick, pale green leaves that clasp the stem are 2 to 3 inches long.

HOW TO GROW. Calendulas thrive in night temperatures of 40° to 50° and day temperatures 10° to 15° higher. They need full sun and a well-drained commercial potting soil. Sow seeds in a cool place, preferably a cold frame, in late August or September for continuous blooms from November to May. Transfer the seedlings to benches in the greenhouse when they are about 1 inch high, spacing them 8 to 12 inches apart. When the plants are 4 to 6 inches tall, pinch back the tips to encourage branching, and feed them every two weeks with a liquid fertilizer diluted to half the strength recommended on the label. Water sparingly, just enough to moisten the soil; provide good air circulation and prevent stem rot. For many small flowers, allow the buds to develop naturally; for larger flowers, pinch off all but the main bud on each stem. Provide the plants with supports to keep their stems from falling over.

CAMELLIA
C. japonica (common camellia); *C. reticulata* (netvein camellia); *C. sasanqua* (sasanqua camellia)

The dark, evergreen leaves of the camellia, coupled with its large, beautifully formed flowers, make this native of China and Japan an attractive addition to the cool greenhouse. The flowers, which bloom from fall to spring, are pink, white, red or multicolored and range from 2 to 7 inches wide, depending on the variety and species; the leaves are up to 4 inches long. Outdoors, camellias grow into small trees but in the greenhouse they are normally pruned back to a height of 2½ to 3 feet, and are grown in 8- to 14-inch pots or tubs. The common camellia has big, 2- to 5-inch-wide blossoms shaped like roses or peonies, and comes in both single and double varieties; the blossoms often have dense clusters of yellow stamens in the center; the leaves are shiny. The netvein camellia has immense blossoms, 3 to 7 inches across; its leaves are dull green and leathery. The sasanqua camellia is a dainty, somewhat straggly plant with slender 1½- to 2-inch glossy leaves. Its single or semidouble flowers are 1½ to 2 inches across and look like wild roses.

HOW TO GROW. Camellias need variable temperatures during the year, depending on their stage of growth. From fall to spring, when they are in flower, they need night temperatures of 40° to 45° and day temperatures of no more than 68°; in fact, unlike most plants, camellias bloom most abundantly when night temperatures are barely above freezing. During the summer, when the buds are forming but before they become visible, the plants need night temperatures of 60° to 65°. Throughout the year, they do best in filtered sunlight, high humidity and good air circulation. Plant them in a commercial potting soil recommended for African violets, with a pH of 4.5 to 5.0. Keep the soil constantly moist and feed the plants three times each year—in early spring, late spring and midsummer—with an acid fertilizer recommended for camellias, azaleas and rhododendrons. Prune the plants after they have finished flowering to encourage branching or to reduce their size. For larger flowers, remove all except the main bud in each flower cluster when buds are about the size of peas. To keep camellias from becoming too large, repot them only when absolutely necessary. To propagate additional plants, take stem cuttings of new firm growth in the summer or fall and root them in a mixture of equal parts of moist peat moss and sand, heated from below to 70°. Camellias can also be propagated from seeds sown in the

NETVEIN CAMELLIA
Camellia reticulata 'Buddha'

spring, but seed-grown plants will not reach flowering size for four to seven years and are likely to be inferior to the named varieties sold by nurserymen.

CAMPANULA

C. isophylla (Italian bellflower)

The Italian bellflower, a late-summer- and fall-blooming perennial, succumbs to frost in northern gardens but will live for several years in the intermediate greenhouse. Its trailing stems, 6 to 12 inches long, and cascades of blue or white blossoms, 1 to 1½ inches across, make it a favorite plant for hanging baskets or for flowerpots placed at the edge of the greenhouse bench.

HOW TO GROW. Italian bellflowers do best in night temperatures of 50° to 55° and day temperatures of 68° to 72°. Place them in the sunniest part of the greenhouse during the winter; in the summer they should have partial shade or filtered sunlight. Grow them in a commercial potting soil recommended for African violets. Water well during the growing season, keeping the soil constantly moist but not soggy, and feed once a month with liquid fertilizer diluted to the strength recommended on the label. After the flowering season has passed, cut back the plants to about 2 inches from the base and allow the soil to become somewhat dry between waterings; do not feed the plants during this resting period. When new growth appears resume the regular schedule of feeding and watering. For abundant branching and more flowers, nip off the stem tips during the early stages of growth. Propagate from stem cuttings taken in the spring; root the cuttings in moist sand, perlite or vermiculite heated from the bottom to 65° to 75°. Italian bellflowers can also be propagated by dividing root clumps in the early spring.

CANDYTUFT See *Iberis*
CAPE COWSLIP See *Lachenalia*
CAPE JASMINE See *Gardenia*
CAPE PRIMROSE See *Streptocarpus*
CARDINAL FLOWER See *Rechsteineria*
CARNATION See *Dianthus*

CATTLEYA

C. hybrids (cattleya orchid)

The cattleya orchid, long associated with delicate corsages, is known for its spectacular, 5- to 7-inch blossoms which last on the plant for as long as six weeks. Originally from Central and South America, the various cattleya species have adapted so easily to the warm greenhouse that there are now literally thousands of hybrids, not only within the genus but with other genera as well, giving rise to such man-made genera as *Brassocattleya, Brassolaeliocattleya, Laeliocattleya* and *Sophralaeliocattleya*. They vary in color from pink to lavender, white, yellow, orange, red, green or even blue, and also come in versions that combine one color on the upper petals with another on the lower petal, or lip; sometimes the lip itself is bicolored and greatly ruffled. The flowers appear singly or in clusters atop stalks 10 to 18 inches tall, and bloom at various times of the year, depending on the variety. Cattleya orchids grow from swollen stems, or pseudobulbs, and each plant has either a single leaf or two or more leaves; the two versions are called unifoliates and bifoliates. They are all aerial plants, or epiphytes, clinging naturally to tree bark, but in the greenhouse they can be grown in pots.

HOW TO GROW. Cattleya orchids do best in night temperatures of 55° to 65°, day temperatures of 68° or higher, a humidity of 50 to 60 per cent and bright indirect sunlight. (If the foliage becomes dark green and the flowers do not devel-

MAY'S ITALIAN BELLFLOWER
Campanula isophylla 'Mayi'

CATTLEYA HYBRID ORCHID
Cattleya Bow Bells 'Christmas Chimes'

op, there may not be enough light.) Plant in 3- to 7-inch pots, depending on the size of the pseudobulbs, in a mixture of 2 parts fir bark to 1 part coarse peat moss. Moisten this mixture well before potting, but then water sparingly for two or three weeks (an initial period of semidryness encourages rooting). Mist the foliage daily, two or three times a day. When growth starts, water more frequently, usually two or three times a week in hot weather (smaller plants usually need to be watered more often). Feed the plants every two weeks during the growing season and every month thereafter, using a high-nitrogen orchid fertilizer such as one labeled 20-10-10, diluted in the proportion recommended on the label. Repot plants every two or three years, or when they grow over the edge of the pot. Do this immediately after they have finished flowering. Propagate additional plants by dividing clumps of pseudobulbs from mature plants, keeping four or five pseudobulbs in each clump.

CENTAUREA
C. cyanea (cornflower, bachelor's button)

The cornflower, a summertime favorite, can also be grown as a winter cut flower in the cool greenhouse. It varies in height from 1 to 3 feet, depending on the strain; the ones most suitable for greenhouse culture are the dwarf forms, 10 to 12 inches high with flowers about 1 inch across. The colors range from the traditional blue through shades of pink, red, lavender and white. Usually grown in planting benches by commercial florists, it is also suitable for pots.

HOW TO GROW. Cornflowers do well in night temperatures of 45° to 50° and day temperatures 10° to 15° higher. They need a well-drained commercial potting soil and should be kept rather dry. Feed them very sparingly if at all because of the natural density of their growth. For winter flowers, sow seeds outdoors in late summer or early fall, transplanting the seedlings to the greenhouse just before the first frost. Set them individually in 8-inch pots or space them 12 inches apart in benches. They will begin to blossom in February and continue to May. Alternatively, sow seeds in the greenhouse from November to January for flowers beginning in late March and continuing until June.

CHINESE LANTERN See *Abutilon*
CHRISTMAS HEATH See *Erica*

CHRYSANTHEMUM
C. frutescens (marguerite, Boston or Paris daisy); *C. morifolium,* also called *C. hortorum* (florists' chrysanthemum); *C. parthenium,* also called *Matricaria capensis* (feverfew)

Of the more than 100 species of chrysanthemums three are widely grown in cool greenhouses: marguerites, florists' chrysanthemums and feverfew. Marguerites look like perfectly formed daisies, 2 to 3 inches wide, with yellow centers and petals of white, yellow or pink. They grow in clumps 2 to 3 feet high, but begin to bloom when they are only 6 inches tall. Their lacy, gray-green leaves, 3 to 6 inches long, complement the flowers in cut-flower arrangements. Marguerites bloom chiefly in the spring, summer and fall, but if given additional artificial light will also bloom during the winter. Florists' chrysanthemums, hybrids of a parent species from central China, are 1 to 4 feet high and come in a fascinating array of shapes, sizes and petal configurations. Some are miniature pompon varieties; others have gigantic exhibition blossoms, 6 to 8 inches across. In some varieties the petals are slender and tubular and spring out from the center in rays; in others they curve inward and overlap to form globular flower heads; a third type has tubular petals that spread

CORNFLOWER
Centaurea cyanea

FLORISTS' CHRYSANTHEMUM
Chrysanthemum morifolium

open at the ends like tiny spoons; while others have flat petals like anemones or long, arching petals that end in hooks and look like spider legs. These many versions of the florists' chrysanthemum also come in many colors: white, yellow, gold, bronze, pink, lavender and crimson. The blossoms normally appear in the fall but their period of bloom can be manipulated to provide large quantities of long-lasting cut flowers at almost any time of year. Feverfew comes in only two colors, yellow and white. This small-flowered chrysanthemum, a native of Europe, bears numerous strong-smelling blossoms, each up to 1 inch across, in loose clusters at the ends of stems 1 to 3 feet tall. It comes in single- and double-flowered forms. Feverfew can be brought into bloom during the winter by giving it additional artificial light, but it is usually grown to blossom from early to late summer.

HOW TO GROW. Chrysanthemums do best in night temperatures of 40° to 50°, day temperatures of 68° or lower, and at least four hours of direct sunlight a day. Plant feverfew and marguerites in standard 5- to 8-inch pots, florists' chrysanthemums in 4- to 6-inch pots or in benches fitted with supporting frames. Fill the pots or benches with commercial potting soil. Space bench plants 8 to 12 inches apart, depending on the size. Keep the soil moist but not soggy during the growing season and feed the plants every two or three weeks with a liquid fertilizer diluted to the strength recommended on the label. When the plants are 6 to 8 inches high, pinch off the tips to encourage branching. For bushier plants and more blooms, pinch the tips of the new branches again when they are about 4 inches long. As the buds form on florists' chrysanthemums, a decision must be made concerning the number and size of flowers to be produced. If all the buds are allowed to mature there will be a maximum amount of flowers. If some of the side buds are removed, the flowers will be larger but fewer in number. In growing certain large-flowered varieties, only one bud is left on each stem so as to produce a maximum-sized flower. Stake pot-grown plants to prevent the weight of the blossoms from bending the stems. Chrysanthemums can be forced to bloom at any time of year by increasing or withholding light to match the length of the days and nights in autumn when they normally come into bloom. In general, chrysanthemums make nonflowering, vegetative growth when daylight exceeds 12 hours. When the hours of darkness are greater in number, the plants develop flower buds, no matter how small the plants may be. For that reason, chrysanthemums grown during the short days of winter to flower in the long days of summer must be given artificial light until they reach the appropriate vegetative stage. Then, to shorten the long days for bud production, they must be covered for part of the day with opaque material. This is an exacting cultural method used routinely by professional florists, but it requires unfailing attention to details. To propagate additional plants, take stem cuttings or divide root clumps in the spring. Place cuttings in damp sand to root, then transfer the rooted cuttings to 2½-inch pots or group several to a pot; a 6-inch pot will hold three young plants. Feverfew is often started from seed and should be sown in the early spring for early summer blossoms, and in the late spring for blossoms in the fall.

CITRUS

C. *limonia* (lemon); C. *mitis* (calamondin or Panama orange, dwarf orange); C. *sinensis* (sweet or common orange); C. *taitensis,* also called C. *taintense* (Otaheite orange, Tahiti orange)

All four of these citrus species are evergreen shrubs and trees, suitable for growing in tubs and pots, and prized in the

FEVERFEW
Chrysanthemum parthenium

intermediate greenhouse for their fragrance and their fruit. Their white blossoms, 1 inch wide, flower intermittently throughout the year but most abundantly during spring and fall. After the flowers disappear, their fruits decorate the plants for many months and the dark, leathery oval foliage is beautiful in all seasons. Although some of them grow into medium-sized trees in their native environments, greenhouse citrus plants are generally pruned to be kept under 4 feet. Two varieties of lemon are popular for greenhouse culture: one is *C. limonia meyeri,* or dwarf Chinese lemon, which bears 3-inch fruit that is less bitter than ordinary lemons; the other is *C. limonia ponderosa,* a hybrid that yields fruit weighing as much as 2½ pounds and measuring up to 5 inches long. The calamondin orange from the Philippines seldom grows more than 2 feet high in the greenhouse and bears small, very acid oranges, 1 to 2 inches in diameter, that can be used for marmalade. The sweet orange from Southeast Asia is the parent of many commercial hybrids and even the dwarf varieties produce delicious, full-sized fruit. The Tahiti orange is really from China; a natural dwarf, usually under 3 feet tall, it bears quantities of insipid-tasting flattened oval fruit, 1 to 1½ inches long.

HOW TO GROW. Citrus plants need night temperatures of 50° to 55°, day temperatures of 68° or slightly higher, and at least four to six hours of full sun. Plant them in tubs or pots 8 to 10 inches in diameter in a commercial potting soil recommended for African violets. Keep the soil constantly moist during the summer but allow it to dry out between waterings the rest of the year. Feed three times a year, in the very early spring, the early summer and the late summer with liquid fertilizer diluted to the strength recommended on the label. Prune tip growth at any time to keep the plants a manageable size. Propagate from stem cuttings taken in the late summer or early fall and rooted in moist sand.

CLERODENDRON See *Clerodendrum*

CLERODENDRUM, also called CLERODENDRON
C. fallax, also called *C. speciosissimum; C. fragrans pleniflorum; C. thomsonae* (all called glory bower)

The clerodendrums, a large group of vigorously growing tropical plants and vines, are versatile plants for the warm greenhouse: they can be trimmed to pot size, trained to a trellis or used for hanging baskets. All of them are noted for their colorful clusters of flowers, which, under good growing conditions, are produced throughout the year. Those of *C. fallax,* a 2- to 4-foot-tall Japanese shrub, are brilliant red, 1½ to 2 inches wide, and bloom in pyramidal clusters 6 to 10 inches or more high. The flowers of *C. fragrans pleniflorum,* a 3- to 5-foot-tall shrub from China and Japan, are hyacinth scented and are borne in rounded clusters 4 inches across; the individual 1-inch blossoms are pink and white and are double petaled. *C. thomsonae,* a vine from West Africa that may grow as tall as 12 feet, blossoms when it is only 1 foot tall. It bears a loose floral spray, 2 to 3 inches across, at the end of each stem, and is often called the bleeding-heart vine because its blood-red petals seem to bleed from the heart of its 1-inch snow-white puffy base, or calyx. The foliage of the clerodendrums is downy or hairy, deeply veined, and ranges in size from 3 to 12 inches long. *C. fallax* and *C. fragrans pleniflorum* are generally grown as shrubs in large tubs or 12-inch pots, and are pruned back to any desired height by pinching off the stem tips from time to time. *C. thomsonae* can also be grown in pots, but is especially suited to hanging baskets or for training to grow up a greenhouse trellis from a tub or directly from the ground.

CALAMONDIN ORANGE
Citrus mitis

HOW TO GROW. Clerodendrums need night temperatures of 60° to 65° and day temperatures of at least 70°. They do best in full sun but will tolerate light shade in midsummer. Plant them in a commercial potting soil. To keep them in blossom over the longest possible season, keep the soil moist and feed them every two weeks with a liquid fertilizer diluted to half the strength recommended on the label. After each crop of flowers, cut back the tips of the branches to stimulate new growth and more flowers. For spring and summer flowers only, keep the soil moist during the growing season and fairly dry from late fall through winter, when the plants will rest. During this period it is best to keep the plants in temperatures below 60°. When flowers are desired, raise the night temperature back to 60° to 65°, and increase water. Propagate from stem cuttings of new growth taken at any time and root them in moist sand heated from the bottom to a temperature of 70° to 80°.

COELOGYNE
C. cristata; C. massangeana; C. mooreana (all called coelogyne orchids)

The dainty flowers of the tropical coelogyne orchid, so popular for wedding bouquets, make it a sensational hanging plant for the warm greenhouse. *C. cristata,* a native of India and Ceylon, bears cascading sprays of wavy-petaled flowers, 3 to 5 inches across, that are white tinged with yellow in the centers; it blooms from the late fall to early spring. *C. massangeana,* from Malaysia, produces drooping clusters of fragrant 2-inch yellow flowers with dramatic dark brown markings, from spring through fall. *C. mooreana,* a Vietnamese orchid, produces tall spikes of five to 10 white blossoms streaked with yellow during the winter; the individual blossoms may be 3 to 4 inches wide. All of these coelogyne orchids grow from short, oblong pseudobulbs, or thickened stems, and have two narrow, deeply ribbed, dark evergreen leaves, 9 to 16 inches long. Because they are epiphytic, or air growing, they take naturally to hanging baskets, but they can also be set individually in 5- to 7-inch pots and placed on shelves against the walls of the greenhouse.

HOW TO GROW. Coelogyne orchids do best in night temperatures of 55° to 65° and day temperatures of 60° to 75°, although they will tolerate night temperatures as low as 50° in the winter. They thrive in humidity of 50 to 60 per cent and require bright indirect light during the winter, light shade the rest of the year. Plant them in a mixture of 2 parts fir bark to 1 part coarse peat moss.. Water the plants generously during the growing season, keeping the growing medium constantly damp. After they have flowered, allow the growing medium to become almost dry, giving the plants just enough water to keep the pseudobulbs from withering. Then, when new growth begins, resume regular waterings. Feed the plants every two weeks during the growing season with a high nitrogen orchid fertilizer, such as one labeled 20-10-10 diluted as instructed on the label. Do not feed the plants and give them less water when they are resting. Coelogyne orchids are not readily transplanted and should be repotted only when absolutely necessary. Propagate by dividing the bulb clumps of mature plants, keeping three to four bulbs or more to a cluster.

COLUMNEA
C. affinus; C. gloriosa; C. hybrida banksii; C. linearis (all called columnea)

The columneas are tropical trailing plants from Central and South America for the warm greenhouse. They have exotic-looking tubular flowers, 2 to 4 inches long, in many

GLORY BOWER
Clerodendrum thomsonae

COELOGYNE ORCHID
Coelogyne cristata 'Orchid Hill'

BANKS'S COLUMNEA
Columnea 'Banksii'

LARKSPUR
Consolida ambigua

shades of orange, red and yellow. The flowers, which bloom throughout the year, are often covered with fine hairs. Pairs of waxy or hairy leaves, 1 to 5 inches long, grow from stems up to 4 feet long. Frequently white berry-like fruit, ½ inch in diameter, appears after the flowers. *C. affinus* bears yellow flowers covered with orange hairs; *C. gloriosa* has red blossoms with yellow throats; *C. hybrida banksii,* reddish brown flowers with hairs of the same color; *C. linearis,* pink blossoms with white hairs. All are gesneriads and are epiphytes, growing naturally from the branches of trees. In the warm greenhouse they are excellent for hanging baskets.

HOW TO GROW. Columneas thrive in night temperatures of 65° to 70° and day temperatures of over 75°, but for the most luxuriant blooms they should have a period of semidormancy in the winter, when night temperatures are reduced to 50° to 60°. They need bright light but should be shielded from the direct rays of the sun in the spring and summer. Plant them in a commercial potting soil recommended for African violets. Keep this mixture moist at all times and provide the plants with high humidity. Feed them once a month during their active growing season with a liquid fertilizer diluted to half the strength recommended on the label. To stimulate new growth, prune branches that are no longer in flower. Propagate additional plants from stem cuttings at any time. Start them in moist sand or vermiculite heated from the bottom to 75° to 85°. Columneas can also be propagated from seeds sown in the early spring in moist sand or vermiculite also heated from the bottom to between 75° and 85°. Transplant the seedlings into planting cubes when the first new leaves appear, and then into pots or baskets when the seedlings are 2 to 3 inches high.

COMMON STOCK See *Mathiola*

CONSOLIDA

C. hybrids, also called *Delphinium ajacis* (larkspur)

The tall, graceful larkspurs are grown as bench plants in the cool greenhouse for cut flowers in late spring and early summer. These annuals are often confused with the perennial delphiniums because their flower spikes and feathery foliage are similar, but the larkspurs belong to a separate genus. Larkspurs come in two types: branching varieties with many flower stalks springing from the base of each plant, and hyacinth-flowered types with only one flower spike. The latter variety blooms about a month earlier. Both types grow 3 to 5 feet high and have delicately petaled flowers in shades of pink, blue, purple and white.

HOW TO GROW. Larkspurs need full sun, night temperatures between 50° and 55°, and day temperatures of 55° or higher. Sow seeds in a bench fitted with a supporting frame, in a commercial potting soil. For a continuous supply of flowers from late April through June, sow seeds in September and October. Space rows about 12 inches apart and thin seedlings to stand 12 inches apart. To stimulate long stems, keep the temperature at 50° for the first two months, then raise it to 55° or slightly higher. Feed every two weeks with a liquid fertilizer diluted to half the strength recommended on the label. Allow the soil to become fairly dry between thorough waterings.

CORNFLOWER See *Centaurea*
COWSLIP, CAPE See *Lachenalia*

CROCUS
C. hybrids

When grown in the cool greenhouse, the gaily colored,

cup-shaped blossoms of the early-blooming crocuses, 1 to 2 inches wide, are midwinter reminders that spring is on its way. Flowers are varying shades of purple, blue, yellow and white. Queen of the Blues (dark blue), Striped Beauty (white striped with blue), Remembrance (purple), Snowstorm (white), Vanguard (lilac) and E. P. Bowles (yellow) are among the popular types available. After they flower, these bulb plants send up grasslike leaves 4 to 5 inches high. They are generally planted in groups in shallow pots.

HOW TO GROW. Crocuses do best in full sun, night temperatures of 45° to 50° and day temperatures of 68° or lower when they are in flower. But initially, when the roots are growing, they need moisture, darkness and temperatures between 40° and 45°. Plant the bulbs, or corms, using the largest-sized ones available, in shallow containers in October, putting four to seven corms in a container 5 to 7 inches in diameter. Use a commercial potting soil, adding a teaspoon of bone meal to each pot. Cover the corms with about an inch of soil and place them in a cold frame until roots form, 10 weeks or longer, then bring them into the greenhouse for blooming four to six weeks later. After they have flowered, plant crocuses outdoors, where they will revert to their natural cycle and bloom the following spring; they do not do well when forced to bloom out of season two years in a row.

CRYPTANTHUS
C. bivittatus, also called *C. rosea picta; C. fosteriana; C. zonatus zebrinus* (all called earth star)

The earth star gets its name from the starlike circle, or rosette, made by its stiff, spreading, strangely colored leaves. It is grown for this variegated foliage rather than its central clump of stemless summer-blooming white flowers. A bromeliad from the tropical rain forests and swamps of Central and South America, the earth star grows naturally on trees but adapts easily to pots, and makes a year-round splash of color in the warm greenhouse. All three species listed here have leaves 5 to 9 inches long and 1 to 1½ inches wide. Those of *C. bivittatus* are bronze-green striped with white on top, bronze on the underside, and have spiny edges. The wavy-edged dark brown leaves of *C. fosteriana* are patterned with zigzag streaks of gray-green, purple or red. *C. zonatus zebrinus* has horizontal zebra stripes of silver-gray on reddish brown or copper, with a white underside and crinkled edges.

HOW TO GROW. Earth stars do best in night temperatures of 60° to 65°, day temperature of 70° or higher, and filtered sunlight. They need a humid atmosphere in the summer, less humidity in the winter. Plant them in a commercial potting soil recommended for African violets. They can be anchored on pieces of bark, or placed in pots or baskets. Water until the soil is moist but not soggy, and allow the soil to dry slightly between waterings. Feed plants with a liquid fertilizer diluted to half the strength recommended on the label at monthly intervals from midspring through early fall. Propagate additional plants from the small shoots that appear between the leaves at the center of the plant, or by dividing the swollen roots, the rhizomes, in the spring.

CYCLAMEN
C. persicum (cyclamen, Persian violet)

The distinctive blossoms of the cyclamen, in shades of pink, red, purple and white, hover like butterflies over this plant from midfall to early spring. A native of the eastern Mediterranean, it comes in some 20 different species, of which *C. persicum* is especially suitable for the cool greenhouse. *C. persicum* grows 8 to 14 inches tall, depending on whether the strain chosen is a miniature or full-sized plant. It

DUTCH CROCUS
Crocus hybrid 'Vanguard'

EARTH STAR
Cryptanthus bivittatus 'Ti'

CYCLAMEN
Cyclamen persicum

has long-stemmed kidney-shaped leaves, sometimes with silver markings. The flowers, sometimes scented, are 2 to 3 inches wide, and in addition to decorating the greenhouse make long-lasting cut flowers.

HOW TO GROW. Cyclamens need night temperatures of 40° to 55°, day temperatures of 60° to 70°, and good ventilation and humidity. They should have full sun except during the summer, when the plants should be kept in partial shade. Grow them in a commercial potting soil with a pH of 5.8 to 6.5. During the flowering season, keep the soil constantly moist and feed every two weeks with liquid fertilizer diluted to half the strength recommended on the label. After flowering, reduce the frequency of watering, providing just enough moisture to keep the soil from drying out, and allow plants to rest until midsummer. Then repot in fresh soil, allowing the beetlike root, called a corm, to stick halfway out of the potting soil. Cyclamens are usually propagated from seed sown directly in shallow boxes of potting soil 1 inch apart. Keep the seedbed moist and shaded until the seeds germinate, which may be seven to eight weeks, and then move them into the sun. Transplant seedlings into 2½-inch pots, and then into larger pots as needed. The seeds of some miniature types of *C. persicum* will reach flowering size in four to six months, but the large-flowering strains require a minimum of 12 to 15 months to reach maturity. Seeds of these types sown in midsummer will begin to blossom in the fall of the following year and will continue to blossom for a six-month period that year and many years thereafter.

CYCNOCHES
C. chlorochilon (swan orchid)

The swan orchid gets its name from the long, curving column that emerges from the center of the flower like an upside-down swan's neck. An epiphytic, or air-growing, orchid from Colombia, Panama, Venezuela and the Guianas, it is easily cultivated in the warm greenhouse in hanging baskets or in pots. The species *C. chlorochilon* bears graceful sprays of two to 10 fragrant chartreuse flowers, 5 to 6 inches wide, during the late fall or winter. Just before blooming, the plant begins to shed its leaves.

HOW TO GROW. Swan orchids do best in night temperatures of 65° to 75°, day temperatures of 75° or higher, bright indirect sunlight and high humidity. Plant them in a mixture of equal parts of fir bark, redwood-bark fiber and coarse peat moss. Put pots on a humidifying tray and spray hanging baskets daily. During the active growing season keep the potting medium barely moist and feed the plants monthly with a high nitrogen orchid fertilizer, such as one labeled 20-10-10, diluted as instructed on the label. After flowering, when plants become semidormant, reduce the light and do not water or fertilize until new growth appears, but mist the swollen parts of the stem, called pseudobulbs, occasionally to keep them from withering. When new growth appears, repot the plants in fresh potting medium, removing any withered bulbs. Propagate additional plants by dividing the pseudobulbs right after the plant has flowered; replant in groups of three to five bulbs to a 5- to 6-inch pot.

CYMBIDIUM
C. standards and miniature hybrids

Cymbidium orchids, from Asia and the Pacific islands, are semiterrestrial plants that grow in soil as well as in bark. Their long, tapering leaves are evergreen, and their waxy flowers bloom in arching sprays that stay fresh for two or three months. The larger types, called standards, bloom during the winter and early spring. Their stems are 1½ to 3 feet

SWAN ORCHID
Cycnoches chlorochilon 'Tinnie'

high and bear sprays of 10 to 20 or more flowers, 3 to 4 inches wide. Originally from the high Himalayas, they are cool greenhouse plants. The miniature cymbidiums, from Japan and China, are rarely more than 12 to 15 inches high, and bear a profusion of flowers, as many as 30 or more to an average-sized plant growing in a 5- or 6-inch pot. Older plants in larger pots may have more than 100 blossoms. The flowers are 2 to 4 inches wide and bloom from fall to spring, depending on the variety. These miniature cymbidiums derive from warm-climate plants and are generally grown in a moderately warm greenhouse although they will tolerate the cooler conditions suited to the larger types. Both standard and miniature cymbidiums come in colors that range from rich mahogany, bronze and maroon to chartreuse, yellow, pink and ivory.

HOW TO GROW. Standard cymbidiums do best in night temperatures of 45° to 50° during the winter and up to 60° during the summer; daytime temperatures should be about 10° higher. Miniature cymbidiums will tolerate the same temperatures but ideally should have night temperatures of 50° to 60° and day temperatures of 68° or higher. They need constantly circulating air and at least four hours of bright filtered sunlight a day, but should be shaded from the hot midday sun to prevent the leaves from turning brown. Plant standard-sized cymbidiums in tubs or pots that are large enough (10 to 12 inches) that they need not be disturbed more often than every two to four years; miniature plants do well in 4- to 6-inch pots. Use a mixture of 2 parts fir bark to 1 part coarse peat moss. Water regularly during the growing season, keeping the potting medium moist but not soggy. When the plants have finished blooming, water less frequently but do not let the potting medium dry out completely. Feed once a month during the growing season with a high nitrogen fertilizer, such as one labeled 20-10-10, diluted ¼ teaspoon to a quart of water. Repot when necessary, immediately after the flowers have finished blooming. For additional plants, separate groups of swollen stems, or pseudobulbs, at the time of repotting, keeping at least four to six bulbs in the new clusters.

CYTISUS

C. canariensis (florists' genista, yellow broom)

The delicately scented genistas, with their bright yellow flower spikes, perfume the greenhouse in spring. They are related to the pea and bear ½-inch pealike blossoms in great profusion. Their clover-like leaves, each segment of which is ¼ to ½ inch long, are covered with silky hairs. These evergreen shrubs grow up to 6 feet tall in their native Canary Islands but they are usually kept pruned back to 3 feet or less in the cool greenhouse, where they are maintained in 5- to 8-inch pots or small tubs.

HOW TO GROW. Genistas do best in night temperatures of 45° to 50°, and day temperatures below 60°; their flower buds will not form unless temperatures remain below 60° for more than four months. They need full sun. Plant them in pots in a mixture of equal parts commercial potting soil and sand. During the growing season, keep the soil constantly moist and feed the plants once a month with a liquid fertilizer diluted to half the strength recommended on the label. When the plants are resting, keep the soil barely damp and do not feed. Genistas do best if placed outdoors in the summer and brought back into the greenhouse in the early fall. Pinch back the stem tips occasionally until early fall to encourage branching. After they have finished flowering, prune them back to about 6 inches from the pot, or at least remove the straggly growth. Repotting should also be done

CYMBIDIUM ORCHID
Cymbidium 'Ivy Fung'

FLORISTS' GENISTA
Cytisus canariensis

CANDLE DELPHINIUM
Delphinium elatum 'Pacific Hybrids'

at this time. For additional plants, take stem cuttings of new growth in the spring and root them in sand heated from the bottom to a temperature of 70°.

D

DAISY, BARBERTON See *Gerbera*
DAISY, BOSTON See *Chrysanthemum*
DAISY, GERBERA See *Gerbera*
DAISY, PARIS See *Chrysanthemum*
DAISY, TRANSVAAL See *Gerbera*
DANCING DOLLS See *Oncidium*
DARLING RIVER PEA See *Swainsona*

DELPHINIUM

D. elatum hybrids (candle delphinium, bee delphinium)

The stately candle delphinium, backdrop of so many garden borders, can be moved into the intermediate greenhouse in the fall to provide spectacular wands of 2- to 3-inch single- or double-petaled flowers in blue, purple, white, mauve and sometimes yellow and red during the winter. These gigantic hybrids may tower 5 to 6 feet or more and make excellent cut flowers. The most commonly grown greenhouse varieties are Pacific hybrids, Blackmore and Langdon hybrids and Wrexham hybrids. They can be grown in pots or planting benches, but because of their height they are more suited to ground-level beds. Though actually perennials, under greenhouse culture delphiniums are treated as annuals.

HOW TO GROW. Delphiniums do best with night temperatures of 50° to 55°, day temperatures of about 60°, and full sun. Delphiniums are usually propagated from seed because seed-grown plants are stronger and healthier. Sow seeds in the spring or early summer in the open garden or a cold frame. They germinate best at temperatures of 50° to 55°. Transplant the seedlings into rows or beds, setting them 6 to 8 inches apart, and leave them there until late fall. Then dig them up, with as much soil as possible clinging to their roots, and store them in a cold frame until midwinter, when they can be brought into the greenhouse. Plant them in pots or benches in commercial potting soil. Water sparingly at first, keeping the soil barely moist until new growth starts. Then increase frequency of watering and feed the plants once a month with a liquid fertilizer diluted to the strength recommended on the label. Stake plants or provide them with wire supports to prevent the tall stems from bending. Flower spikes will be ready for cutting eight to 10 weeks after planting, and frequent cutting will stimulate the plant to produce second and sometimes third crops.

DENDROBIUM

D. aggregatum majus; D. chrysotoxum; D. nobile; D. phalaenopsis (all called dendrobium orchid)

The dendrobium orchids, natives of Asia and the South Pacific, are epiphytic, or air growing, and fall into two distinct groups: cool-growing deciduous species whose two-year-old stems lose their leaves just before a period of flowering, and warm-temperature, evergreen species that keep their leaves year round. The dendrobiums also have two distinct habits of growth: in some, the flowers are borne in long graceful sprays from the upper end of a jointed, canelike stem; in others, the blossoms cluster at the joints, or nodes, of the stem itself. The spring-flowering A. *aggregatum majus* from Burma, India and south China, is a dwarf evergreen species, about 3 to 4 inches high, whose squat pseudobulb produces only one leaf. Its orange- or pink-tinged yellow flowers, 2 inches across, hang in clusters of 10 to 30 blooms along an arching stem. The orchid *D. chrysotoxum* from

Burma, also evergreen, rises 15 inches high and produces six to eight thick leaves. Its deep-yellow flowers, 2 inches across, bloom in the spring in clusters of seven to 15 at nodes along arching stems 6 to 12 inches long. One of the most popular dendrobiums, *D. nobile,* is a deciduous species from the Himalayas. It bears drooping clusters of two or three flowers at the upper joints, or nodes, of its 18- to 24-inch-tall cane-like stems. The velvety flowers, 2 to 4 inches across, are white with purple tips and dark red or purple centers. Often grown commercially for corsages, they bloom from late winter to early summer and are long lasting. *D. phalaenopsis,* an evergreen species from the jungles of New Guinea, Australia and the Pacific islands, bears flowers throughout the year. The flowers appear on long, arching sprays of 10 to 15 blossoms at the end of the 18- to 24-inch-tall canelike stems. The individual flowers, 2 to 4 inches across, vary in color from pale violet to deep purple to white tinged with rose, and last as long as three months. Often two or three crops of flowers will bloom on the same cane.

HOW TO GROW. The evergreen dendrobiums do best at night temperatures of 60°, and day temperatures about 10° higher. The deciduous dendrobiums need night temperatures of about 50° during the winter, when they are dormant, and 55° to 60° during the growing and flowering seasons; day temperatures should be about 10° to 15° higher. They require indirect or filtered sunlight. Plant them in pots in a mixture of 2 parts fir bark to 1 part coarse peat moss. As air plants, they may also be grown on a slab of tree fern. During the growing season, keep the potting mixture moist and feed the plants once a month with a high-nitrogen orchid fertilizer, such as one labeled 20-10-10, diluted as instructed on the label. When the deciduous species have flowered, stop feeding and cut down on water, giving them only enough to keep the pseudobulbs from shriveling. Resume normal watering and feeding when new growth appears. Evergreen species should be watered and fed year round. Repot mature plants only when absolutely necessary, approximately every two or three years; the time for repotting is after flowering or when new growth begins. Propagate by dividing pseudobulbs at the time of repotting, keeping three or four bulbs to a cluster. Or propagate from offsets that form at the joints, or nodes, along the canelike stem; root these offsets in sand.

DIANTHUS

D. caryophyllus (carnation)

The carnation is second only to the rose in popularity as a greenhouse-grown cut flower. It is especially suited to growing in benches in the cool intermediate greenhouse, although in small greenhouses it is sometimes practical to grow a few in pots. Standard carnations are up to 3 feet tall and bear 1- to 3-inch-wide double blossoms in yellow, red, pink, white and bicolor mixtures; miniature carnations are the same height but produce flowers half this size. The flowers bloom continuously for 10 months or more, from fall until late spring or early summer, a few at a time on each plant. The foliage is blue-gray and the fragrance is clovelike.

HOW TO GROW. Carnations do best in full sun, in night temperatures of 50° to 55° and day temperatures of 10° to 15° higher. Greenhouse carnations are generally propagated vegetatively. Although it is sometimes possible to buy seeds for them, the resulting plants will be vastly inferior to plants grown from cuttings of named varieties. These can be purchased from nurseries, rooted or unrooted (sometimes you can use side shoots of carnations purchased from florists as cuttings). The best time to take cuttings is from December through February; given good growing conditions, these will

DENDROBIUM ORCHID
Dendrobium nobile 'Oroville'

CARNATION
Dianthus caryophyllus

develop into sturdy, many-stemmed plants by early June. Plant the rooted cuttings in commercial potting soil and, when they are 4 to 5 inches tall, pinch off the tip growth to produce side shoots. Continue to pinch off tips as the plant develops, to encourage branching. When the plants are about 6 inches high, set them in planting benches, spacing them 8 inches apart and setting them the same depth at which they were previously growing. Feed them every two weeks with a liquid fertilizer diluted to the strength recommended on the label. For flowers beginning in early fall, do not pinch the plants after early June, but allow the stems to elongate. Provide the stems with wire and string supports to keep them from bending. Ideally, new plants should be started each year, but some growers allow the plants to flower a second season. If the plants are cut back in early summer and all weak or straggly growth is removed, flowers will appear again in early fall.

To produce the large-flowered carnations sold by florists, it is necessary to start with a large-flowered variety and then disbud the stems so that only the terminal bud matures. Do not disbud miniature carnations, which have a more graceful, open habit of growth and should be allowed to develop naturally, producing many small flowers on one stem.

DIPLADENIA

D. amoena, also called *Mandevillea amabilis; D. rosacea* hybrid

A native of Brazil, the dipladenia is a tropical vine that bears handsome trumpet-shaped blossoms, 2½ to 3½ inches wide. *D. amoena's* blossoms are pink shading into rose; those of *D. rosacea* are rose-pink with a deeper border. The plants bloom for six months, from early spring until fall, and when not in bloom they ornament the warm greenhouse with their glossy evergreen foliage. The dipladenia is usually grown as a pot plant, and its twining stems are trained to a trellis or a shaped wire form, such as a globe or a cone. Its ultimate height of 10 feet is easily controlled by pruning. Plants often begin to blossom when they are only 1 foot tall.

HOW TO GROW. Dipladenia does best in night temperatures from 60° to 65° and day temperatures of at least 70°. It needs bright sunlight in the fall and winter, and light shade during the late spring and summer. Plant in commercial potting soil. Allow the soil to become dry on the surface between waterings, and feed the plant every two weeks during the growing season with a liquid fertilizer diluted to half the strength recommended on the label. Do not feed the plants when they have completed their period of bloom until new growth starts. Pruning should also be done just as the new growth starts. Repot the plants in early spring to larger containers, as needed. Propagate new plants from stem cuttings removed while pruning in the early spring, and root them in coarse sand, kept moist and heated from the bottom to 70°. Shade the cuttings until the roots form, usually in three or four weeks, then transplant them into pots.

DOUBLE-DECKER PLANT See *Rechsteineria*

E

EARTH STAR See *Cryptanthus*
EDELWEISS, BRAZILIAN See *Rechsteineria*

EPIDENDRUM

E. cochleatum (clamshell orchid); *E. fragrans; E. mariae,* also called 'Mariae Ames'; *E. O'brienianum* (all called epidendrum orchids)

Epidendrum orchids grow naturally in the American trop-

DIPLADENIA
Dipladenia hybrid 'Rosacea'

ics from Florida to Brazil, and come in more than 500 varieties. Most of them are epiphytic, forming large clusters on the branches of trees and sending out aerial roots for food and support. Adapted to both warm and intermediate greenhouses, they are best displayed in hanging baskets where they can get the fresh air and good drainage they require. *E. cochleatum,* the clamshell orchid, bears its delicately scented flowers upside down in clusters of three to 10 at the ends of 10-inch stems. It has spidery yellow-green petals, 2½ to 3½ inches long, and a distinctive shell-shaped lower lip with purplish-black and green markings. This species is nearly everblooming and flowers may appear at any time of the year. Spicy-scented *E. fragrans* resembles *E. cochleatum* in its habit of growth, but its 2-inch flowers have creamy white curling petals and a heart-shaped lip striped in red or purple. The flowers bloom from late summer and early fall. The tiny *E. mariae* grows only 6 to 8 inches tall but bears one to four blossoms at the end of the flower spikes; the slender petals are yellow-green and surround the 2-inch ruffly lip, which is snowy white with green veins. It blooms in midsummer. *E. O'brienianum* is often called a reed-stem epidendrum because of its slender stems, 2 or 3 feet tall, topped by clusters of 1- to 1½-inch bright orange-red flowers with touches of yellow on the lip. It blooms year round.

HOW TO GROW. Epidendrums are less particular about temperatures than some orchids. They do well in night temperatures of 50° to 65°, and day temperatures of 65° to 75°. Most of the epidendrums need bright indirect sunlight, but *E. O'brienianum* needs full sunshine. Plant them in a mixture of 2 parts fir bark to 1 part coarse peat moss. Water the newly potted plants lightly, until the growing medium is barely damp to the touch, and mist them frequently until the new roots are established. During their period of lush growth, drench the plants, then allow them to become almost dry before watering them again. Feed them monthly during the growing season with a high-nitrogen orchid fertilizer, such as one labeled 20-10-10, diluted as instructed on the label. Repot epidendrums when aerial roots creep over the edges of pots, usually every year or two.

EPIPHYLLUM

E. ackermannii, also called *Nopalxochia ackermannii* (red orchid cactus); *E. oxypetalum,* also called *Phyllocactus latifrons* (queen of the night); *E.* hybrids (all called orchid cactus)

The epiphyllum is a jungle cactus, more at home in the company of orchids than with the more familiar desert-type cacti. It is a plant for cool, intermediate and warm greenhouses and is effective in hanging baskets because it is epiphytic, growing naturally among the branches of trees in Brazilian rain forests. It has soft, flattened stems that look like leaves with scalloped edges, and from the edges of these leaf-stems spectacular flowers grow. Most of the flowers appear in late winter and spring, blooming at various times of day: some blossom in the daylight hours, others bloom only at night. *E. ackermannii,* which blooms in the daytime, has curving stems as much as 3 feet long, and bears 4- to 6-inch-wide scarlet flowers with greenish-yellow throats. *E. oxypetalum* is a rambling plant that grows to 20 or 30 feet in the wild, but as a pot plant can be kept to any desired size. Each powerfully perfumed white flower blooms for only one night, but the plant produces the 4- to 6-inch star-shaped blossoms continually throughout the spring. The many hybrid varieties, some of which flower at night and some during the day, bear blossoms in white, cream, yellow, pink, rose, red, orange, bronze, purple, orchid or combinations of these colors.

EPIDENDRUM ORCHID
Epidendrum mariae

ORCHID CACTUS
Epiphyllum hybrid

FLAME VIOLET
Episcia cupreata 'Chocolate Soldier'

CHRISTMAS HEATH
Erica canaliculata

HOW TO GROW. The epiphyllums do best in a greenhouse with night temperatures of 50° to 55°, and day temperatures of 65° to 70°; but they tolerate a wider temperature variation. They need bright indirect sunlight, high humidity and more frequent waterings than their desert-blooming cousins. Plant them in commercial potting soil recommended for African violets. Water newly potted plants lightly and let the soil become almost dry before watering them again. After the roots are established, in a week or two, keep the soil barely moist. Feed every two weeks from April to August with a low-nitrogen fertilizer, such as one labeled 5-10-10, diluted to the strength recommended on the label. During the rest of the year, keep the soil on the dry side and do not fertilize. To control the length of stems, pinch back the tips when flowering has ceased. Propagate additional plants from stem cuttings taken at any time. Cut the stems into 3- to 4-inch pieces, inserting their lower ends into damp coarse sand. Plants can also be started from seed but may take three years or more to reach blooming size. When epiphyllums become rootbound, repot them immediately after the blooming season. During the summer the plants can be hung outside in the shade of trees and will fare even better there than in the hot greenhouse.

EPISCIA
E. cupreata; E. dianthiflora; E. lilacina; E. punctata (all called episcia or flame violet)

Episcia is a gesneriad with the typically lobed flowers of that plant family but it is most admired for its dramatic foliage, which combines a puckery texture with colorings of red, purple, bronze, copper and silver, as well as the customary green. In the tropical jungles of Central America, episcias are creeping ground covers, but in the warm greenhouse they are especially suited to hanging baskets. Their tiny tubular flowers are 1 to 2 inches long, ½ to 1 inch wide, and bloom continuously from early spring to early fall. *E. cupreata* has vivid orange-red flowers and downy leaves, 2 to 3 inches long, variously marked with copper-, bronze- or silver-colored areas; its stems are seldom more than 6 inches high. *E. dianthiflora* has 1½-inch oval, velvety, green leaves with purple midribs and white blossoms; it forms a mound about 4 inches high. *E. lilacina*'s 3- to 4-inch-long leaves are dark bronze-green and its 1- to 1½-inch flowers are lavender. *E. punctata*'s 3-inch hairy leaves are green with red-purple midribs, and its 1-inch yellow-white flowers are spotted with purple.

HOW TO GROW. Episcias do best in night temperatures of 65° to 70° and day temperatures of 75° or higher. They need high humidity and bright indirect light rather than full sun; the latter will bleach and burn their delicately marked foliage. Good air circulation is essential. Plant them in pots or hanging baskets in commercial potting soil recommended for African violets. Keep the soil moist but not soggy, and feed the plants once a month during the growing season with a liquid fertilizer diluted to the strength recommended on the label. Pinch growing stems to encourage branching, and cut back any straggly stems when they have stopped blooming to encourage fresh growth. Propagate additional plants from runners or from stem cuttings taken at any time. Root the cuttings in damp sand, perlite or vermiculite.

ERICA
E. canaliculata (Christmas heath)

Christmas heath is an evergreen South African shrub that blooms in the fall and winter, and is often cut and sold by florists as heather, although heather actually belongs to a different genus. It is a pot plant for the cool greenhouse, growing 1 to 2 feet high, with immense quantities of bell-shaped ⅛-inch flowers that cluster along the delicate, densely branched stems. The stems are covered with ¼-inch-long needle-like dark green leaves.

HOW TO GROW. Heath does best in night temperatures between 40° and 50°, and day temperatures no higher than 65°. The plants should be kept lightly shaded through the summer but need direct sun from fall through spring. They are related to azaleas and rhododendrons, and grow in a similarly acid soil, a commercial potting soil recommended for African violets, with a pH of 4.5 to 5.5. The soil for heath should never be allowed to dry out between waterings. Feed twice a year, once in the early spring and then again about a month later with a light dusting of cottonseed meal or rhododendron-azalea-camellia fertilizer. Do not cultivate the soil around heath because its shallow roots are easily damaged. Propagate additional plants from stem cuttings taken from November through January; root them in a damp mixture of equal parts of sand and peat moss heated from the bottom to 60° to 65°. Roots take six to eight weeks to form; two years are required for plants to reach blooming size.

EUPHORBIA
E. fulgens, also called *E. jacquinaeflora* (scarlet plume); *E. pulcherrima* (poinsettia)

The poinsettia and its less well-known relative, the scarlet plume, are winter-blooming tropical shrubs from Central America, suitable for the warm greenhouse. Both have evergreen leaves and inconspicuous yellow flowers surrounded by brilliantly colored bracts, or flower-leaves, that are often mistaken for the flowers themselves. The flowers of the poinsettia are at the end of the stems, while those of the scarlet plume are clustered at intervals along the stem. The poinsettia has leaves and bracts 4 to 7 inches long; in mild climates it is a shrub that reaches a height of 10 feet, but in the greenhouse it is grown as a decorative pot plant. The scarlet plume, a smaller plant, has arching stems 2 feet long and slender willow-like leaves; great numbers of the ½-inch orange-scarlet blossoms line the stems during the winter months. Like the poinsettia, scarlet plume can be used for cut flowers in addition to being grown as a pot plant.

HOW TO GROW. Both the poinsettia and the scarlet plume do best in night temperatures of 50° to 65° and day temperatures of 68° or more. They should be grown in the sunniest part of the greenhouse in a commercial potting soil with a pH of 5.0 to 6.0. Allow the soil to become almost dry between waterings, and feed the plants every two weeks during the growing season with a liquid fertilizer diluted to the strength recommended on the label. When the flower buds form, stop feeding. Pinch back the stems to control the size of plants and produce more flowers. The flower buds of poinsettias and scarlet plume normally form in late October when the days grow shorter and the plants are without light for at least 14 hours each day. This daily period of darkness must be uninterrupted and must continue for nine to 11 weeks; otherwise the plants send out only leaves, not flowers. Their period of bloom can be manipulated by reproducing this condition artificially. Thus, in latitudes of the temperate zones, plants can be forced to bloom in early September by shading them with opaque cloth for enough hours a day from early July onward to account for the necessary 14 hours of uninterrupted darkness. For Christmas blooms the shading treatment should start in early October. Modern varieties of poinsettias have long-lasting floral bracts that often remain colorful for six months or more. For additional plants, take

SCARLET PLUME
Euphorbia fulgens

POINSETTIA
Euphorbia pulcherrima

FREESIA
Freesia hybrid 'Super Giant'

FUCHSIA
Fuchsia hybrid 'Springtime'

stem cuttings in the spring and summer. Root them in moist sand heated from the bottom to 65°, and transfer the rooted cuttings to 6- or 8-inch pots.

F

FEVERFEW See *Chrysanthemum*
FLAME VIOLET See *Episcia*
FLAMINGO FLOWER See *Anthurium*
FLORISTS' GENISTA See *Cytisus*
FLOWERING MAPLE See *Abutilon*
FORGET-ME-NOT See *Myosotis*

FREESIA
F. hybrids

The freesias, native to South Africa, are grown in the cool greenhouse for their fragrance and as a source of long-lasting winter and early spring cut flowers. Their trumpet-shaped blossoms, 1¼ inches long, bloom in graceful sprays at the ends of the 12- to 18-inch stems; the slender, sword-shaped leaves are 12 to 18 inches high. Hybridizers have interbred the original wild freesia species to produce flowers in subtle pastel colors that range through blends of pink, mauve, lilac, blue, yellow and orange. The plants rise from corms, or bulb-like roots, and are most often grown in pots although they can also be grown in planting benches.

HOW TO GROW. Freesias do best in night temperatures of 45° to 50°, day temperatures 10° to 15° higher. They do best in commercial potting soil to which ground limestone is added at the rate of 3 to 5 ounces per bushel. Plant the corms in pots, 2 to 4 inches apart, at two-week intervals from August through December for flowers from December through March. Cover the corms with 1 inch of soil and water lightly, keeping the soil barely moist until growth starts. Then keep the soil constantly moist to the touch; the foliage of freesias will turn brown at the tips if the soil is allowed to dry out. Place the plants in a sunny, well-ventilated part of the greenhouse and provide their weak stems with strings and stakes for support. Feed them once a month until the flower buds show color, using a liquid fertilizer diluted to the strength recommended on the label. After flowering, water freesias less frequently and let the foliage die back; then remove corms and store them in a cool, dark place until the following fall. Propagate additional plants by dividing corms, or from seeds. Sow seeds in flats outdoors in the spring; in early fall bring the flats indoors and reduce watering so that the foliage withers and dies. After about a month, dig up the corms and replant them for winter flowers.

FRENCH MARIGOLD See *Tagetes*
FRENCH PINK See *Centaurea*

FUCHSIA
F. hybrids (fuchsia, lady's eardrop)

Fuchsias, which grow wild in the forests of the Central and South American highlands, are among the most versatile of intermediate greenhouse plants. They bloom in shade as well as sun and can be grown in hanging baskets, trained on trellises or pruned to the shape of small trees. Their pendulous flowers, 1½ to 3 inches long, are enclosed by colorful bracts shaped like bells or hoop skirts and come in pink, red, purple, orange and white, as well as combinations of these colors. The plants themselves range from erect or trailing varieties, 1 to 3 feet high, to others, grown in mild-climate gardens, that reach a height of 6 to 10 feet. Some varieties bloom from spring through fall; others bloom all year long.

HOW TO GROW. Fuchsias do best in night temperatures of

50° to 55° and day temperatures of 60° to 70°. Plant them in pots, hanging baskets or tubs in a commercial potting soil, pH 5.5 to 6.5. Place them in a sunny part of the greenhouse from fall through spring, but give them light shade in the summer. Fuchsias thrive on humidity; keep the soil moist but not wet. Feed them every two weeks during the growing season with a liquid fertilizer diluted to the strength recommended on the label. During the fall and winter, when most varieties do not blossom, feed monthly and keep the soil somewhat drier. For bushier plants, pinch back the tips during the growing season; to train fuchsias into small trees, cut or rub off the side shoots until the main stem reaches the desired height. Repot, when necessary, in the spring as new growth appears. Propagate additional plants from stem cuttings taken at any time; root them in moist sand.

G

GARDENIA
G. jasminoides veitchii (gardenia, Cape jasmine)

Few owners of warm greenhouses can resist the challenge of growing this fragrant evergreen shrub from tropical Asia. This particular species of gardenia, suitable for tubs, reaches a height of 1 to 3 feet and has shiny dark green leaves, 4 to 6 inches long. Its waxy white flowers, about 3 inches across, bloom intermittently throughout the year, and certain varieties of gardenia, such as Belmont, Mystery, Hadley and McLellan 23, produce blossoms measuring as much as 5 inches in diameter.

HOW TO GROW. Gardenias do best in night temperatures of 60° to 65° and day temperatures of 70°. The most important key to flower production is a night temperature of 65° or lower. In parts of the country where these temperatures are not possible during the summer months, plants will not make flower buds until cooler weather arrives. They also need full sunshine for the best flower production; shaded plants have lovely foliage but few blossoms. Plant gardenias in a commercial potting soil recommended for African violets, with a pH of 5.0 to 5.5. Keep the soil moist but not soggy and mist the plants daily; they need high humidity. Feed once a month with an acid fertilizer formulated for azaleas, camellias and gardenias. Repot gardenia plants whenever they become potbound. For additional plants, take stem cuttings of mature growth at any time of the year. Root the cuttings in damp sand or peat moss heated from the bottom to 75°; then transfer the rooted cuttings to 2¼-inch pots and shift them to larger pots as required.

GENISTA, FLORISTS' See *Cytisus*
GERANIUM See *Pelargonium*

GERBERA (GERBERIA)
G. jamesonii (gerbera daisy, Barberton daisy, Transvaal daisy)

The spectacular gerbera daisy from South Africa is a perennial grown in the intermediate greenhouse for long-lasting cut flowers sold in florists' shops at premium prices. Its colors range from white through cream, yellow, orange, pink, salmon or rose to red, and each flower grows 3 to 5 inches across on a leafless stem, 10 inches tall or more. The flowers may be singles, with one ring of petals, or doubles, with many layers of petals. The wavy-edged 10-inch leaves, growing up from the plant's base, are hairy and woolly on the underside. Gerberas bloom most prolifically from midwinter into late spring, but will also produce occasional flowers throughout the year.

HOW TO GROW. Gerbera daisies need full sun with night

GARDENIA
Gardenia jasminoides veitchii

temperatures of 55° to 60° during the winter months, but with the arrival of spring, night temperatures of 65° to 70° are acceptable. They can be grown in benches but do best in deeper soil in large pots or tubs. Grow single plants in 8- to 10-inch pots or space clumps 12 to 15 inches apart in benches. Gerberas should have slightly acid soil, pH of about 6.0. Use a commercial potting soil, adding 1½ teaspoons of 20 per cent superphosphate to each gallon pailful of this mixture. Do not feed newly potted plants for six months; feed established blooming plants biweekly using a liquid fertilizer diluted to half the strength recommended on the label. Water young or recently divided plants sparingly; keep established ones moist so that the soil feels damp to the touch, but provide good drainage, as they are easily damaged by overwatering. Propagate from seed or by root division. Gerbera seeds take almost a year to make blooming-sized plants, but this is an inexpensive way to get choice healthy plants. Buy seeds of double-flowered varieties, some of which will be single-flowered nevertheless. When propagating from root division, divide mature, three- to four-year-old plants in early summer for flowering the following winter. These divisions can be set outdoors in pots and returned to the greenhouse the following fall, before frost.

GLADIOLUS

G. hortulanus (miniature gladioluses)

The miniature gladioluses are a favorite source of winter cut flowers when grown in a cool greenhouse. They are just as lovely as the larger varieties and take up far less room. The plants grow from swollen, underground stems, called corms, and they reach a height of only 2 feet. They have sword-shaped leaves and graceful flower spikes composed of a dozen or more individual open-faced flowers 2½ inches wide. The variety of colors and color combinations is broad, ranging from white through green, cream, yellow, buff, orange, salmon, scarlet, pink, red, rose, lavender, purple and blue, to smoky tan and brown.

G. hortulanus is an inclusive name given to the large group of commonly cultivated garden gladioluses with complex ancestry and no specific botanical names. In some bulb catalogues, they are classified by flower size and color using a three-digit numbering system that is explained in the catalogues. In most catalogues, however, they are simply called miniature gladioluses.

HOW TO GROW. Gladioluses need full sun, night temperatures of 50° to 55°, and day temperatures of 10° to 15° higher. Since gladiolus corms are usually sold in the spring rather than the fall, it will probably take a special request to a gladiolus specialist to get corms for fall planting. Because of the shorter winter days, gladioluses planted in midwinter will not begin to bloom until mid-April, some four and a half months later. The closer the planting date to spring, the faster the plants will grow. Gladioluses planted in February, for example, come into blossom in about three and a half months. Plant the corms in commercial potting soil in planting benches or pots. Space bench-planted corms 4 inches apart in rows 12 inches apart, setting the corms 2 inches deep. When grown in pots place three corms in a 6-inch pot, setting them at least 1 inch deep. Keep the soil moist and feed the plants once a month with a liquid fertilizer diluted to the strength recommended on the label. Provide stakes to support plants as they grow. When cutting flower spikes leave three to four leaves on the plant and allow this foliage to die back naturally so that the corms will mature, producing new corms on top of old ones with small cormels at the base. Dig up corms and allow them to dry for about two

GERBERA DAISY
Gerbera jamesonii

GLADIOLUS
Gladiolus hortulanus miniature

weeks, then break off new corms and cormlets, and store them at 45° in a well-ventilated area. Discard the shriveled old corms. To propagate gladioluses, plant the tiny cormels in the garden the following spring and dig them up in the fall; follow this procedure for two or three years, until the cormels reach flowering size.

GLORY BOWER See *Clerodendrum*
GLORY BUSH See *Tibouchina*

GLOXINERA
G. hybrids, also called *Sinningia* hybrids

The gloxinera is a man-made gesneriad, a cross between two other gesneriads, gloxinia and rechsteineria. Like them, it grows from tuberous roots and needs the tropical conditions of a warm greenhouse. First generation gloxineras tend to be as tall as their rechsteineria forebears, 6 to 10 inches high, with 2- to 3-inch flowers; plants of succeeding generations grow more compactly, 3 to 6 inches high, and they bear ½- to 1-inch flowers. Some blooms are tubular; some, like the variety Melinda, are slipper shaped. Their colors range from bright pink to deep orange or lavender blue, and some varieties combine two colors with stripes or speckled markings of still a third color. The foliage also varies, from glossy and heart shaped to furry and oval. Gloxineras bloom in the greenhouse at any time of year, depending on when their tubers are planted.

HOW TO GROW. Gloxineras need filtered sunlight, a relative humidity of 60 to 70 per cent and grow best when night temperatures are 65° to 70°, rising to 75° and higher during the day. Plant them in a commercial potting soil recommended for African violets. Feed growing plants once a month with a liquid fertilizer diluted to half the strength recommended on the label. Keep the soil moist but not soggy; good drainage is important. After flowering water less, stop fertilizing, and let foliage die back. Keep tubers in their pots, barely moist, for two or three months, until new sprouts appear. Then repot in fresh soil. Gloxineras begin to bloom about two months after the tubers are planted and continue to bloom for varying lengths of time; some even bloom continuously. By cutting off old stems when their flowers wither, the period of bloom can often be prolonged; new stems rise, bearing new blooms. For additional plants, propagate from stem or leaf cuttings or seeds. Seed-grown gloxineras take as little as three to four months to flower.

GLOXINIA See *Sinningia*

GODETIA
G. hybrids (satinflower)

The godetia, an annual that normally blooms outdoors in the spring, will flower at any time of year in the intermediate greenhouse, providing clusters of satin-textured, cup-shaped blossoms, 3 to 5 inches across, for cutting or simply for decoration. The flowers come in both single and double forms, and in solid colors of white, pink, red or lilac, as well as in multicolored versions with striated markings. They cluster along stems that range from 10 to 30 inches tall, depending on the variety. The leaves are narrow and vary in length from 2 to 4 inches.

HOW TO GROW. Godetias need full sun and night temperatures ideally from 50° to 55°, rising no higher than 65° to 70° during the day. Sow the seeds in shallow flats or pots, allowing four to five months for the plants to reach flowering size. Use commercial potting soil. Thin the seedlings to stand 6 to 12 inches apart. Do not feed during the growing season, and

GLOXINERA
Gloxinera hybrid 'Melinda'

SATINFLOWER
Godetia hybrid

ANNUAL BABIES'-BREATH
Gypsophila elegans 'Covent Garden'

CHINESE HIBISCUS
Hibiscus rosa-sinensis 'Toreador'

keep the soil barely moist; fertilizer and too much water produce floppy growth. Pinch tips of stems when they are 4 to 5 inches tall to encourage bushiness, and provide support as plants increase in height.

GOLDEN CUP See *Allamanda*
GOLDFISH PLANT See *Hypocyrta*

GYPSOPHILA

G. elegans (annual babies'-breath)

The airy flower heads of babies'-breath, a stand-by for summer bouquets, are also available for winter flower arrangements when grown in the cool greenhouse. The clusters of dainty blossoms, ¼ inch wide, are borne at the ends of 12- to 18-inch-tall stems, and are available in shades of pink, rose and crimson as well as the traditional white.

HOW TO GROW. Babies'-breath does best in night temperatures of 45° to 50° and day temperatures 10° to 15° higher. Sow seeds in rows spaced 6 inches apart in flats or benches, or scatter seeds thinly in a 6- to 8-inch pot. Use a sandy, well-drained soil, weak in nutrients. Thin seedlings to stand 1 inch apart; this ensures straight stems, good for cut flowers. Seeds that are planted in September will produce blooms three months later, in December; successive sowings will provide cut flowers through the winter. From September to April, the plants need four hours per day of artificial light to compensate for the short winter days.

H

HAIRY WATTLE See *Acacia*
HEATH, CHRISTMAS See *Erica*

HIBISCUS

H. rosa-sinensis (Chinese hibiscus, rose of China)

A native of East India and China, and a popular ornamental shrub in tropical climates, the Chinese hibiscus is a plant for warm greenhouses. The pointed, oval leaves, 3 to 4 inches long, have scalloped edges and a lustrous sheen that would give the plant decorative value even without flowers; in some varieties the leaves are marked with streaks of white and red. The large funnel-shaped flowers, 4 to 6 inches in diameter, bloom continuously throughout the year. They may be red, yellow, pink, white, cream or orange and come in both single- and double-flowered varieties. In a greenhouse, the Chinese hibiscus is a long-lived evergreen shrub, usually kept at 3 to 4 feet in height by pruning.

HOW TO GROW. Chinese hibiscus does best in full sun but will tolerate light shade. It needs night temperatures of 60° to 70° and day temperatures of 70° or higher. Use a commercial potting soil and keep the soil constantly moist. Feed the plant once a month with a liquid fertilizer diluted to the strength recommended on the label. Prune the plant at any time to keep its size and shape under control. Propagate from stem cuttings taken at any season from the tips of new growth; root the cuttings in moist sand heated from the bottom to 65°. Transfer the rooted cuttings to pots.

HIPPEASTRUM

H. hybrids (amaryllis)

The hybridized amaryllis, derived from interbreeding several South American species, blooms from winter into spring in the warm greenhouse, putting forth spectacular lily-like blossoms as much as 8 to 10 inches across. The flowers are borne in clusters of three to five at the tops of thick leafless stalks, 18 to 24 inches tall, and come in various hues and combinations of red, pink, white and orange. The flowers are followed by fleshy, sword-shaped leaves, 1½ inches wide and 18 inches long, and often by a second flower stalk.

HOW TO GROW. Amaryllis does best in night temperatures of 60° to 65° and day temperatures of 70° or above. It needs sunshine but should be moved to a cooler, less bright part of the greenhouse when the buds begin to open, to keep the flowers from fading too quickly. Plant one bulb to a pot, selecting a pot 2 inches wider than the diameter of the bulb. Use a well-drained commercial potting soil, positioning the bulb so that half of it is visible above the soil; press the soil firmly around the roots. Water well, then keep the soil barely moist until growth starts. Thereafter, keep the soil constantly moist. Continue watering after flowering, while the foliage is still growing, and fertilize once a month until the leaves turn yellow in the early fall, using a liquid fertilizer diluted to the strength recommended on the label. Then reduce watering gradually until the soil is nearly dry. Cut off the foliage even with the top of the bulb and store the pot in a warm spot for two or three months to rest. When buds begin to appear, return to a sunny, warm place and start the watering cycle again. Amaryllis may be left in the same pot for three or four years if the surface soil is washed away carefully, so as not to damage the roots, and replaced with fresh soil each year just as the new growth starts; add a teaspoon of bone meal each time. Plant in succession from October to December for late January, February and March blooms. Propagate from side bulbs that form around the main bulb. Amaryllis may also be grown from seed but may take three to four years to reach blossoming size.

HOYA

H. australis; H. bella, also called *H. paxtonii; H. carnosa* (all called wax plant)

The wax plants are twining, climbing evergreen vines from Southeast Asia and Australia that are grown in the warm greenhouse for their ornamental foliage and fragrant long-lasting flowers. Their perfectly formed, waxy, star-shaped blossoms, of pink or white with darker centers, are borne on spurs in neat, round clusters at the junctions of the leaves with the stems. The fall-blooming *H. australis* is an 8- to 10-foot-tall vine that bears clusters of honeysuckle-scented white flowers, ½ inch across, with red centers. Each flower cluster holds up to 55 blossoms, and all of the plant tends to bloom at once. The leaves are thick and oval, 3 to 4 inches long; they are dark on the top, paler on the bottom, and occasionally marked with silver blotches. The plant is usually trained to a trellis. *H. carnosa* bears ½-inch-wide pale pink flowers in large pendant clusters, 3 to 4 inches across, that look like inverted parachutes; it blooms in late spring and summer. The elliptical leaves, 2 to 3 inches long, are thick, fleshy and in varieties such as Exotica are marked with pink and creamy white areas. The slender branches grow 8 to 10 feet tall and will cling by their aerial roots to the interior wall of a lean-to greenhouse: usually, however, it is grown on a trellis. *H. bella* is a miniature species, 1 to 2 feet high, with arching stems and thick, triangular, pointed leaves, 1 to 1½ inches long. The flowers are pure white with purple or deep red centers and bloom in clusters 2 to 3 inches across in the summer. This species is usually grown in hanging baskets, hung above eye level for the best effect.

HOW TO GROW. The wax plant does best in night temperatures of 60° to 65° and day temperatures of 70° or over. It does well in full sunshine or partial shade. Plant it in commercial potting soil. Keep the soil moist while the plant is in flower, but after flowering reduce the watering to match the slower growth rate; in the winter when the plant is dormant,

AMARYLLIS
Hippeastrum hybrid 'Ludwig's Goliath'

WAX PLANT
Hoya carnosa 'Exotica'

keep the soil almost dry. Feed every other month during the growing period with a liquid fertilizer diluted to the strength recommended on the label; do not feed when the plants are resting. Prune in the spring, cutting out old unwanted shoots and cutting back other shoots to encourage growth. But do not remove conelike spurs on old flower stems as these will flower again. Propagate from stem cuttings taken at any time and rooted in moist sand, perlite or vermiculite.

HYACINTH-FLOWERED CANDYTUFT See *Iberis*

HYACINTHUS
H. orientalis (large-flowered hyacinth, Dutch hyacinth); *H. orientalis albulus* (French-Roman hyacinth)

Hyacinths are looked upon as harbingers of spring, yet gardeners with cool greenhouses can enjoy their sweet perfume and colorful flowers in the winter months too by growing bulbs especially prepared for forcing. Both the Dutch hyacinth, originally from the eastern Mediterranean, and the French-Roman hyacinth, from southern France, have many forcing varieties: they are generally labeled as such; be sure to purchase so-called top-size or exhibition bulbs. The flowers bloom in dense clusters at the ends of columnar stems and are surrounded by slender, strap-shaped foliage. The Dutch hyacinth produces one or two flower spikes covered with bell-shaped, 1-inch-long blossoms; the flower stem is 6 to 10 inches high and the foliage is 8 to 12 inches long and ½ to 1½ inches wide. Its flowers come in shades of red, blue, purple, pink, white and yellow. The French-Roman hyacinth is extremely fragrant and produces three or four smaller spikes per bulb, 6 to 8 inches high, with graceful, nodding flowers, usually white, but sometimes pink or blue. The flower spikes are less compact, and leaves are narrower. Hyacinths are grown as decorative pot plants.

HOW TO GROW. Hyacinths need night temperatures of 40° to 50° and day temperatures as cool as possible. They are usually grown in pots, one bulb to a 4-inch pot or three to a 6-inch pot, in commercial potting soil. But they can be grown hydroponically, in bowls filled with pebbles or in water-filled vases. When grown in water, the bottom of the bulb should barely touch the water; when grown in a pot, the bulb should be buried so that only its top shows above the soil.

Pot up bulbs as early in the fall as they are available, usually in late September or early October. Place them in a cool dark place, about 40°, for a minimum of 12 weeks, until roots have formed. A protected cold frame is ideal for this purpose. After the new growth is 2 inches tall, the bulbs may be brought into the greenhouse, a few pots at a time at 10-day intervals, for a continuous succession of blossoms. Keep the soil uniformly moist during the growing period, but avoid splashing water inside the leaves, as this may cause the flower buds to rot. Stake the plants to provide support for the heavy blooms. Bulbs grown in soil can be allowed to die back after flowering, then removed and stored for replanting in the garden in the fall. Propagation of hyacinths is an exacting, complicated process, requiring four or five years, and few amateur gardeners bother with it.

HYDRANGEA
H. macrophylla, also called *H. hortensis* (common bigleaf hydrangea, house hydrangea)

The bigleaf hydrangea that blooms in mild-climate gardens in the spring and summer is also an intermediate greenhouse plant. Given the proper preliminary care, it will flower in early to late spring, producing dense globular clusters of flowers, 8 to 10 inches across, in shades of blue, pink, red or

LARGE-FLOWERED HYACINTH
Hyacinthus orientalis 'Princess Margaret'

white. The clusters form a canopy over the 18- to 24-inch woody stems and are sometimes so heavy that it is necessary to stake the stems to keep them from bending. The jagged-edged, oval leaves grow 2 to 6 inches long. Greenhouse hydrangeas are grown in pots or tubs as ornamental shrubs. The blossoms stay fresh for one to two months.

HOW TO GROW. Hydrangeas grow best in night temperatures of 55° to 60° and day temperatures of 68° to 72°, but they need a preliminary cold period to be forced into midwinter bloom. In the fall, after a summer outside, while the fat terminal buds at the tips of the branches are forming, they should be kept at temperatures no higher than 65° for about six weeks until the buds have formed. After the buds are formed the plant becomes dormant, loses its leaves, and should be kept at temperatures just above freezing, 35° to 45°, for another six weeks. Brought into the greenhouse at the end of this period and given night temperatures of 60°, it will bloom about three months later, in late winter or early spring. Flowering can be delayed until late spring by holding the plant just above freezing until late winter.

Hydrangeas need sunlight during the growing period, but should be given partial shade after the flowers appear, as bright sunlight bleaches their color. The plants wilt quickly and should be watered frequently, but should not be waterlogged. Feed them every two weeks during the summer growing season as well as the winter forcing period with a liquid fertilizer diluted to the strength recommended on the label. Do not feed them after the flowers show color.

Except for white varieties, the color of hydrangeas is controlled by the soil acidity. If hydrangeas are grown in a neutral or slightly acid soil, pH 6.5 to 7.0, the flowers will be pink or red. If grown in an acid soil, with a pH of 4.5 to 5.5, the flowers will be blue.

Forced hydrangeas can be kept growing for several years by shifting plants to ever-larger pots. Additional plants can be propagated from stem cuttings taken in the spring from shoots on flowering plants. Root the cuttings in moist sand heated from below to 70° and transfer the rooted cuttings to pots. Pinch back the central stem in midsummer to encourage branching. Then allow the plant to develop naturally; buds will form at the ends of new growth.

HYPOCYRTA

H. nummularia, also called *Alloplectus nummularia; H. strigillosa*, also called *Nematanthus strigillosa; H. wettsteinii*, also called *Nematanthus wettsteinii* (all called goldfish plant)

Originally from the tropical regions of Central and South America, the goldfish plants are fibrous-rooted gesneriads bearing puffy red-orange flowers that bloom almost continuously in a warm, humid greenhouse. All of them have drooping or trailing stems from 1 to 2 feet long. *H. nummularia* has red hairy stems and oval leaves ¾ to 2½ inches long. Its blossoms are scarlet with small yellow mouths outlined in purple. It flowers throughout the year, but most abundantly in summer, fall and winter. *H. strigillosa* has narrow, tapering, dark green leaves covered with bristly hairs. The 1-inch long flowers are crimson and yellow, and bloom most abundantly in the winter and spring. The diminutive *H. wettsteinii* has tiny orange flowers less than an inch long, but it blooms profusely, especially in the summer and fall. The 12- to 18-inch-long trailing stems are thickly covered with shiny elliptical leaves, ¾ inch long. Goldfish plants may be grown in pots, but are most effective in hanging baskets.

HOW TO GROW. Goldfish plants grow best in night temperatures of 65° to 70° and day temperatures of 75° or above. They need bright light but must be protected from the direct

COMMON BIGLEAF HYDRANGEA
Hydrangea macrophylla 'Strafford'

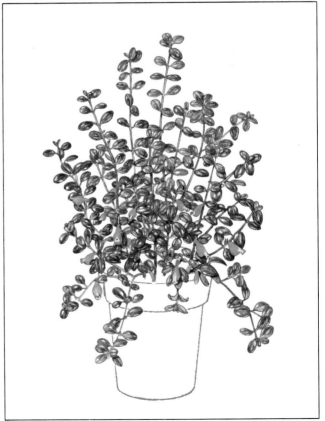

GOLDFISH PLANT
Hypocyrta wettsteinii

HYACINTH-FLOWERED CANDYTUFT
Iberis amara coronaria 'Iceberg'

PATIENT LUCY
Impatiens wallerana 'Zig Zag Scarlet'

rays of the sun. Plant them in commercial potting soil. Keep the soil moist but not soggy and feed the plants once a month with a liquid fertilizer diluted to the strength recommended on the label. If plants become too large or straggly, prune the stems after flowering to keep the plants compact. For additional plants, take stem cuttings at any time and root them in moist sand, perlite or vermiculite.

I

IBERIS

I. amara coronaria, also known as *I. coronaria* (hyacinth-flowered candytuft, rocket candytuft)

The crown-shaped blossom spikes of the hyacinth-flowered candytuft, a familiar garden annual, are also a source of winter cut flowers when grown in the cool greenhouse. The fragrant white blossoms, ¾ to 1 inch in diameter, are borne in clusters about 6 inches tall and 4 inches in diameter. Ball Giant White is a variety especially suited to greenhouse culture, and grows 18 to 24 inches tall.

HOW TO GROW. Candytuft does best in night temperatures of 45° to 50°, day temperatures as cool as possible, and full sun. Sow seeds four to five months before flowers are wanted, in planting benches filled with commercial potting soil; thin seedlings to stand 6 inches apart. Keep soil moist but not soggy, and feed every two weeks with a liquid fertilizer diluted to the strength recommended on the label. To assure straight stems, provide wire-and-string supports as the plants increase in size.

IMPATIENS

I. wallerana, also called *I. holstii* and *I. sultani; I.* New Guinea hybrids (all called patient Lucy)

The impatiens' tolerance of shade and its tendency to flower continuously and prolifically make it a favorite plant for year-round culture in a warm greenhouse. An annual when grown outdoors, it lives indefinitely in a greenhouse. Its flowers range in size from 1 to 2½ inches in diameter, come in both single- and multipetaled forms, and are available in solid colors of pink, red, orange, purple or white as well as subtle shadings and combinations of these. Two particularly decorative types are the relatively new upright-growing, large-flowered New Guinea hybrids and the common *I. wallerana,* known to gardeners for generations and now available in a multiplicity of colors and plant sizes. The former, 2 to 3 feet high, are bred either for their abundant blossoms, like Red Magic, or for their variegated foliage, like Brandywine. The smaller *I. wallerana* comes in compact forms, some only 6 inches high but spreading to a foot in diameter; other versions are 1 to 2 feet tall, like Zigzag Scarlet, which is notable for its bicolored flowers and its glossy red and green foliage. New Guinea hybrids are most suitable for planting in pots, but common patient Lucy is particularly attractive grown in hanging baskets.

HOW TO GROW. Impatiens does well in night temperatures of 60° to 65° and day temperatures of 70° or over. It thrives in commercial potting soil and in light shade; it cannot tolerate bright sun. Keep the soil moist but not soggy and feed the plants twice a month with a liquid fertilizer diluted to the strength recommended on the label. New Guinea hybrids are seldom available as seeds and must be propagated from stem cuttings. Root the cuttings in moist sand heated from below to a temperature of 70°. Patient Lucy can be propagated either from stem cuttings or from seeds. Sow the seeds in midsummer to provide early winter blossoms, or in midwinter for spring flowers. Transplant the seedlings into individual 2½-inch pots, and when they are 2 to 3 inches tall, pinch off the tips to encourage branching. Transfer them to larger pots as they increase in size.

IRIS
I. hybrids (Dutch iris)

Of the more than 200 species of iris, the Dutch iris is the most successful for forcing into winter bloom, but it needs a cool greenhouse. Often called the poor man's orchid for its dramatic color and the arrangement of its petals, the Dutch iris bears one or two flowers, 2½ to 4 inches across, on each 12- to 18-inch stem; the foliage is stiff and sword-shaped. Two particularly good varieties for greenhouse culture are Wedgwood and Imperator, medium and dark blue respectively. Other favorites are White Perfection, White Excelsior, Yellow Queen and Golden Lion. Dutch irises are usually grown in pots or movable boxes in the greenhouse because the bulbs must be subjected to a period of cold temperatures, usually in a cold frame, as part of the forcing process. They are excellent cut flowers, lasting a week to 10 days.

HOW TO GROW. Dutch iris does best in night temperatures of 45° to 55° and day temperatures no higher than 65°. For midwinter flowers, plant bulbs in the early fall, allowing three months to reach the flowering stage. Plant bulbs in pots or boxes in commercial potting soil, setting the bulbs 1 inch deep and 2 to 3 inches apart. Water them thoroughly. Store the pots or boxes at least six weeks in a cold frame with temperatures of 50° or lower, then bring them into the greenhouse at staggered intervals, allowing an additional six weeks for the plants to flower. Place them in a sunny location and keep the soil moist at all times. Feed them every three weeks during the growing season with a liquid fertilizer diluted to the strength recommended on the label. Because iris bulbs used for forcing will have exhausted most of their strength, they are not usually saved. However, they can be planted outdoors as garden flowers in areas where the Dutch iris is hardy, roughly south of a line running from the District of Columbia through Charlotte, North Carolina, Memphis, Tennessee, Dallas, Texas and Phoenix, Arizona, to the Pacific Coast, and north along the coast to British Columbia.

ITALIAN BELLFLOWER See *Campanula*

J

JASMINE See *Jasminum*
JASMINE, CAPE See *Gardenia*

JASMINUM
J. gracile magnificum, also called *J. simplicifolium* and *J. volubile* (royal jasmine, angelwing jasmine); *J. officinale grandiflorum*, also called *J. officinale affine* and *J. grandiflorum* (poet's jasmine, Spanish jasmine); *J. polyanthum; J. sambac* (Arabian jasmine)

A single jasmine plant can perfume the intermediate or warm greenhouse with the rich, spicy fragrance of its flowers, and most of them have obligingly long blooming seasons. Natives of India, Kashmir, China and Australia, they are plants that eventually can occupy large pots or tubs; some have a twining habit of growth while others are straggly shrubs that must be pruned or trained to a trellis. When cultivated in mild-climate gardens, some are naturally deciduous, but they all grow as evergreens in the greenhouse. Winter-flowering royal jasmine, a vigorous shrub, may reach a height of 10 feet or more and bears star-shaped white blossoms, 1 inch across, in clusters at the ends of its stems; its shiny teardrop-shaped leaves are 1½ to 3 inches long. Poet's jasmine bears clusters of ⅞-inch star-shaped white flowers

DUTCH IRIS
Iris hybrid 'Imperator'

from early summer through fall; it is a rambling semiclimber with compound leaves made up of five to seven leaflets and can easily attain a height of 10 feet or more unless cut back occasionally. *J. polyanthum* is a robust climber that reaches a height of 20 feet and produces panicles of ¾-inch flowers, white on the inside, pink on the outside, from late winter to late spring; its compound leaves contain five to seven leaflets, 3 to 5 inches long. Arabian jasmine is a twining plant that blooms from early spring to late fall. Its 1-inch white blossoms, borne in small clusters, turn purple with age and can be single- or double-flowered, depending on the variety.

HOW TO GROW. Except for Arabian jasmine, these jasmine species need night temperatures of 50° to 55° and day temperatures between 68° and 72°; Arabian jasmine needs warmer temperatures of 60° to 65° at night and 72° or higher during the day. All four species require at least four hours of direct sun a day all year round. Grow them in commercial potting soil, kept moist at all times, and feed them every two weeks except when they are resting, using a liquid fertilizer diluted to the strength recommended on the label. Prune the plants when they have finished flowering, to keep them a manageable size; provide climbing varieties with wire or trellis supports. Propagate additional plants from stem cuttings taken at any time and rooted in moist sand, perlite or vermiculite heated from below to 70°. Transfer rooted cuttings to 4-inch pots and then into successively larger pots and tubs as the plants become root bound.

JUSTICIA See *Beloperone*

K

KALANCHOE

K. blossfeldiana; K. hybrids (all called kalanchoe)

These particular kalanchoes are tropical perennials usually treated in the greenhouse as annuals. They flower naturally in midwinter but can be manipulated to bloom at any time. In the intermediate greenhouse they are often forced to produce flowers for a particular holiday—Valentine's Day, Thanksgiving, Christmas. All of the kalanchoes are succulents, with fleshy leaves, and all have round flower heads that rise above the foliage, forming masses that sometimes obscure the leaves entirely. Each flower head is composed of great numbers of ¼- to ½-inch four-petaled blossoms. One familiar favorite, *K. blossfeldiana,* is a dwarf type with 8- to 12-inch stems and red or yellow flowers; the oval leaves are 1 to 2 inches long. Other popular varieties are Hummel's Hybrids, with varicolored flowers, and the long-stemmed Swiss Strains, which are useful for cutting.

HOW TO GROW. Kalanchoes need full sun, night temperatures of 50° to 60° and day temperatures of 68° to 72°. Sow seeds any time from January to July in commercial potting soil heated from below to 65° to 70°; they should germinate in 10 to 14 days and reach the flowering stage the following January and February. The earlier the seeds are planted, the larger the plants will be when they bloom. Transplant seedlings into 2½-inch pots and then into 6-inch azalea pots, grouping plants three to a pot. Allow the soil to become almost dry between waterings, but then water thoroughly. Feed the growing plants every two weeks until the flower buds form with a liquid fertilizer diluted to the strength recommended on the label. Give them full sun except in midsummer when they should be lightly shaded from the sun's most intense rays. Kalanchoes can also be propagated from stem or leaf cuttings taken from mature plants, rooted in moist sand heated from below to 65° to 70°.

Left alone, kalanchoes will bloom in midwinter. To delay

POET'S JASMINE
Jasminum officinale grandiflorum

blossoming, lower the greenhouse temperature to 50° to slow the rate of growth. To accelerate blooming, shade the plants for six to nine weeks during the period of vegetative growth by placing an opaque cloth over them from 5 p.m. to 7 a.m., in effect shortening the day to 10 hours, a necessary condition for the formation of the flower buds. Before the buds open but after the flower color can be seen, stop the shading treatment and allow the plants to continue to grow in the normal amount of light. To have flowering plants for December, shade the plants from mid-August to early October. The entire length of time from the start of shading to the appearance of flowers will average about three months.

KANGAROO THORN See *Acacia*

KOHLERIA
K. amabilis; K. bogotensis; K. eriantha; K. hybrids; K. lindeniana

The kohlerias, native to Central and South America, are long-blooming pot plants for the warm greenhouse. They are gesneriads with the velvety leaves and tubular, five-petaled flowers typical of their family. The flowers come in many different colors and are usually spotted with darker colors. *K. amabilis* is a trailing species with scallop-shaped leaves veined with reddish brown; its plentiful rose-colored blossoms, 2 inches long, are dotted with dark red and bloom continuously for at least six months, from late winter through the spring and sometimes into the summer. *K. bogotensis* and *K. eriantha* are species that bloom during the winter and spring. *K. bogotensis* grows 2 feet high and has dark green leaves tinged with brown; its 1-inch-long flowers are yellow spotted with red. *K. eriantha* can reach a height of 4 feet if it is not confined to a small pot. It has dark green leaves edged with conspicuous red hairs and 1½- to 2-inch-long orange-red flowers with yellow throats and dark red spots. *K. lindeniana* has weak stems about 1 foot long and is especially attractive in hanging baskets. It has bright, velvety, green leaves that are mottled and veined with silver, and fragrant, 2-inch-long bell-shaped purple and white flowers with yellow throats that bloom from late fall to spring. In addition to these species there are many kohleria hybrids that are bred to bloom throughout the year. Among the most popular are Carnival, red flowers with yellow spots; Longwood, white flowers with red throats and red spots; and Rongo, purplish pink flowers spotted with darker pink.

HOW TO GROW. Kohlerias need night temperatures of 65° to 70°, day temperatures of 75° to 80°, and filtered sunlight. (If the leaves seem pale, there is too much light, but spindly growth indicates too little light.) Plant them in a commercial potting soil recommended for African violets. Keep the soil moist during the growing season and feed the plants monthly with a liquid fertilizer diluted to the strength recommended on the label. Species kohlerias become semidormant after they flower; cut them back at this time to stimulate new growth, and withhold both fertilizer and water, keeping the soil moderately dry. Resume regular watering and feeding when new growth appears. Hybrid kohlerias that blossom year round should be fed and watered continuously, according to the regular schedule. Propagate additional plants from stem cuttings of new growth rooted in moist sand, perlite or vermiculite heated from below to 70°. Or propagate from seeds sown at any time.

L
LACHENALIA
L. aloides aurea, also called *L. aurea; L. aloides luteola*, also

KALANCHOE
Kalanchoe blossfeldiana 'Tom Thumb'

KOHLERIA
Kohleria hybrid 'Rongo'

CAPE COWSLIP
Lachenalia aloides aurea

called *L. tricolor luteola; L. bulbifera,* also called *L. pendula* (all called cape cowslip, leopard lily)

Cape cowslips are cool greenhouse plants, originally from South Africa, that send up colorful spikes of waxy, slender, bell-shaped flowers during the winter and early spring. As many as 25 of these 1-inch blossoms are produced on a single 9- to 10-inch stem, and they last for two months or more. *L. aloides aurea* bears yellow flowers; *L. aloides luteola* has yellowish green flowers tipped with red; and *L. bulbifera* bears multicolored flowers with bands of pinkish orange, yellow and purple. The straplike leaves of all three species grow 6 to 8 inches long and are sometimes spotted with purple. Cape cowslips are bulb plants. They are usually grouped in 4- or 5-inch pots but they can also be grown successfully in hanging baskets.

HOW TO GROW. Cape cowslips do best in night temperatures of 40° to 45° and day temperatures of 60° or less. They need full sun. Start bulbs in the late summer in commercial potting soil, placing five bulbs in a 6- to 7-inch pot. Set bulbs about 1 to 2 inches apart just below the soil surface. Keep the newly potted plants in a cold frame or under a planting bench until growth begins, and keep soil barely moist. When leaves appear, move the plants into the light and increase frequency of watering, keeping the soil constantly moist. Feed once a month with a liquid fertilizer diluted to the strength recommended on the label. When the plants stop flowering, gradually reduce the amount of water until the leaves die back; then allow soil to dry out completely. Store the pots in a hot, sunny spot until late summer so that the bulbs ripen fully. Repot the bulbs in fresh soil to begin a new growth and flowering cycle. Propagate additional plants by separating new bulbs from old ones at the time of repotting. Cape cowslips can also be propagated from seeds sown in the fall. About three years are needed for plants grown from seed to reach flowering size.

LADY'S EARDROP See *Fuchsia*
LADY'S POCKETBOOK See *Calceolaria*

LAELIA

L. anceps; L. autumnalis; L. flava; L. lundii, also called *L. regnellii* (laelia orchids)

Laelia orchids are prized for their rich, deeply colored flowers that bloom in the fall and winter. They are often crossed with cattleya orchids for brilliant, large hybrids and, like the cattleyas, are plants for the warm greenhouse. The most popular species, *L. anceps,* from Mexico, bears arching flower spikes up to 3 feet long with purple and yellow-centered flowers, 3 to 4 inches wide, often striped with thin red or purple lines. The flowers bloom in midwinter and remain beautiful for two or more months if left on the plant, but die quickly when cut. *L. autumnalis,* also from Mexico, blooms in the fall and has rose and purple flowers with lips composed of two white outer lobes spotted with purple and one inner yellow lobe. Its flowers, too, are 3 to 4 inches across and are borne on stems up to 2 feet long. *L. flava,* a smaller orchid from Brazil, bears clusters of four to eight deep yellow blossoms, 2 to 2½ inches wide, on 12-inch-high stems. This relatively dainty plant, each of whose pseudobulbs produces a solitary purple-tinged leaf, blossoms in the fall and winter. *L. lundii,* another Brazilian orchid, is even tinier, rarely reaching more than 4 to 5 inches tall. Its 1- to 1½-inch lilac-pink flowers have ruffled lips veined in red and appear singly or in pairs in midwinter, before the plant's leaves are fully formed.

HOW TO GROW. Laelia orchids do best in night tempera-

LAELIA ORCHID
Laelia flava

tures between 55° and 65° and day temperatures of 68° or higher. They need the brightest possible light, with only enough shade to prevent the leaves from becoming sunburned. Plants grown in shade have dark green leaves but few flowers. Grow them in 3- to 7-inch pots in a mixture of 2 parts fir bark to 1 part peat moss. Allow the potting medium to become fairly dry between thorough waterings. Feed monthly with a high-nitrogen orchid fertilizer such as one labeled 20-10-10, diluted ¼ teaspoon to a quart of water. After it has flowered, the laelia orchid goes through a period of rest; do not water it during this time unless the pseudobulb shrivels markedly, in which case spray it lightly. Propagate new laelia orchids by dividing the pseudobulbs just as the new growth begins after a period of rest, keeping three or four bulbs to a cluster.

LARKSPUR See *Consolida*

LATHYRUS
L. odoratus (sweet peas)

The same sweet peas that grace the summer garden also come in winter-flowering varieties specifically developed to bloom in the cool greenhouse. These fragrant, delicately hued flowers, with their fluttering petals, resemble tiny sunbonnets and are available in practically all the colors of the rainbow and in strains with bicolored, mottled or striped petals. The flowers are 1 to 2 inches across and are borne on multiflowered stems that are excellent for cutting. Unlike garden sweet peas, winter-flowering types do not form side shoots until their first flowers appear; then they develop side shoots and produce more blossoms. Winter-flowering sweet peas are rampant climbers, growing as high as 10 to 14 feet tall in ground beds where they will climb by means of tendrils up strings or netting supports until they reach the roof. Plants of lesser height but with equally lovely flowers can be grown in large pots on the greenhouse floor. Sweet peas make delicate, sweet-smelling winter cut flowers.

HOW TO GROW. Sweet peas do best in night temperatures of 45° to 50° and day temperatures between 55° and 60°. They need full sun and good ventilation. Sow seeds in commercial potting soil in pots or ground beds at least 10 inches deep, setting seeds 1 inch apart in rows 7 inches apart. Alternatively, sow individual seeds in 3-inch peat pots and transplant them, pots and all, when they are about 3 inches high. To help the plants take in free nitrogen from the air, dust the seeds with a legume inoculant, available at garden supply centers. For flowers beginning in November, sow seeds in mid-July; for flowers beginning in January sow seeds in September; for flowers in February sow in October. Each of these crops will stay in bloom at least three months. When seedlings are 2 inches tall, thin them to stand 3 inches apart. Keep the soil moist, but water less on cloudy days. Feed plants once a month with a liquid fertilizer diluted to the strength recommended on the label. Provide sweet peas with string or wire netting supports connected to overhead rafters. To encourage more flowers, prevent the plants from setting seeds by pinching off all blossoms as they fade; this will prolong the flowering season.

LEMON See *Citrus*
LEOPARD LILY See *Lacheralia*
LIGURIAN BELLFLOWER See *Campanula*

LILIUM
L. Mid-Century hybrids; *L.* Oriental hybrids; *L. longiflorum* varieties (Easter lily). (All called lily)

SWEET PEA
Lathyrus odoratus 'Multiflora'

Of the hundreds of species and varieties of lilies, among the best for greenhouse culture are the Mid-Century hybrids, Oriental hybrids and Easter lilies. All three can be planted in the fall for blossoming during the winter and spring, bringing both color and fragrance to the cool greenhouse. Mid-Century hybrids typically bear flowers ranging in color from white to yellow and orange-red, and from pink through various shades of red to maroon. They come with both upward-facing and outward-facing blossoms. Good varieties of the former are Cinnabar, 2 feet tall, deep crimson; Enchantment, 2 feet tall, orange-red; Joan Evans, 3 feet tall, golden yellow; Pepper, 3 feet tall, deep red; and Tabasco, 2 feet tall, maroon. Three excellent outward-facing varieties are Corsage, 3 feet tall, pink; Paprika, 2 feet tall, deep red; and Prosperity, 2 feet tall, lemon yellow. The Oriental hybrids, derived from crosses in which the gold-band lily *L. auratum* was the dominant parent, usually grow 5 to 6 feet tall. Their outward-facing flowers are 8 to 10 inches in diameter, and most varieties have petals that curl backward. They range in color from white to pink to crimson, and many of them have a deep-colored stripe down the center of each petal. Typical varieties are Allegra, white; Jamboree, crimson; and the Imperial strain, with pink, crimson, yellow or white flowers. The Easter lily is always white, with trumpet-shaped blossoms that face outward. Two good lily varieties for forcing are Ace and Nellie White, both of which grow about 2 feet tall.

HOW TO GROW. Lilies do best in night temperatures of 40° to 50°, and daytime temperatures of 68° or lower. They need bright sun until the flowers open, but then they should be given light shade to prolong the life of the blossoms. Lilies are susceptible to root rot and therefore they need excellent drainage. Use commercial potting soil, but put an inch of coarse gravel in the bottom of the pot. Set each bulb deeply enough so that it will be covered by at least 2 inches of soil. Water the soil thoroughly, and keep it moist thereafter, throughout the life cycle of the plant.

Although precooled lily bulbs are occasionally available for forcing, most greenhouse gardeners do not have access to them, nor are they needed. (Precooled bulbs have been refrigerated to shorten their forcing time, and are normally sold only to commercial growers in case lots.) By planting standard bulbs a little earlier and waiting a little longer, the amateur greenhouse gardener can also produce midwinter blooms. Pot up the bulbs in the early fall, and set them in a cool place to make underground root growth. Because greenhouse space is usually at a premium, the potted bulbs are often placed in a cold frame during this rooting period and brought inside at intervals through the late fall and winter so as to spread their blossoming time over several months. The cold frame should be insulated to keep the temperature above freezing. During the growing period, feed the plants monthly with a liquid fertilizer diluted to the strength recommended on the label. After flowering, allow the foliage to mature and die back. When the outdoor temperature rises above 40°, plant the bulbs in the garden, where they will revert to their normal season of flowering. Forced bulbs can seldom be forced successfully a second time.

LILY See *Lilium*
LILY, LEOPARD See *Lachenalia*

LIMONIUM

L. sinuatum (notchleaf statice); *L. suworowii* (rat-tail statice, Russian statice)

The decorative spurs and spires of notchleaf and rat-tail

ASIATIC HYBRID LILY
Lilium hybrid 'Cinnabar'

statice, one planted in the fall, the other in late winter, bloom as easily in the intermediate greenhouse as they do in the garden and provide cut flowers from midwinter to spring. The papery blossoms of notchleaf statice, ⅜ inch wide, come in white and bright shades of blue, lavender and rose that look as though they had been dipped in dye; they bloom in clusters along the many-branched ends of 18-inch flower stems. Rat-tail statice, also 18 inches high but very different in appearance, bears its tiny lilac-colored blossoms in cylindrical spires, ⅜ inch wide and often more than 1 foot long.

HOW TO GROW. Statice thrives in night temperatures of 50° to 55°, day temperatures under 75°, and bright sun. Use a commercial potting soil and sow seeds in 6-inch pots or in planting benches, thinning the plants to stand 8 inches apart. Sow notchleaf statice seeds in late winter for spring flowers; sow Russian statice seeds in the fall for flowers in midwinter. Water the plants just enough to keep the soil barely moist, and keep them in the sunniest part of the greenhouse. Feed them once a month with a liquid fertilizer diluted to the strength recommended on the label. Statice will be ready for cutting about 20 weeks from the time seeds are sown.

LIPSTICK PLANT See *Aeschynanthus*
LUPINE See *Lupinus*

LUPINUS
L. annual hybrids derived from *L. hartwegii; L.* Russell hybrids (lupine)

The stately lupines, with their tall flower spikes, can be grown in the cool greenhouse for cut flowers from midwinter through spring, depending on when the seeds are sown. The annual hybrids, 1 to 2 feet tall, are prized for their strong, clear colors, while the perennial Russell hybrids, 2 to 3 feet tall, are valued for their closely packed flower spikes. The individual flowers of both hybrid types are about 1 inch across and are tightly set along their stems; both types have attractive compound leaves of seven to nine leaflets. The blossoms come in shades of blue, pink, lavender, orange and yellow, as well as in white and bicolors. Annual lupines are most easily grown in planting benches, while the perennial Russell hybrids are usually grown as pot plants.

HOW TO GROW. Lupines do best in night temperatures of 40° to 50° and day temperatures under 75°. They need bright sunlight, good ventilation and a dry atmosphere. Use a well-drained commercial potting soil. Annual and Russell hybrid lupines are handled differently. Sow the seeds of annual lupines in groups of three seeds, spacing the groups 12 to 15 inches apart. When the seedlings are 3 inches tall, clip off all but the strongest specimen in each group. Keep the temperature at 60° to 65° while the seeds are germinating, then gradually lower it. Keep the soil moist while the plants are young, but allow it to become moderately dry in between waterings when they are full grown. Feed plants once a month during the growing season with a liquid fertilizer diluted to the strength recommended on the label. Provide the plants with wire-and-string supports. Annual lupines develop from seed to flower in five to six months. After the first flower stalks are cut, secondary stalks will develop to prolong the flowering season. Seeds that are sown in the fall will begin flowering in the early spring; seeds sown in midwinter will provide blossoms in June.

Sow the seeds of Russell hybrid lupines in the spring, no later than June, putting three seeds in each pot; if possible, keep the pots outdoors. Thin out the seedlings, leaving the strongest specimen in each pot. Shift the plants to larger pots during the summer, as needed, so that by fall they are husky

NOTCHLEAF STATICE
Limonium sinuatum

LUPINE
Lupinus Russell hybrid

LYCASTE ORCHID
Lycaste aromatica 'Joe'

COMMON STOCK
Mathiola incana annua 'Ball Column'

specimens in 6- to 8-inch pots. Put the pots in a cold frame and keep them just above freezing, to be brought into the greenhouse at any time during the winter, where they will come into bloom about three months later.

LYCASTE

L. aromatica; L. skinneri, also called *L. virginalis* (lycaste orchids)

Though their blossoms look superficially like tulips, lycaste orchids are true orchids from the mountains of Central and South America. In the intermediate greenhouse their extremely fragrant long-lasting flowers bloom from winter to spring, appearing singly on erect 10- to 16-inch stems that arise from the base of a swollen stem called a pseudobulb. *L. aromatica,* a Mexican species, bears yellow-green flowers, 1½ inches across, with spotted orange lips. *L. skinneri,* from Guatemala, has rose-tinged white flowers, 4 to 6 inches wide, with mottled purple lips. The leaves of *L. aromatica* are 8 inches long, while those of *L. skinneri* are as much as 2 feet long. Lycaste orchids are epiphytes, or air plants, clinging to trees, but in the greenhouse they are usually grown in pots or hanging baskets.

HOW TO GROW. Lycaste orchids do best in night temperatures of 50° to 55° and day temperatures of 60° to 65°. They need light shade and a moist atmosphere. Plant them in 3- to 7-inch pots in a mixture of 2 parts fir bark to 1 part peat moss. Feed them once a month until they begin flowering with a high-nitrogen orchid fertilizer, such as one labeled 20-10-10, diluted as recommended on the label. Keep the medium moist but not soggy while the plants are growing and in flower, but when the flowering period is over, reduce watering, allowing the growing medium to become almost—but not completely—dry until new growth starts. Then resume watering. Propagate lycaste orchids by dividing their pseudobulbs after flowering, allowing at least four pseudobulbs to remain in each cluster.

M

MAGIC FLOWER See *Achimenes*
MARGUERITE See *Chrysanthemum*
MARIGOLD See *Tagetes*
MARIGOLD, POT See *Calendula*

MATHIOLA

M. incana (common stock)

The dense flower spikes of common stock, an annual, will bloom in the cool greenhouse from January until June, depending on when the seeds are sown. They make fragrant cut flowers. The spikes are composed of 1-inch single or double flowers in varying shades of white, buff, rose, lilac and purple. Two types especially suited to greenhouse culture are the single-stemmed, non-branching varieties such as Column or Ten-week stock, which grow 1 to 3 feet high and may have either single or double flowers, and the multi-branched, double-flowered Trysomic stock, which comes in both dwarf and standard strains, ranging in height from 12 to 30 inches. Ten-week stock, as its name implies, flowers 10 to 12 weeks after sowing. Double- and single-flowered plants may be distinguished by the color of their foliage at the seedling stage: doubles have light green leaves, singles have dark green foliage. Stocks are excellent for growing in planting benches, but if only a few plants are desired they can be grown instead in pots.

HOW TO GROW. Stocks do best in night temperatures of 45° to 50° and day temperatures under 65°. They need full sun and good ventilation. Fill 6-inch-deep benches with well-drained commercial potting soil; for flowers from January to June sow seeds at intervals from late July until early February. Seeds sown in the fall take slightly longer to reach the flowering stage than those sown in the late winter. Seeds of single-stemmed varieties should be sown in rows 6 inches apart; rows for branching varieties should be 8 inches apart. Thin seedlings of single-stemmed stocks to stand 4 inches apart; branching varieties, 6 to 8 inches apart. Allow the soil to become moderately dry between thorough waterings and water only in the morning, taking care to keep the foliage dry. Feed the plants every two weeks with a liquid fertilizer diluted to half the strength recommended on the label. When thinning remove all dark-leaved plants, since only pale green leaves will produce double-flowering plants. Pinch off the top of branching types to encourage further branching. Stake tall-growing single-stemmed varieties of common stock with wire-and-string supports.

MILTONIA
M. spectabilis; M. vexillaria; M. hybrids (pansy orchid)

The pansy orchids, with their flat, pansy-shaped flowers and pansy-like masks, or markings, are aptly named. These small pot plants, with their velvety blossoms, grow in an intermediate greenhouse, producing many slender flower stems, 6 to 20 inches long, surrounded by yellow-green foliage. *M. spectabilis,* from Brazil, blooms in the fall and is grown for its spectacular floral display, producing as many as 50 single blossoms simultaneously on separate 10- to 20-inch-high stems. The large white flowers, 3 to 4 inches across, have scalloped, rose-purple veined lips. *M. vexillaria,* from Colombia, is also prized for its abundant quantities of large flowers, 4 or more inches wide, which appear in clusters of two to seven during the spring and summer. The rose-colored flowers, sometimes rimmed with white, have a gigantic, two-part lip striped in yellow and red and flanked by two hornlike projections. The many beautiful hybrids of the pansy orchid come in white, pink, pale orange or yellow with center markings of red, purple or brown. The hybrids bloom at different times throughout the year, depending on the variety, and their flowers last a month or more. Species varieties last nearly a month.

HOW TO GROW. Pansy orchids do best in night temperatures of 50° to 60°, day temperatures of 75° or less, and a humidity of about 60 per cent. They are difficult to grow in areas that have hot summers, and require rather deep shade during the summer months to hold down temperatures. In fall and winter, however, they should have only light shade. Plant pansy orchids in 4- to 5-inch pots in a mixture of 2 parts fir bark to 1 part coarse peat moss; provide the pots with good drainage. Keep the soil moist at all times, taking particular care to water thoroughly during the hot summer months. Fertilize once a month during the growing season with a high-nitrogen orchid fertilizer, such as one labeled 20-10-10, diluted as recommended on the label. Repot plants to slightly larger containers every year or two immediately after flowering. Propagate pansy orchids by dividing pseudobulbs into groups of four or more at the time of repotting.

MIMOSA See *Acacia*
MONKEY-FACED FLOWER See *Achimenes*

MUSA
M. acuminata 'Dwarf Cavendish' (Chinese or Jamaican banana); *M. arnoldiana,* also called *M. ensete, Ensete ventricosum* (Abyssinian banana)

With their large, paddle-shaped leaves, purplish-red flow-

PANSY ORCHID
Miltonia hybrid

BANANA PLANT
Musa acuminata 'Dwarf Cavendish'

FORGET-ME-NOT
Myosotis sylvatica

er buds and upright rings of seedless fruit, banana trees give any warm greenhouse a truly tropical character. Although called trees, bananas are really herbaceous plants with tall stems. Some species grow as high as 40 feet in the tropics, but the ones recommended here as tub plants seldom grow more than 8 feet high. The Chinese or Jamaican banana averages about 6 feet tall and produces delicious edible 5-inch fruit. Its smooth, leathery blue-green leaves are about 4 feet long and 2 feet wide and are often blotched with red markings when the plant is young. The Abyssinian banana, 5 to 8 feet high, has larger, bright green leaves with red midribs and purple edges and is grown as an ornamental plant only: its fruit is inedible.

HOW TO GROW. Banana trees do best in a very warm greenhouse with a minimum night temperature of 60° in the winter and 70° in the spring and fall. They adapt to either full sun or light shade. Plant them in commercial potting soil and keep the soil very moist, almost soggy, except during the winter when the plant is at rest and needs less water. Feed monthly during the growing season with a liquid fertilizer diluted to the strength recommended on the label. Propagate the Chinese banana from offshoots that form at the base of the stem after the fruit has ripened; each of these offshoots eventually becomes a fruiting stem. Cut away the offshoots and plant them in separate containers. Abyssinian banana trees are propagated from seed sown in moist potting soil and given bottom heat of 70° or more.

MYOSOTIS

M. sylvatica, also called *M. oblongata* (woodland forget-me-not)

Although these dainty forget-me-nots are only 9 to 12 inches high, they remain fresh as cut flowers for a very long time and in the cool greenhouse are in bloom 12 to 14 weeks after they are sown. The natural color of the species is blue, and the blue-flowered variety Ball Early is especially good for greenhouse culture because it flowers so abundantly, but other varieties have white or pink blossoms. They can be grown in pots for a spot of color or in planting benches for a full-scale display.

HOW TO GROW. Forget-me-nots do best in night temperatures of 45° to 50° and day temperatures under 75°. They need sun but should be given partial shade during the hottest part of the day in the spring and summer. Sow seeds at six-week intervals from August to January for flowers from November to June. Sow them directly into pots or planting benches filled with commercial potting soil. Keep the soil moist. Thin seedlings to stand 10 inches apart. Feed them monthly with a liquid fertilizer diluted to the strength recommended on the label.

N

NARCISSUS

N. trumpet-flowered hybrids (daffodils); *N. tazetta* hybrids (narcissus, poetaz narcissus)

Narcissus, the outdoor herald of spring, blooms as much as three months ahead of time in the cool greenhouse. Of the many species and varieties, two types are especially recommended for greenhouse culture: the large trumpet-flowered ones called daffodils, and the smaller cluster-flowered tazetta species and hybrids. Both types have gray-green lance-shaped leaves, 10 to 12 inches long, and stand 12 to 18 inches high. The blossoms of the trumpet-flowered daffodils are borne one to a stem and are as much as 4 inches across with trumpets of equal or greater depth. They have yellow or white petals with trumpets of the same or a second color—

yellow, white, buff, pink or orange. Typical examples are King Alfred, solid yellow; Music Hall, white with yellow trumpets; and Mount Hood and Beersheba, all white. Tazetta hybrids bloom in clusters of four to eight flowers on a stem. The fragrant flowers, 1 to 2 inches across, are usually white or yellow with shallow cups in contrasting shades of yellow, orange or red. Typical examples are Cragford, white with scarlet cups; Geranium, white with orange cups; Laurens Koster, white with yellow cups; and Cheerfulness, an all-yellow variety with double flowers. All of these are hardy varieties, often grown out of doors in the coldest parts of the country. Other tazetta narcissuses, also grown in greenhouses, come from a group of tender varieties. They include Chinese Sacred Lily, white with deep yellow cups; Paper White, completely white; and Soleil d'Or, yellow flowers with orange cups. Both trumpet-flowered narcissus and tazetta hybrids are suitable for cutting.

HOW TO GROW. Narcissus does best in night temperatures of 45° to 50°, day temperatures of 68° or lower, and full sun until the flowers appear, when they should be given partial shade to prolong their life. Daffodils and hardy tazetta narcissuses are usually grown in shallow 8-inch pots, called pans. Bulbs for greenhouses are sold in late September and early October, and should be potted immediately and put into a cold frame at about 40°, for at least 15 weeks, until the roots are formed. Then they can be brought into the greenhouse at intervals, and will flower in about two weeks. Use any kind of soil for potting, preferably one that holds moisture. Place the bulbs in the pot so they nearly touch one another, and so that their tips barely protrude above the soil. Water them thoroughly and keep them moist during the rooting and flowering period. After the plants have flowered, water less frequently until the foliage has matured and died. The bulbs cannot be forced a second year but may be stored for planting outside the following fall.

Tender tazettas are traditionally grown in pebbles, but they can also be grown in soil. The usual advice for growing tender tazettas indoors calls for a period of darkness while the roots develop, but this is unnecessary and leads to weak, overly tall stems. Simply place the potted bulbs in full sun and keep the soil moist, or keep sufficient water around the base of pebble-grown bulbs to barely touch the base of the bulbs. In areas where the ground does not freeze, tender tazettas can also be stored and planted outdoors the following fall. None of the forced narcissuses need to be fertilized.

NASTURTIUM, COMMON See *Tropaeolum*

NERIUM

N. oleander (oleander, rosebay)

The delicately scented old-fashioned oleander, an evergreen shrub from the Mediterranean, decorates both warm and cool greenhouses with its clusters of 1- to 2-inch-wide rose-shaped flowers. It comes in both single- and double-flowered varieties, and in yellow, pink, red or white. Normally it blossoms from early summer until fall, but occasionally plants will blossom continuously if kept in a tropical atmosphere. Although oleander reaches a height of 10 feet or more in the garden, when grown in containers its height is often 5 feet or less. It begins to blossom when it is only 2 feet tall. Oleanders can be grown as bushy, many-branched shrubs, or they can be trained into treelike shapes with single trunks and crowns of numerous flower-laden branches. Although oleander has been grown as an ornamental plant for thousands of years, it is important to note that all parts of it are poisonous to eat but not to touch.

TRUMPET DAFFODIL
Narcissus 'Unsurpassable'

TAZETTA NARCISSUS
Narcissus tazetta 'Cragford'

HOW TO GROW. Oleanders need full sun but will grow in a wide range of temperatures. In cool greenhouses, with night temperatures of 45° to 50°, they will rest during the winter months; in warm greenhouses, with night temperatures at or above 60°, they will blossom intermittently all winter. Plant them in commercial potting soil and keep the soil moist during the spring and summer, when the plants are in bloom, and somewhat dry during the winter when they are resting. Feed them monthly during the period of active growth with a liquid fertilizer diluted to the strength recommended on the label; do not feed them when they are resting. Propagate from 4- to 5-inch stem cuttings of mature wood taken at any time except when the plant is dormant. Root them in a mixture of equal parts of peat moss and sand. Oleanders can also be grown from seed, but the color of seed-grown plants may not be the same as that of the parent plant.

NOTCHLEAF STATICE See *Limonium*

ODONTOGLOSSUM

O. grande (tiger orchid); *O. pulchellum* (lily-of-the-valley orchid); *O. schlieperianum,* also called *O. insleayi macranthum*

Most of the beautifully marked odontoglossum orchids are native to the mountains of Central and South America, and those found above 12,000 feet can be grown only in air-conditioned greenhouses: they cannot stand heat. But these three species, from the lower slopes, will survive in the cool greenhouse. The odontoglossums have wide-spreading flowers that bloom as sprays on arching stems. *O. grande* has golden yellow flowers with white lips and is striped and spotted with brown. The flowers are huge, 5 to 9 inches wide, and appear in clusters of four to seven blossoms on a single stem during the fall and winter; they last for two to three weeks. *O. pulchellum* bears graceful sprays of five to 10 waxy, white flowers with yellow lips, 1½ inches wide. These fragrant flowers, whose scent resembles the lily-of-the-valley, bloom in the spring, remaining fresh for six or seven weeks. *O. schlieperianum* looks like a small version of *O. grande;* its 3-inch-wide yellow-green flowers are streaked and sometimes spotted with brown or gold. The flowers bloom in clusters of eight to 15 blossoms on each stem and appear during the fall, lasting into early winter.

HOW TO GROW. Odontoglossums do best in night temperatures of 45° to 55° and day temperatures no higher than 60°. They need rather dense shade and a highly humid atmosphere, 70 to 75 per cent, especially during the summer. Plant them in a mixture of 2 parts fir bark to 1 part coarse peat moss. The pot size is a matter of choice. Some orchid fanciers plant odontoglossums in rather small pots because the plants flower most profusely when their roots are crowded. But this means repotting them annually instead of at the usual two- to three-year interval. Water generously during the growing season but let the soil become almost dry between waterings. After flowering, until new growth appears, water only enough to keep the plant from drying out. Feed once a month during the growing season with a high-nitrogen orchid fertilizer, such as one labeled 20-10-10, diluted as recommended on the label. Propagate by dividing the pseudobulbs when they become crowded.

OLEANDER See *Nerium*

ONCIDIUM

O. varicosum (dancing lady orchid)

Of the hundreds of species and varieties of the oncidium

OLEANDER
Nerium oleander

TIGER ORCHID
Odontoglossum grande

orchid, this winter-blooming species with its fluttering skirt-like lip is especially popular. A native of Brazil, it flourishes in the intermediate greenhouse, bearing as many as 100 blossoms on long arching sprays that last up to four weeks and make excellent cut flowers. The blossoms are yellow or yellow-green with brown bands and spots and sometimes contain pink or purple markings. Usually they are small, ranging in width from 1 to 1½ inches, but the variety *O. varicosum rogersii* has flowers with huge flared lips, up to 2 inches across. They are often grown in combination with cattleya orchids, and like them are epiphytes with aerial roots. They can be planted in hanging baskets or pots, or can be mounted on slabs of bark.

HOW TO GROW. Oncidiums do best with night temperatures of 55° to 65° and daytime temperatures of 68° or higher. They need bright filtered light, with only enough shade to keep the foliage from being sunburned. Plant them in a mixture of 2 parts fir bark to 1 part coarse peat moss. During the growing season, water them only when the potting medium becomes slightly dry to the touch, but then water them until the potting medium is thoroughly moist. After flowering, when plants are at rest, give them just enough moisture to keep the pseudobulbs from shriveling. Feed monthly during the growing season with a high-nitrogen orchid fertilizer, such as one labeled 20-10-10, diluted as recommended on the label. Repot every two to four years, as needed, after flowering. Propagate just as new growth starts by dividing the pseudobulbs, keeping three or four bulbs to a cluster.

ORANGE See *Citrus*
ORCHID, BRASSAVOLA See *Brassavola*
ORCHID CACTUS See *Epiphyllum*
ORCHID, CATTLEYA See *Cattleya*
ORCHID, CLAMSHELL See *Epidendrum*
ORCHID, COELOGYNE See *Coelogyne*
ORCHID, CYMBIDIUM See *Cymbidium*
ORCHID, DANCING LADY See *Oncidium*
ORCHID, DENDROBIUM See *Dendrobium*
ORCHID, EPIDENDRUM See *Epidendrum*
ORCHID, LADY-OF-THE-NIGHT See *Brassavola*
ORCHID, LADY'S-SLIPPER See *Paphiopedilum*
ORCHID, LAELIA See *Laelia*
ORCHID, LILY-OF-THE-VALLEY See *Odontoglossum*
ORCHID, LYCASTE See *Lycaste*
ORCHID, MILTONIA See *Miltonia*
ORCHID, MOTH See *Phalaenopsis*
ORCHID, NUT See *Achimenes*
ORCHID, ODONTOGLOSSUM See *Odontoglossum*
ORCHID, ONCIDIUM See *Oncidium*
ORCHID, PANSY See *Miltonia*
ORCHID, POOR MAN'S See *Schizanthus*
ORCHID, SOPHRONITIS See *Sophronitis*
ORCHID, SWAN See *Cycnoches*
ORCHID, VANDA See *Vanda*

P

PAINTED TONGUE See *Salpiglossis*
PANSY, WINTER-FLOWERING See *Viola*

PAPHIOPEDILUM, formerly called CYPRIPEDIUM
P. callosum; P. glaucophyllum; P. hybrids; *P. maudiae* (all called lady's-slipper orchids)

These mottled-leaved lady's-slipper orchids are among the easiest orchids to grow in the warm greenhouse. They are prized for their exotic, waxy blossoms, which last at least a month as cut flowers and as long as three months on some

DANCING LADY ORCHID
Oncidium varicosum rogersii

plants. The 3- to 5-inch flowers, on stems 15 inches or less, are characterized by a highly modified lower petal or lip that is shaped like a pouch or dainty slipper. Opposite this lip is a distinctive leaflike sepal, a greatly enlarged petal at the back of the flower. The narrower side petals are frequently hairy or warty. The leathery, evergreen leaves are sometimes mottled with silver markings and grow directly from the ground.

P. callosum has 10- to 15-inch flower stems bearing one or two 4-inch blossoms during the spring and summer. The sac-like lip is purple; the huge sepal, sometimes as much as 3 inches wide, is white with purple and green veins; and the narrow, pale green petals are tipped with purple and dotted with dark black warts along their upper edges. *P. glaucophyllum* produces flowers atop stems up to 2 feet tall. The long mauve pouch is spotted pink or red; the dark green sepal is edged with white; and the hairy, white, 2-inch-long petals streaked with maroon are twisted and spread horizontally.

Paphiopedilum hybrids, which rarely grow taller than 15 inches, bloom throughout the year depending on the variety grown. Their magnificent 3- to 5-inch-wide flowers range from white, yellow and green to pink, red, brown and purple with several hues sometimes often combined in one flower. *P. maudiae* is a hybrid recommended for beginning orchid growers. It has marbled green foliage and bears 3-inch wide green and white striped flowers on 15-inch stems two or three times a year.

HOW TO GROW. These four species of lady's-slipper orchids need night temperatures between 65° and 70° and daytime temperatures of 75° or higher. Lowering the temperature a few degrees after flower stems have reached their full length and the buds are almost completely developed will delay the opening of the blooms; lowering temperatures a few degrees after the plants are already in full bloom will preserve the flowers longer. Lady's-slippers tolerate humidity as low as 30 per cent but they do best when it ranges from 55 to 60 per cent. Shade lady's-slippers from direct sunlight; yellowish leaves indicate there is too much light. Pot lady's-slippers ½ inch deep in a mixture of 4 parts fine fir bark to 1 part coarse sand, covering the top of the plant with ½ inch of this mixture. Water lightly after potting, keeping the growing medium just damp until new growth starts; once new growth appears, keep the growing medium moist. Spray the leaves lightly once a day but do not allow water to stand on the leaves or collect between them, as this may cause rot. Feed monthly using a high-nitrogen orchid fertilizer such as 20-10-10 or 30-10-10, diluted as recommended on the label. Lady's-slippers are injured by overfeeding and by the accumulation of fertilizer salts around their roots; if this happens water thoroughly until water drains from the bottom of the pots in order to flush salts out. After plants have flowered for two or three years, repot them in spring when new leaves begin to form at the bases of old leaf clusters. Propagate at repotting time by dividing the roots with your fingers, keeping three or four leaf clusters in each division.

PARIS DAISY See *Chrysanthemum*

PASSIFLORA
P. alato-caerulea, also called *P. pfordtii; P. caerulea; P. coccinea* (all called passionflower)

Growing up a greenhouse wall on stakes, string supports, or trellises, a passionflower vine provides a dramatic display with its large, intricate flowers. These fragrant blossoms appear in spring and summer; each has 10 petals surrounding several rings of threadlike filaments called the corona. From

LADY'S SLIPPER ORCHID
Paphiopedilum maudiae

the center projects a distinctive stalk carrying the flower's reproductive parts. The three species listed all thrive in a warm greenhouse. *P. alato-caerulea* has 4-inch flowers with pink petals and a purple, white and blue corona. Its deeply lobed, smooth leaves are 4 to 6 inches long. *P. caerulea* has 3- to 4-inch flowers with white or pink petals and a corona of purple, white and blue filaments. The leaves are 4 to 5 inches long. *P. coccinea* bears 4- to 5-inch flowers with scarlet petals and a purple, pink and white corona; its oval leaves are 3 to 6 inches long.

HOW TO GROW. Passionflowers grow best in a greenhouse where the night temperature is 55° to 65° and the day temperature is 65° or higher. They need full sun and a trellis, netting or string support on which to climb. Plant passionflower seeds in commercial potting soil. Keep the soil evenly moist and feed every two weeks during the growing season with a liquid fertilizer diluted to the strength recommended on the label. When growth slows in the fall, stop fertilizing. Let the soil become slightly dry between waterings until new growth starts. Early the next year, cut the vine back to 6 inches to force new growth. Passionflowers are usually propagated from 4- to 6-inch cuttings taken at any time of active growth, but they can also be propagated from seeds, although germination may be slow and uncertain.

PASSIONFLOWER See *Passiflora*
PATIENCE See *Impatiens*
PATIENT LUCY See *Impatiens*
PEA, DARLING See *Swainsona*
PEA, GOAT'S RUE SWAINSON See *Swainsona*

PELARGONIUM

P. domesticum (Lady Washington or show geranium); *P. hortorum* (common or zonal geranium); *P. peltatum* (ivy geranium)

Geraniums, one of the most popular of all flowering plants, are simple to grow in the cool greenhouse. Among those recommended for the greenhouse are the spring-blooming Lady Washington geraniums, which are often grown for show specimens. They reach 2 feet in height, with large clusters of 3- to 4-inch pansy-like flowers in shades of white, pink, red or purple. Two or three colors are often combined in the single or double blossoms. Common or zonal geraniums range from 3 inches to 3 feet or more in height. They blossom continuously in the greenhouse, bearing red, pink, white or lavender flowers in clusters up to 4 inches across. The 2- to 3-inch wide, rounded leaves have deep horseshoe-shaped markings of white, yellow, red or brown. Ivy geraniums have trailing stems up to 4 feet long, making them an excellent choice for planting in hanging baskets. They have succulent, shiny leaves similar in shape to those of English ivy and bear 2- to 3-inch flower clusters in white, pink, red or lavender from spring through fall.

HOW TO GROW. Geraniums need full sun and do best with night temperatures of 45° to 50°, day temperatures of 68° to 72°. They thrive when their roots are slightly crowded, but repot plants in successively larger pots before they become root bound. Use a commercial potting soil that is slightly acid, pH 6.5 to 7.0, and feed every two weeks while the plants are growing and blooming, monthly at other times, with a liquid fertilizer diluted to the strength recommended on the label. Water plants thoroughly but allow the soil to dry slightly between waterings. Be very careful not to over-water in the winter. Potted geraniums can be moved outdoors in summer and returned to the greenhouse in fall.

Geraniums can be propagated from seeds or stem cuttings,

PASSIONFLOWER
Passiflora caerulea

COMMON GERANIUM
Pelargonium hortorum

MOTH ORCHID
Phalaenopsis Diane Rigg 'Pink Mist'

although seeds germinate erratically. To propagate plants from cuttings, take 3- to 4-inch tips of firm, new growth that have several stem joints or nodes. Remove the lower leaves and place the stems 2 inches deep in moist sand, perlite or vermiculite. Cuttings take three to four weeks to develop roots, and an average of 10 weeks to form flower buds. As cuttings develop, pinch off the growing tips to encourage side shoots, then pinch off side shoots to encourage branching and a bushier appearance. Pinching can also be used to time bloom; each pinch will delay flowering a month or more.

Lady Washington geraniums usually bloom only in late spring and summer because they need temperatures below 60° to initiate flower buds; only high mountains or coastal areas normally have summer temperatures this cool. Propagate new plants from stem cuttings taken in late summer. Place them in a cold frame or other cool place until late fall, when they should be brought into the greenhouse for the winter. For blooms in late spring, pinch off tips of new growth once during the winter; for summer blooms, where temperatures are low enough, pinch twice. After summer cuttings have been taken from plants, cut the parent plants back to 3 to 4 inches above the pots and allow the soil to dry almost completely. Mist the plants daily to encourage new growth. Repot in fresh soil when growth begins, and resume regularly scheduled watering and feeding.

Common geraniums will bloom continuously, given proper growing conditions. Start them from cuttings taken any time, but hold the cuttings for 24 hours before planting to allow a protective skin or callus to form over the cut. Cuttings taken in early fall will grow fast enough to provide another crop of cuttings in early winter; cuttings taken in early spring will provide smaller plants. For the most abundant winter blooms, place geraniums outdoors for the summer and pinch back the tips of branches, removing any flower buds until the end of summer. Move them into the greenhouse in the fall and allow buds to develop into winter blooms.

Culture of ivy geraniums is similar to that of common geraniums except that cuttings do not need to be held overnight to develop a callus.

Geraniums can be grown as standards, tall tree-shaped straight plants with single stems topped by compact heads of growth by the techniques described on page 54. Geranium standards are usually started in winter for blooms in spring of their second year.

PERSIAN VIOLET See *Cyclamen*

PHALAENOPSIS
P. hybrids (all called moth orchid)
Some gardeners consider moth orchids the most beautiful flowers in the world. This warm-greenhouse plant, whose blooms are favorites for bridal bouquets, bears as many as 30 broad, flat ½- to 4-inch flowers along an arching 2- to 4-foot stalk. Each long flower stalk rises from a cluster of lustrous leaves rarely more than a foot high. The larger hybrids have velvety, round petals in shades of white, pink, or sometimes yellow that are often tinged with rose, purple or yellow. The smaller hybrids sometimes have waxy, star-shaped flowers and can be found in shades of yellow, peach, pink and white. Often several colors are combined in the same flower, or the petals are spotted or striped. Some of the recommended hybrids include Palm Beach, with 3-inch white blooms; Alice Gloria, also with white flowers about 3 inches across; Doris, with white 3½- to 4-inch-wide blossoms; Texas Star, with 2-inch lavender-speckled white blooms; Zada, with pink flowers 2 to 3 inches wide; Golden Sands, with about 2½-inch

yellow flowers; Diane Rigg, with pink blossoms; and Golden Louis, a yellow hybrid with 2- to 3-inch-wide blooms. Moth orchid species generally grow new leaves and roots from spring through fall, then send out flower stalks from late fall through spring; the hybrids, however, may bloom in any season. Most moth orchids will bloom two or three times a year, and some bloom year round. As the first flowers fade, other blooms continue opening along the stalk. After they begin flowering, stalks may have some open flowers along their length for up to a year.

HOW TO GROW. Moth orchids thrive in a warm greenhouse where night temperatures are 65°, day temperatures are 75° or warmer, and the relative humidity is 60 per cent or higher. Provide good ventilation but avoid drafts or sudden temperature changes. Moth orchids need dim light during the summer growing season, when they form new leaves and roots, more as they enter their winter and spring period of bloom. To prolong the blooming period, cut the flower stalk just below the point where the lowest flower first appeared; this will sometimes force the stalk to branch and go through a second complete blooming cycle. As new leaves form, lower leaves drop off and old roots die. When 1 or 1½ inches of the old stem is bare, repot the orchids in spring when new leaves and roots begin forming; cut off any dead lower portion of the stem and place the living portion in a pot or hanging basket. Use a potting mixture of 2 parts fir bark to 1 part coarse peat moss. Feed monthly during the blooming period with a high-nitrogen orchid fertilizer, such as one labeled 20-10-10, diluted as recommended on the label. Keep the roots constantly moist, but provide good drainage. Moth orchids are difficult to propagate. Most are grown from seed under sterile conditions by highly skilled specialists. A few species produce young plants along their flower stalks, others on their roots. Allow these plantlets to form roots of their own, then remove them and plant them in individual pots filled with potting mixture.

PIGTAIL PLANT See *Anthurium*

PLUMBAGO

P. capensis, also called *P. auriculata; P. capensis alba* (both called leadwort, Cape plumbago)

Leadwort produces masses of blue or white blossoms from summer into fall in the cool to intermediate greenhouse. The large, loose clusters of inch-wide flowers are borne at the tips of the current year's growth from trailing branches up to 8 feet long that may be tied to wires, trained to trellises, or allowed to cascade from hanging baskets. *P. capensis* is a blue variety; *P. capensis alba* is white. Leadwort loses its 2- to 3-inch oval leaves during a period of winter dormancy.

HOW TO GROW. Leadwort needs full sun and will grow in a greenhouse with night temperatures of 45° to 50° and a day temperature of 60°. But it will flower earlier and longer in the warmer temperatures of the intermediate greenhouse. Use a commercial potting soil. Keep the soil evenly moist while plants are growing and blooming. Feed monthly with a liquid fertilizer diluted to the strength recommended on the label. When the plants cease flowering, stop fertilizing and let the soil become dry between waterings. Cut back one third to one half of each plant in late winter just before new growth begins. Repot the plants at that time in fresh potting soil. Pinch off the growing tips of young plants to prevent straggly growth and encourage branching. For additional plants, propagate leadwort from stem cuttings taken in the spring or from seeds; if seeds are started in the winter they will produce 4-foot plants by late summer.

LEADWORT
Plumbago capensis

OBCONICA PRIMROSE
Primula obconica

DOUBLE-FLOWERED PERSIAN BUTTERCUP
Ranunculus asiaticus Tecolote hybrids

POCKETBOOK FLOWER See *Calceolaria*
POINSETTIA See *Euphorbia*
POT MARIGOLD See *Calendula*
PRIMROSE See *Primula*

PRIMULA

P. malacoides (fairy primrose, baby primrose); *P. obconica* (obconica primrose); *P. polyantha* (polyanthus primrose)

Annual and perennial primroses can provide a wide range of color almost year round in the cool greenhouse. Fairy primroses are annuals that can be grown for blooms in winter through early spring. The clusters of single or double flowers in shades of purple, pink, red or white are carried on 8- to 10-inch stalks in tiers above tight rosettes of broad, hairy leaves. Obconica primroses, also annuals, have large clusters of 2-inch flowers in shades of red, pink, salmon, lavender or white; however, the glandular hairs on their leaves release secretions to which some persons are allergic. The polyanthus primrose, a spring-flowering perennial, bears 1½- to 2-inch blossoms ranging in color from white through cream, yellow, pink and red, to lavender and purple. The plant grows 6 to 8 inches tall.

HOW TO GROW. Primroses grow best in cool temperatures, 40° to 50° at night, 68° or lower by day. Germinate fresh seeds with bottom heat at 70°, then move the seedlings to cooler temperatures. Grow them in successively larger pots, up to 6 inches, using commercial potting soil. Feed every two weeks with a liquid fertilizer diluted to the strength recommended on the label. Primroses need bright light but should be shielded from direct sun. In winter, lower temperatures will prolong the life of the blooms.

Sow fairy primroses in summer to early fall for blooms in winter through early spring. Successive sowings of obconica primroses from winter through early spring will provide blossoms the following fall and winter; sow seeds in fall for late-spring blooms. Obconica primroses will tolerate slightly higher temperatures than other primroses when they are growing, up to 55° at night. Sow polyanthus primroses in the garden in spring. Pot plants in fall and place them in a cold frame. Move them into the greenhouse in succession for blooms throughout the winter. Discard annual primroses after they flower. Polyanthus primroses can be returned to the garden after blooming.

PRINCESS FLOWER See *Tibouchina*

Q

QUEEN-OF-THE-NIGHT See *Epiphyllum*

R

RAGGED SAILOR See *Centaurea*

RANUNCULUS

R. asiaticus (Persian buttercup, French buttercup, Dutch buttercup, Scotch buttercup, turban buttercup, double buttercup)

Persian buttercup, a favorite florist's cut flower in the winter and spring, provides abundant, long-lasting blossoms when grown in a cool greenhouse. Each of the plant's erect, 18-inch stalks carries several double-petaled, 2- to 5-inch flowers that resemble camellias. A plant blooms for three to four months, bearing up to 75 flowers in a single season. The flowers come in a wide range of colors, usually shades of yellow, orange, pink, red or white. Persian buttercups grow from thick, tuberous roots that can be stored after flowering and grown again another year.

136

HOW TO GROW. Persian buttercups do best with night temperatures of 45° to 50°, and day temperatures no higher than 68°. The plants can be started from tubers or from seed. Clawlike tubers are usually planted in fall for winter-to-spring blooms in the greenhouse. They can be potted and put in a cold frame, kept from freezing, and moved into the greenhouse at intervals for a succession of blooms. Persian buttercups can also be planted in summer for fall blooms, or in early spring for summer blooms, although flowering is restricted by high temperatures. Plants can also be moved to the garden when there is no longer any danger of frost.

Before planting the tubers, soak them in water for three or four hours. Plant them, claws down, about 2 inches deep in a mixture of equal parts of commercial potting soil, peat moss and builder's sand. Add a teaspoon of bone meal to each 5- to 6-inch pot to help the tuber recover its strength after blooming. Provide light shade and water sparingly until new growth begins, then give the plants full sun and keep the soil evenly moist but not soggy. Good drainage is essential for Persian buttercups; the soil around their crowns should be kept quite dry. Feed the plants monthly with a liquid fertilizer diluted to the strength recommended on the label. After flowering ceases, gradually reduce watering until the foliage dies back. Two weeks later, dig the tubers and store them at 50° in a dry, well-ventilated place until you are ready to replant them and start the growth cycle again. Seeds sown in the spring will produce flowering plants in two years.

RAT-TAIL STATICE See *Limonium*

RECHSTEINERIA
R. cardinalis, also called *Sinningia cardinalis* (cardinal flower); *R. leucotricha,* also called *S. leucotricha* (Brazilian edelweiss); *R. verticillata,* also called *S. verticillata* (double-decker plant)

Rechsteineria, a tuberous-rooted gesneriad from Central America, thrives in the warm greenhouse. It grows 12 to 18 inches high and produces clusters of tubular flowers, 1 to 2 inches long, at the center of rosettes of hairy, heart-shaped leaves, 4 to 6 inches long. The cardinal flower has intense red flowers covered with fine hairs and can be induced to bloom year round if the old flower stems are removed as they fade. Brazilian edelweiss has remarkable leaves, thickly covered with long silky white hairs when they are young; this covering becomes thinner as the plant grows older. The salmon-pink flowers are hairy, too. It blooms nine months after the tuber is planted and stays in bloom for six months, but the foliage continues to ornament the greenhouse even during the plant's period of dormancy. The double-decker plant has tiers of pink flowers spotted and streaked with purple and dark green velvety leaves; as many as 20 flowers appear in a single cluster. The tuber takes seven months to reach the flowering stage, and the plant, like the Brazilian edelweiss, has a six-month period of dormancy.

HOW TO GROW. Rechsteinerias grow best in night temperatures of 65° to 70° and day temperatures of 75° or higher. Give them 50 per cent or more relative humidity. They will tolerate direct sun during the winter, but should be shielded from the sun's direct rays during the rest of the year. Pot the thick tubers in a commercial potting soil recommended for African violets. Water sparingly until growth begins, gradually increasing the amount. Allow the soil to become slightly dry between waterings, and do not allow water to stand on the foliage. Fertilize monthly during the growing season using a liquid fertilizer diluted to the strength recommended on the label. When the plants become dormant, reduce the

BRAZILIAN EDELWEISS
Rechsteineria leucotricha

amount of water and omit fertilizer. Store tubers in their pots at 50° to 55° before returning them to the warm greenhouse for repotting and another growth cycle. Propagate additional plants from stem cuttings or seeds; cardinal flowers, when they are grown from seed, reach flowering size in one year; the double-decker plant and Brazilian edelweiss take two to three years to reach flowering size.

RHODODENDRON (AZALEA)

R. kurume and hybrids (kurume azalea); *R. pericat* and hybrids (Pericat azalea); *R. rutherfordiana* and hybrids (Rutherford azalea); *R. simsii* hybrids, also called *R. indicum* (Indian azalea)

Gaily colored azalea blossoms brighten the cool greenhouse from late winter to early spring. These evergreen shrubs from Japan and the Himalayas come in varying hues of white, pink and red, and in both single- and double-flowered varieties. The flowers range in size from 1 to 4 inches across, and the plants from 6 inches to 2 feet tall. All of them are grown in pots. The kurume azalea and its hybrids bear dense masses of relatively small single or double blossoms, ½ inch to 1½ inches across, which almost completely hide the foliage. In its native Japan, this species reaches a height of 7 feet, but in the greenhouse it rarely exceeds 2 feet in height. The Pericat azaleas are medium-sized hybrids, seldom more than 2 feet tall in greenhouses, with single and semidouble blossoms, 1½ to 2¾ inches across; they are often cultivated for Easter flowering. The Rutherford hybrids, also usually under 2 feet in height in greenhouses, are known for their long-lasting, spectacularly colored 2- to 3-inch-wide flowers. The Indian azalea spreads wider than its height, as much as 3 feet across but only 18 inches tall; it bears flowers 2 to 3 inches across. All these azaleas live for many years and may be pruned to almost any size, regardless of their age.

HOW TO GROW. Azaleas require night temperatures of 40° to 55° and day temperatures between 60° and 68°. Place them in the sunniest part of the greenhouse in the winter, but give them bright indirect light the rest of the year. They need plenty of air around them; do not crowd azalea plants. They do best in a coarse peat moss, often called "poultry litter" grade, with a pH of 4.5 to 5.5. For winter flowers, buy azaleas with well-formed buds in the fall. Soak the root balls in water until they are thoroughly moist, then set the root balls in 5- or 6-inch azalea pots. Keep the potting medium constantly moist; it is essential that the roots of azaleas never become dry. Prune branches after flowering and snip off dead blossoms. After the flowers have faded in spring, they can be kept in the greenhouse or moved outdoors for the summer. Feed the plants every two weeks until new buds appear in late summer with an acid fertilizer recommended for azaleas, camellias and rhododendrons. Then stop feeding them and subject them to a six-week period of cold storage at 40° to 50°. Keep them fairly moist during this period. Bring them into the greenhouse for flowers six weeks later. Do not feed the plants when they are in bloom. Repot azaleas every second or third year, after flowering, if the plants outgrow their pots. If the leaves become pale and develop dark green veins, water monthly with a solution of 1 ounce iron sulfate dissolved in 2 gallons of water; or use iron chelate following the directions given on the label. If the leaves start to fall off, plants are either too dry or they do not have enough light. Azaleas can be propagated from 3-inch stem cuttings taken during the summer and fall, but they do not root easily and are so readily available as nursery stock that most people prefer to buy them.

KURUME AZALEA
Rhododendron 'Coral Bells'

ROCKET CANDYTUFT See *Iberis*

ROSA
R. hybrids (rose)

Many modern roses such as hybrid teas, grandifloras and floribundas bloom year round in the warm greenhouse, but since most home greenhouses are small, it may be best to grow miniature roses rather than the taller-growing types. Miniature roses, despite their size, also bloom throughout the year and offer all the decorative potential of their larger counterparts. Their penny- to quarter-size blooms are borne on thin stems amid proportionately small three- to five-leaflet leaves, and come in myriad shadings of white, pink, red or yellow. Most varieties develop into bushes from 12 to 15 inches high.

HOW TO GROW. Miniature roses do best in night temperatures of 55° to 65°, rising to 70° or more during the day. They need full sun and a relative humidity of 60 to 70 per cent. In winter they should be placed on high shelves close to the greenhouse roof where they will get the maximum amount of light.

Miniature roses are usually sold in small pots, although they sometimes come with bare roots. Plant them or repot them in 4- to 6-inch pots filled with commercial potting soil, firming it well around the roots. Water them thoroughly and then keep the soil just barely moist until growth begins. Thereafter keep the soil moist, never soggy, and feed the plants every two weeks with rose food or a liquid fertilizer diluted to the strength recommended on the label. Cutting the flowers for indoor bouquets will automatically induce branching, but miniature roses can also, if desired, be pruned and shaped like full-size roses. The plants can be placed outdoors in the summer, and returned to the greenhouse in the fall. Propagate roses from stem cuttings of new growth. Placed in moist sand and heated from the bottom to 70°, they should form roots in about four weeks.

ROSE See *Rosa*
ROSEBAY See *Nerium*
ROSE OF CHINA See *Hibiscus*
RUSSIAN STATICE See *Limonium*

S

SAINTPAULIA
S. grotei; S. ionantha (African violet)

The African violet, long a popular house plant, does even better in the warm greenhouse, where the added humidity makes its year-round blossoms remarkably abundant and beautiful. Available in many species and hybridized varieties, with new ones developing all the time, the African violet can be divided into two main types, according to its habit of growth. *S. grotei* is a trailing species suitable for hanging baskets. It has pale violet flowers, two or three to a stalk, and glossy leaves that are pale green above, almost white underneath. *S. ionantha* is the familiar pot plant whose leaves grow outward in a rosette. The flowers are five-petaled or multipetaled, and come in shades of blue, pink, white, plum and purple. Some varieties are bicolored. The velvety flowers are 1 to 2 inches across and grow in clusters above hairy, oval leaves 2 to 4 inches across, on plants 4 to 6 inches tall.

HOW TO GROW. African violets need night temperatures of 65° to 70° and day temperatures of 75° or higher. They thrive in relative humidity of 60 to 75 per cent. Unlike many flowering plants, they do not need full sun except in midwinter; during the rest of the year they should have partial shade. Pale or off-color leaves indicate too much light; leaves

MINIATURE ROSE
Rosa hybrid 'Yellow Doll'

AFRICAN VIOLET
Saintpaulia ionantha 'Ballet series'

that are too green or that grow up instead of out, or lack of blooms indicate too little light.

Plant African violets in the commercial African violet soil formulated especially for them. Water them with tepid water when the top inch of soil becomes dry. Cold water causes leaf spots. Place them on humidifying trays, and give them an occasional misting with water warmer than the air temperature if the air in the greenhouse becomes dry. Feed the plants monthly with a liquid fertilizer diluted to half the strength recommended on the label.

When African violets become crowded, divide them into single rosettes of leaves and replant them. Propagate additional plants from leaf cuttings or seeds. Cut leaves with about 1 inch of stalk and root them in moist sand, perlite or vermiculite. Keep the rooting medium warm, about 70°, and when roots develop plant them in 2-inch pots. Sow seeds on top of African violet soil and when seedlings develop, transfer them to 2-inch pots. Seed-grown plants do not run as true to type as plants propagated from cuttings, and may vary considerably in flower size and leaf configuration.

SALPIGLOSSIS
S. sinuata (painted tongue)

Painted tongue is an annual, normally grown in the garden, but equally adaptable to the intermediate greenhouse, where it is easily grown as a cut flower or for ornamental display. Its velvety, trumpet-shaped blossoms are 2 to 2½ inches across and resemble petunias, to which they are related. The brilliantly colored red, yellow, blue or purple flowers, streaked and veined with contrasting color, stand out vividly above the pale green, hairy leaves. Their slender, wiry stems grow 1½ to 3 feet tall.

HOW TO GROW. Painted tongue needs full sun, night temperatures of 50° to 60° and day temperatures of 65° or higher. Propagated from seed, plants require five to seven months to reach maturity, depending on the time of year they are planted. For flowers in April and May, sow seeds in a cold frame in September, and transplant the seedlings into 3-inch, then 6-inch pots for transfer to the greenhouse before the arrival of freezing weather. September-sown seeds can also be brought into bloom in midwinter by giving the plants five to six hours of supplementary artificial light each night in late fall, until the stems become elongated and flower buds form. For late spring blossoms, sow seeds in the greenhouse in January. Use a commercial potting soil, and keep the soil moist at all times. Feed the plants every month until flower buds appear with a liquid fertilizer diluted to the strength recommended on the label. Pinch off the leading stem to encourage bushiness, and provide support for the plants so they will not straggle.

SCARLET PLUME See *Euphorbia*

SCHIZANTHUS
S. wisetonensis hybrids (butterfly flower, poor man's orchid)

The butterfly flower is an annual with pansy-like, usually bicolored blossoms on slender stems that bloom profusely in the cool greenhouse. The flowers, with deeply cleft petals, are excellent for cutting and arranging. Hybrids of this species grow 2 to 4 feet tall with flowers in combinations of purple, red and white, veined with yellow. *S. wisetonensis compactus* is a smaller variety that grows only 18 inches tall. The plants normally come into bloom in the spring, but can be made to blossom ahead of schedule, in midwinter, if they are root bound.

HOW TO GROW. The butterfly flower grows best in night

PAINTED TONGUE
Salpiglossis sinuata

140

temperatures of 45° to 50°, rising to 60° by day. Grow it from seed, making successive sowings from late summer to winter for blooms from midwinter through late spring. Later sowings produce smaller plants than earlier ones. Transplant seedlings into 3-inch pots, then gradually move them into larger pots, up to 7 inches, keeping in mind that the plants must become root bound to produce early blooms. Plant them in a commercial potting soil and feed them monthly with a liquid fertilizer diluted to the strength recommended on the label. Water sparingly in the winter, increasing the amount of moisture in spring and summer. Good ventilation is essential for strong growth. When seedlings are about 3 inches high, begin pinching off the tips to encourage the development of side shoots. Stake tall-growing plants. After the butterfly flower blooms, the plant should be discarded, since its life cycle ends with seed production.

SHRIMP PLANT See *Beloperone*

SINNINGIA
S. pusilla; S. speciosa (both called gloxinia)

Gloxinias, one of the most familiar tuberous-rooted gesneriads, bloom profusely in the warm greenhouse, bearing 3- to 6-inch bell- or slipper-shaped erect or nodding flowers with ruffled edges. The plants themselves are compact, about 1 foot tall and equally wide. The five-lobed single blossoms or multilobed double flowers of *S. speciosa* are often edged or spotted with contrasting colors in red, purple, blue, lavender, pink or white. Their hairy, 4- to 6-inch oval leaves form a tight rosette at the plant base. Among the popular named varieties of *S. speciosa* are Princess Elizabeth with white-throated blossoms edged with a broad blue band, Switzerland with scarlet flowers edged with white ruffles, Emperor Frederick with deep crimson flowers edged in white, and Tigrina with red or blue edges and white throats speckled red or blue. *S. speciosa* will bloom at any time of the year. After plants have flowered, their leaves will wither and they will go through a period of dormancy before new growth begins. *S. pusilla* is a miniature species scarcely 2 inches high. It bears tubular-shaped ½-inch purple flowers with yellow throats continuously throughout the year.

HOW TO GROW. Gloxinias do best with night temperatures of 65° to 70° and day temperatures of 75° or higher. They need indirect, filtered sunlight. Plant the tubers or thickened underground stems of *S. speciosa* ½ inch deep in a commercial potting soil recommended for African violets; plant the fingernail-sized tubers of *S. pusilla* so that the tops rest at the soil surface. While they are growing and until flower buds form, keep large-flowered gloxinias moist and feed monthly with a liquid fertilizer diluted to the strength recommended on the label. When the flowers start to fade, withhold fertilizer and gradually reduce the amount of water until the leaves wither. Do not water at all until new growth appears two to four months later. Repot in a fresh soil mixture and resume regular watering and fertilizing. Flowering will begin in three to four months. The delicate everblooming miniature gloxinia, *S. pusilla*, needs different care. Give it moisture and fertilizer throughout the year and set the pots on a humidifying tray to keep the soil from drying out. Propagate additional gloxinia plants from leaf cuttings or from seed. Take leaf cuttings any time and root them in sand, perlite or vermiculite. Cuttings take about a year to develop into flowering plants. Plants grown from seed will produce blossoms in six to seven months.

SLIPPERWORT See *Calceolaria*

BUTTERFLY FLOWER
Schizanthus wisetonensis hybrid

GLOXINIA
Sinningia speciosa hybrid

TEMPLE BELLS
Smithiantha 'Orange King'

SMITHIANTHA, formerly known as **NAEGELIA**
S. hybrids (temple bells)

Temple bells are gesneriads native to Central America that provide blooms from late summer through early winter in the warm greenhouse. Handsome 8- to 24-inch spires of nodding, 1½-inch slipper-shaped flowers rise from rosettes of dark green, heart-shaped leaves that are usually mottled deep red or purple and covered with downy red hairs. Much hybridized from five species, the flowers come in many combinations of yellow, red, pink, orange and white, and are often marked with contrasting streaks and speckles.

HOW TO GROW. Temple bells do best with night temperatures of 65° to 70°, daytime temperatures of 75° or higher and 45 to 60 per cent relative humidity. Give them bright filtered sunlight. For late summer to early winter blooms, pot the thick underground stems, or rhizomes, in early spring using a commercial potting soil recommended for African violets. Keep the soil moist but never soggy and feed monthly during the growing season with a liquid fertilizer diluted to the strength recommended on the label. When plants are dormant during the late winter, do not fertilize, and water just enough to keep the large, scaly rhizomes from drying out. Rhizomes may also be shaken from their pots and stored in barely damp peat moss or vermiculite until repotting time. Propagate by dividing the rhizomes at the time of repotting, or by taking leaf cuttings at any time. Temple bells can also be started from seed at any time; seeds sown in the spring produce flowering plants six to eight months later.

SNAPDRAGON See *Antirrhinum*

SOPHRONITIS
S. grandiflora, also called *S. coccinea* (sophronitis orchid)

This miniature intermediate-greenhouse orchid from Brazil grows 2 to 3 inches high and bears 1½- to 3-inch blossoms during the winter. The long-lasting flowers are vivid scarlet or orange with yellow, red or purple markings. Each year, as new growth is produced, a single leathery leaf and a flower rise from each tiny oval pseudobulb—a thick, aboveground stem. These pseudobulbs are closely spaced along a horizontal rootstock, the rhizome. The sophronitis orchid is often crossed with laelia or cattleya orchids to obtain red colorings in these orchids, which do not normally have red flowers.

HOW TO GROW. The sophronitis orchid can be difficult to grow because of its diminutive size: it is easy to overlook among larger plants. It does best in night temperatures of 50° to 55° and daytime temperatures of 60° or higher. Give it bright indirect or filtered sunlight and 60 to 70 per cent humidity. Plant it in shallow 4- to 5-inch pots in a mixture of 2 parts fir bark to 1 part coarse peat moss. Keep the medium evenly moist and well drained. Feed monthly during its period of active growth with a high-nitrogen orchid fertilizer, such as one labeled 20-10-10, diluted as recommended on the label. Do not feed during and after flower production. Repot every two or three years. Propagate by dividing the rhizomes as new growth starts, allowing at least four pseudobulbs per division.

STATICE See *Limonium*
STOCK, COMMON See *Mathiola*

STRELITZIA
S. reginae (strelitzia, bird-of-paradise flower)

This perennial from South Africa usually blooms during the summer and fall in the intermediate greenhouse and occasionally at other times. Its striking orange petals and

SOPHRONITIS ORCHID
Sophronitis grandiflora

tonguelike blue petals fan out of 6-inch-long purple canoe-shaped bracts. The spear-shaped leaves are 12 to 15 inches long and about 3 inches wide. New leaves have red midribs. The plants grow 2 to 3 feet high.

HOW TO GROW. Strelitzias do best with night temperatures of 50° to 55°, daytime temperatures of 68° to 72°. To produce good blooms, plants need direct sun except during the hottest days of midsummer. Plant in tubs or pots in commercial potting soil. Water until the soil will absorb no more water, then let the soil become slightly dry between waterings. Feed every two weeks from early spring until fall with a liquid fertilizer diluted to the strength recommended on the label. Do not feed during the winter and keep the soil slightly drier than at other seasons. Propagate by dividing the plant's rhizomes in the spring, planting new divisions in 6-inch pots and gradually increasing the container size. Divide plants only when necessary; the divisions often take two to three years to reach flowering size. Plants can be started from seeds but require five to 10 years to bear flowers.

SWAINSONA
S. galegifolia (winter sweet pea, Darling River pea, red sweet pea, swan flower)

Winter sweet peas bear sprays of up to 30 red, white or purple flowers, each blossom about an inch long, from summer through fall and winter in a cool greenhouse. The flowers resemble those of its distant relative, the garden sweet pea, but are not fragrant; they grow at the tips of branches above evergreen foliage. The plants are 1 to 3 feet tall and sprawling in their habit of growth; they can be treated like climbers and supported by stakes or trained to trellises.

HOW TO GROW. Winter sweet peas do best with night temperatures of 45° to 50° and daytime temperatures of 60° to 65°. Give them full sun and good ventilation. Grow the plants in pots, using a commercial potting soil with 1 teaspoon of lime added to each 6-inch pot. While the plants are growing and blooming, keep the soil evenly moist and feed monthly, using a liquid fertilizer diluted to the strength recommended on the label. Pinch off the growing tips to stimulate branching. When flowering stops, gradually withhold water to allow the plant to rest. Cut plants back to about half their height early in spring, when new growth starts. The plants will bloom best when the roots are a bit crowded in the pot, so delay repotting as long as possible. For best winter blooms, remove all flower buds that appear in summer and do not allow the plant to begin flowering until late fall. Propagate from cuttings taken in the spring and rooted in sand heated from the bottom to 70°. Winter sweet peas can also be grown from seed.

SWEET PEA See *Lathyrus*

T

TAGETES
T. erecta (African marigold); *T. patula* (French marigold); *T.* hybrids

Marigolds, so popular in the summer garden for their abundant quantities of brightly colored blossoms, are easy to grow in the intermediate greenhouse as annuals for blooms at any time of year. Particularly suited to greenhouse culture are the Jubilee series, with 4-inch double-petaled orange, gold or yellow flowers atop sturdy 18- to 26-inch stems, and French marigolds, with smaller flowers that have flatter petals and grow only 16 to 18 inches tall. The latter's 1- to 2-inch single or double blossoms come in yellow, orange, red or combinations of these colors. Hybrid marigolds made by

STRELITZIA
Strelitzia reginae

DARLING RIVER PEA
Swainsona galegifolia

AFRICAN MARIGOLD
Tagetes erecta 'Orange Jubilee'

GLORY BUSH
Tibouchina semidecandra

crossing *T. erecta* and *T. patula* grow 8 to 12 inches tall and blossom continuously for many months; their seeds, however, are sterile and they must be grown from purchased nursery stock. All marigolds make excellent cut flowers.

HOW TO GROW. Marigolds do best with night temperatures of 50° to 60°, daytime temperatures of 65° to 75°. They need full sun and good ventilation. Sow seeds in commercial potting soil at intervals for flowers year round, germinating seeds at 60° to 65°. Seed-grown marigolds will bloom in two to three months. When seedlings show their first true leaves, transplant them to greenhouse benches or pots; or set purchased plants directly into greenhouse benches, spacing them 8 to 10 inches apart. Allow the soil to become slightly dry between thorough waterings and feed monthly with liquid fertilizer diluted to the strength recommended on the label. Pinch off the tips of 3- to 4-inch seedlings to get bushy free-flowering plants. Although commercial growers disbud marigold stems to produce single enormous flowers, most home greenhouse gardeners usually let all the flower buds develop normally. Discard plants after they bloom.

TAILFLOWER See *Anthurium*
TEMPLE BELLS See *Smithiantha*

TIBOUCHINA, also called PLEROMA
T. semidecandra, also called *T. urvilleana* and *P. grandiflora* (glory bush, princess flower)

The glory bush is an abundantly flowering shrub, 3 to 10 feet tall, that can be grown as a bush or as a semiclimber in an intermediate or warm greenhouse. Although its clusters of flaring, royal purple, velvety 3- to 5-inch flowers last for only a day or two, they are quickly replaced with new ones so the plants are almost constantly in bloom through summer, fall and early winter. The blossoms first appear as red buds, later developing long, black stamens resembling spider legs. The 2- to 4-inch oval evergreen leaves are covered with silvery hairs; the leaves turn red as they age.

HOW TO GROW. Give the glory bush night temperatures of 55° to 60°, daytime temperatures 10° to 15° higher. Grow the plants in pots in a commercial potting soil. During the growing season, spring through early winter, keep the soil thoroughly moistened at all times and feed monthly, using a liquid fertilizer diluted to the strength recommended on the label. Pinch off the tips of young growth to stimulate compact branching. Tie older plants to trellises or other supports. When the plants stop blooming, gradually withhold water and permit them to rest. Cut the plants back halfway when new growth starts in the spring, and repot to larger containers when the roots become crowded. Plants flower best when they are less than three years old; they should be replaced with new ones every two or three years. Propagate in the spring from stem cuttings rooted in sand, perlite or vermiculite, heated from the bottom to 70°.

TRACHYMENE
T. caerulea, also called *Didiscus caerulea* (blue lace flower)

This sky-blue annual resembles Queen Anne's lace, the wild carrot. Blue lace flowers can be grown year round in an intermediate greenhouse for long-lasting cut flowers. They bear 2- to 3-inch-wide umbrella-shaped clusters of tiny, sweet-scented flowers on 2½-foot stems with finely divided foliage. Lace Veil is a white variety.

HOW TO GROW. Blue lace flower grows best with full sun and varying temperatures, depending on the plant's stage of growth. Use commercial potting soil and sow seeds directly where they are to grow, since seedlings are not readily transplanted. Seeds sown in late summer and grown at a night temperature of 50° for two months, followed by 60° at night, will flower through the winter. Sow in fall for spring blooms, in spring for summer flowers. When leaves are well established, thin seedlings so that there are 6 to 8 inches between plants and 10 to 12 inches between rows. Plants bloom best when slightly crowded. Keep soil evenly moist but not soggy. Grow plants without using fertilizer unless they appear stunted, then feed monthly with a liquid fertilizer diluted to half the strength recommended on the label. Overfertilization causes lush foliage at the expense of flowers. Discard plants when flowering ceases.

TRANSVAAL DAISY See *Gerbera*
TRICHOSPORUM See *Aeschynanthus*

TROPAEOLUM
T. majus (common nasturtium)

Nasturtiums, which grow wild in Peru, bear brightly colored single or double 2-inch flowers among long-stemmed, shield-shaped leaves. They can be grown year round in a cool greenhouse and make excellent cut flowers. The funnel-shaped flowers have inch-long spurs and come in shades of white, yellow, orange, pink, salmon, scarlet, dark red and mahogany. Dwarf varieties usually remain under a foot tall, but climbing varieties develop stems up to 10 feet long, which make them suitable for growing on trellises or in hanging containers. Young nasturtium leaves are often used to flavor salads.

HOW TO GROW. Nasturtiums do best with night temperatures between 40° and 55° and daytime temperatures of 68° or lower. Give them full sun and good ventilation. Grow them in pots, using a commercial potting soil. Keep the soil moist to slightly dry. Feed plants monthly, using a liquid fertilizer diluted to half the strength recommended on the label. Too much fertilizer or water causes lush foliage growth but fewer flowers. Propagate from seed at any time. Those sown in the late summer produce winter flowers. Plants flower for three or four months, then should be discarded. Double-flowered nasturtiums, which do not always produce seed, can be propagated from cuttings.

TULIP See *Tulipa*

TULIPA
T. hybrids (tulips)

Tulips, familiar heralds of spring in the garden, brighten the cool greenhouse in midwinter with their colors ranging from pure white to cream, yellow, orange, pink, red, lavender, blue, purple, brown and almost black. Blooms last seven to 10 days on the plant and are excellent for cutting.

The most popular tulips for forcing are the early single and double tulips. Both average 9 to 12 inches tall with flower cups that are 2 to 4 inches deep and 1 to 7 inches wide. Early single tulips bear six-petaled blossoms that are often pleasantly fragrant. Among the recommended varieties for growing under glass are Brilliant Star, scarlet; Diana, white; Bellona, golden yellow; and Pink Perfection, pale pink with a white base. Early double tulips have multipetaled flowers, and all varieties of them will bloom during the winter, but Peach Blossom, rosy pink; Scarlet Cardinal, orange scarlet; and Thunderbolt, yellow, are especially good choices.

Other types of tulips include Mendel and Darwin tulips, cottage tulips and varieties and hybrids of the species known as *T. kaufmanniana* and *T. fosteriana*. These are more difficult to force than the early tulips, and not all of each

BLUE LACE FLOWER
Trachymene caerulea

COMMON NASTURTIUM
Tropaeolum majus

type are forceable, but they do offer the greenhouse gardener an extended variety of bloom shapes and colors to choose from. Mendel tulips grow 16 to 26 inches tall and are notable for blossoms in many tonalities of red—from pale pink to crimson. Recommended varieties for forcing include Apricot Beauty, a pink tulip with overtones of yellow; Golden Olga, deep red with yellow edges; Olga, red with white edges; and Van der Erden, bright red. Darwin tulips, 22 to 30 inches tall, have large, deep-cupped flowers. Recommended varieties for forcing include Blizzard, white; and Niphetos, ivory yellow. Cottage tulips, 16 to 36 inches tall, produce egg-shaped flowers. Mrs. John T. Scheepers, with enormous soft-yellow blooms, is one variety recommended for forcing.

T. kaufmanniana varieties, sometimes called waterlily tulips because of their horizontal, pointed petals, grow only 4 to 8 inches tall. Shakespeare, with salmon-apricot-orange petals, and Stressa, a red tulip with yellow edges, are recommended for forcing. *T. fosteriana*, large 4-inch flowers on 8- to 20-inch stems, has several forcing varieties: Pinkeen, a blend of orange, red and pink; Red Emperor, also called Madame Lefeber, varied red with a black base; White Emperor and Purissima, also called White Empress, with white flowers; Orange Emperor, apricot-orange; and Yellow Emperor, also called Summit, with pale yellow flowers.

HOW TO GROW. Tulips last longest in night temperatures of 40° to 45° and day temperatures of 68° or lower. For winter blooming, pot them in the fall, five or six bulbs to a 5-inch bulb pan. Use a commercial potting soil, preferably one that is heavy and holds moisture. Water the newly potted bulbs thoroughly, and thereafter keep the soil constantly moist. Place the pots in a cool dark place, such as a cold frame, at 40° for at least 12 to 15 weeks while roots develop. Bring the pots into the greenhouse at weekly intervals, allowing about three weeks for the flowers to bloom. Give the plants bright indirect light until they are 4 to 6 inches high, and keep the temperature between 50° and 55°; this will elongate their stems. Then move the pots to a cool spot in the sun. After the flowers fade reduce watering, keeping the soil barely moist until the leaves wither. Store the bulbs in a dry, well-ventilated place at 60° to 70° until the fall when they may be planted outdoors for possible bloom the following spring. Do not attempt to force bulbs two years in a row. Tulips can be propagated from the offsets that grow alongside older bulbs, but the exacting growing conditions needed for successful propagation are difficult for the amateur greenhouse gardener to duplicate.

V

VANDA

V. rothschildiana and other strap-leaved *V.* hybrids (vanda orchids)

The strap-leaved vanda orchids, so called because their leaves are flat rather than cylindrical, bear graceful spikes of fragrant, long-lasting flowers in the warm greenhouse. The vanda hybrids bloom two to three times a year, and sometimes continuously. Flower size, color and plant height are extremely variable. Shaped like a pinwheel, each 1- to 6½-inch blossom has five almost equal-sized round petals surrounding a small, short lip or modified petal. Three to 80 flowers are carried on each of the flower spikes, which rise from the joints between the leaves and the stem on alternate sides of the plant. Colors range from white to yellow, pink, purple, red, blue, tan and brown, often with several hues blended in a single flower. Vandas vary from a few inches to 7 feet or more in height at maturity and develop thick, fleshy, aerial roots between their leathery leaves. *V. roth-*

TULIP
Tulipa hybrid 'Bellona'

schildiana, a popular strap-leaved hybrid, bears clusters of 3- to 6-inch lavender blue flowers checkered with deeper blue.

HOW TO GROW. Vanda orchids do best with night temperatures between 55° and 65° and daytime temperatures between 68° and 80°; a few of the hybrids will do well in cooler temperatures. Place vanda orchids where they will receive bright indirect or filtered sunlight. They need 40 to 50 per cent relative humidity and good ventilation. Pot them in shallow pans or hanging baskets using a mixture of 2 parts fir bark to 1 part peat moss. After potting, water very little until the roots are established, then water generously so that the soil is kept constantly moist. Brown or black spots along the leaf edges indicate that the humidity is too high or there is excess water around the roots. Feed every two weeks with a high-nitrogen orchid fertilizer, such as one labeled 20-10-10, diluted ¼ teaspoon to a quart of water. When a plant grows too tall, cut the stem in half, making sure that both parts have a number of roots. Wet the roots of the top half so they are flexible and gently wind them inside their new pot, planting the division about 2 inches deep. Stake the plant until it becomes established. Repot the remainder of the original plant and keep it in a damp place until buds along the stem show new growth. Propagate vandas by removing the small plantlets that form along the stem after they have developed roots of their own, or by air layering. Small plants take several years to grow to blooming size.

VIOLA
V. wittrockiana, also called *V. tricolor hortensis* and *V. tricolor maxima* (pansy)

The low-growing pansy is prized for its wide range of colors and its distinctive markings. The fragrant, 2- to 3-inch blossoms composed of five overlapping petals resemble huge violets and come in shades of brown, purple, white, blue, dark red, pink or yellow, combined in hundreds of variations of stripes, blotches and delicate streakings. The flowers are carried on square stems in clumps about 8 inches tall, and can be used for small bouquets. So-called tall, climbing or winter-flowering pansies grow to a height of 3 to 4 feet if planted in ground beds and given supports over which the weak stems can clamber. They make welcome cut flowers, with stems as much as 12 inches long. Pansies are perennials, but they are cultivated in the cool greenhouse as winter- or spring-flowering annuals because they bloom best as young plants and do not tolerate midsummer temperatures well.

HOW TO GROW. Pansies grow best with night temperatures of 40° to 55° and daytime temperatures under 60°. Give them good ventilation and full sun. For winter blooms, sow seeds outdoors in July or early August. Bring the plants into the greenhouse in fall, transplanting them into 6- to 8-inch pots or setting them 8 inches apart in benches. Use a commercial potting soil and allow the soil to dry slightly between thorough soakings. Feed monthly with a liquid fertilizer diluted to the strength recommended on the label. If flowers are picked before they set seeds, they will bloom all winter.

VIOLET, AFRICAN See *Saintpaulia*
VIOLET, EPISCIA See *Episcia*
VIOLET, FLAME See *Episcia*
VIOLET, PERSIAN See *Cyclamen*

W
WAX PLANT See *Hoya*

Y
YELLOW BROOM See *Cytisus*

VANDA ORCHID
Vanda rothschildiana

WINTER-FLOWERING PANSY
Viola wittrockiana

Appendix

Greenhouse pests and diseases

In the closed, protected world of the greenhouse many pests and diseases are nonexistent. But those that do strike meet no natural enemies and multiply year round in the even, gentle climate. The best preventive is good housekeeping: use sterilized soil; keep tools and containers clean; dispose of refuse promptly; destroy any equipment that may have been in contact with infected plants; immediately isolate plants that are afflicted; maintain good air circulation.

If preventive methods fail, the sovereign remedy in the

PEST	SYMPTOM
	APHIDS Leaves and stems are pale and shriveled. The aphids may be seen on stems and the undersides of leaves, as on the rose bush at left. The plant has sooty mold, attractive to ants. VULNERABLE: PRACTICALLY ALL GREENHOUSE PLANTS ALL YEAR ROUND
	CYCLAMEN MITES Foliage turns purplish or black and is distorted, like the cyclamen leaf at left. Buds may not bloom, or, if they do, may look streaked and blotchy. VULNERABLE: BEGONIA, CHRYSANTHEMUM, CYCLAMEN, FUCHSIA, GERANIUM, SNAPDRAGON
	GREENHOUSE LEAF TIERS or LEAF ROLLERS A webbing of silk wraps together several leaves or parts of one leaf, making a cocoon. The underside of the foliage is punctured with small holes. VULNERABLE: AZALEA, CALCEOLARIA, CALENDULA, CARNATION, CHRYSANTHEMUM, GARDENIA, GERANIUM, ROSE, SNAPDRAGON, SWEET PEA
	MEALY BUGS Cottony dabs nestle along the forks of branching stems, as on a begonia at left. The infested plant looks stunted. VULNERABLE: AFRICAN VIOLET, AMARYLLIS, AZALEA, BEGONIA, CHRYSANTHEMUM, CITRUS, FUCHSIA, GARDENIA, GERANIUM, KALANCHOE, LANTANA, ORCHID
	CHRYSANTHEMUM MIDGES Tiny oval galls, or swellings, appear on the stems and leaves of a plant, as on the leaf shown at left. Leaves become distorted and curl up, and stems may grow crooked. VULNERABLE: CHRYSANTHEMUM
	NEMATODES Wilted, yellowing leaves and gnarled swollen roots, far left, indicate soil nematodes. Foliar nematodes cause brown and yellow blotches on leaves, as on the African violet at left, and may stunt leaf growth. VULNERABLE: PRACTICALLY ALL GREENHOUSE PLANTS
	SCALES Colonies of brown or gray, round or oval shells crowd the stems and undersides of leaves, as on the oleander at left. The plant may become stunted, and leaves may yellow or drop off. VULNERABLE: ABUTILON, CITRUS, FERN, OLEANDER, ORCHID, POINSETTIA
	SNAILS AND SLUGS Ragged holes puncture the foliage, as on the snapdragon leaf, near left, and a trail of slimy fluid across the leaves marks the creatures' passing. VULNERABLE: GERANIUM, MARIGOLD, ORCHID, SNAPDRAGON
	SOWBUGS Stems of young plants such as the zinnia at left are attacked at soil level. If the plant is dug up, the roots show similar feeding. In the greenhouse, the bugs may be found hiding near the soil level or under clods of earth. VULNERABLE: PRACTICALLY ALL GREENHOUSE PLANTS

greenhouse is spray, safer to use there than outdoors. Many experienced gardeners regularly spray with an all-purpose fungicide/insecticide to stop trouble before it starts (*page 31*). To help you watch for early warning signs, the pest and disease charts here and overleaf begin with a description of the symptoms. The remedies recommended are those especially suited to the greenhouse. In every case it is important to read the label carefully to make sure an insecticide that may save one plant will not damage its neighbors.

CAUSE	REMEDY
Aphids are pear-shaped, soft-bodied plant lice less than ⅛ inch long and may be green, black, brown, yellow or pink. Some are winged, others wingless, and some species eject a shiny, sticky fluid called honeydew that enables a harmless but unsightly black fungus to grow.	Wash foliage and stems in warm, soapy water and rinse with clear water. For severe infestations, spray the plants with an insecticide containing malathion or pyrethrum.
Full-grown cyclamen mites are too small to identify with the naked eye. As larvae they have six legs, as adults eight. The mites at both stages nest at the soil level, in the buds and in the foliage of infested plants. They attack the plant by sucking its juices.	Immerse the plant in warm, soapy water and rinse with clear water. Spray with an insecticide containing endosulfan.
The greenhouse leaf tier is shown at near left as a ¾-inch caterpillar, or larva, poised on a snapdragon leaf; in its moth stage, far left, it is ½ inch long. During the day the moths usually remain still; if disturbed, they fly to the undersides of leaves. At night, they make short flights from plant to plant.	Wash off the webs with warm water. Then spray the foliage with an insecticide that contains malathion, pyrethrum or carbaryl.
Mealy bugs are soft-bodied insects, about ¼ inch long, covered with a white waxy coating. They especially favor soft-stemmed plants, which they gradually kill by sucking the sap from the stems. They may also excrete a sticky honeydew fluid that is a host for a harmless but unsightly black fungus.	Lift off the bugs with a cotton swab dipped in alcohol; wash leaves with warm soapy water and rinse. Spray severe cases with an insecticide containing malathion, dimethoate or carbaryl.
The source of the infestation is a tiny orange gnat, about 1/14 inch long, which lays its eggs inside the leaf. As the maggots hatch and leave the eggs, they feed on the leaf, causing the blister-like galls. The adult gnat flies in darkness, generally between midnight and dawn.	Spray midges at the gnat stage, before they lay eggs, with malathion. Remove and destroy parts of plants that are already infested to kill larvae.
Nematodes are microscopic, colorless, wormlike organisms. Some are carried by water and air currents and attach themselves to leaves; others are present in contaminated soils and attack plant roots either by feeding on root hairs or by invading the root structure to cause galls, or root knot, a serious disease.	Spray foliar nematodes with vydate, root nematodes with vydate or methyl bromide. Discard severely infected plants with their soil; treat pots with vydate or methyl bromide; clean tools with alcohol.
As many as 25 species of scale insects are found in greenhouses, all between ⅛ and ¼ inch long. Those with a tough, armored shell attach themselves permanently to one spot; the others, called tortoise scales, have soft shells and may move, but very slowly.	Use a small brush and warm, soapy water to remove scales, then rinse with clear water. Spray young scales, before their shells harden, with an insecticide containing malathion.
Both these fat, legless pests hide during the day under pots and planting benches, and come out at night to feed on leaves, on or near the ground. They lay their eggs in damp areas around greenhouse benches, underneath boards or in the soil itself. Adult snails are ¼ to 1½ inches long; slugs may be as large as 5 inches.	Leave saucers of stale beer to lure and drown the pests. Scatter lime under greenhouse benches to dehydrate them. Spray the soil with metaldehyde or scatter metaldehyde pellets as poison bait.
The sowbug is about ⅜ inch long, with a clearly segmented body on seven pairs of legs; its back is a hard gray shell.	Spray with an insecticide containing malathion or carbaryl.

PEST	SYMPTOM
	SPIDER MITES Leaves are speckled with white, then blotched with larger yellow areas, as on the fuchsia leaf in the left foreground. The undersides of the leaves are threaded with a white webbing, as on the leaf in the background. VULNERABLE: AZALEA, CARNATION, CHRYSANTHEMUM, GARDENIA, ROSE
	GREENHOUSE THRIPS Leaves are flecked on the tops with white, as on the freesia at left, and have black dots on the undersides. There are tiny tears in the leaf tissue. Petals may turn brown and buds may not open. VULNERABLE: PRACTICALLY ALL GREENHOUSE PLANTS
	WHITEFLIES Leaves wilt and are mottled yellow or silvery white; the surface of the leaves may be sticky to the touch and attract a sooty-looking fungus. VULNERABLE: BEGONIA, CALCEOLARIA, CALENDULA, FUCHSIA, GERANIUM, GERBERA, LANTANA

DISEASE	SYMPTOM
	ALGAE An unsightly green scum coats the outside walls of clay pots, wooden surfaces and concrete blocks.
	BOTRYTIS BLIGHT Yellow, orange, reddish or brown areas form, as on the geranium leaves at left. The blotches become slimy, attracting spores which form gray mold. VULNERABLE: AFRICAN VIOLET, AMARYLLIS, BEGONIA, CALENDULA, CARNATION, CHRYSANTHEMUM, GERANIUM, POINSETTIA, PRIMULA, SNAPDRAGON, SWEET PEA
	DAMPING-OFF Healthy seedlings suddenly and without warning topple over and die. Their stems will look waterlogged and rotten at the soil line. VULNERABLE: PRACTICALLY ALL SEEDLINGS
	LEAF SPOT Spots of red, brown or yellow form large blemishes, as on the wax begonia leaves at left. Patches of bacterial ooze or black fungus may appear. Spots may fall out, leaving holes, and the leaves may turn brown and droop. VULNERABLE: MOST GREENHOUSE PLANTS (THERE ARE MANY KINDS OF LEAF SPOT)
	POWDERY MILDEW A whitish granular powder covers the flowers and foliage of the plant, as on the hydrangea leaves at left, and may cause the leaves to turn yellow. VULNERABLE: CHRYSANTHEMUM, ROSE, HYDRANGEA, ANEMONE, GERBERA, LUPINE, ZINNIA
	TOBACCO MOSAIC Leaves are mottled with yellow and green areas, and begin to crinkle up, as on the tomato plant at left. Plants are often dwarfed. Fruit may be small and malformed, and fail to ripen. VULNERABLE: TOMATO, GREEN PEPPERS
	ROT Roots and lower parts of stems turn dry and shreddy, and may become mushy and waterlogged. Growth may be stunted and the top of the plant wilts and collapses, as on the calendula, at left. VULNERABLE: AFRICAN VIOLET, BULB PLANTS, CALENDULA, DELPHINIUM
	RUST The top of the leaf is splotched with brown, the bottom has rusty-looking wartlike pustules, as on the carnation leaves at left. The leaves may curl up and die, and the infected plant may be stunted. VULNERABLE: CARNATION, SNAPDRAGON, LUPINE, ROSE

CAUSE	REMEDY
Spider mites are almost invisible to the naked eye, but can be seen as yellow, green or red dots on the foliage. They usually settle on the undersides of leaves and suck the sap from the plant, causing discoloration on the other side.	Wash foliage with warm water to dislodge webs and mites. For severe infestation, spray with an insecticide containing dicofol, malathion or tetradifon.
Greenhouse thrips are about $1/20$ inch long, with narrow bodies and bristled wings. They attack the plant by scraping across the surface of the leaf with a rasping motion of the mouth.	Spray with an insecticide containing malathion, dimethoate or pyrethrum. Several applications may be necessary, for thrips hide in crevices and buds, and are difficult to reach.
Whiteflies are tiny moths, only $1/16$ inch long and barely detectable. Thousands of them may collect unnoticed on the undersides of leaves until the foliage is disturbed; then they fly off in a swarm, like white powder. As they hatch, whiteflies are transparent, but full-grown flies are opaque.	Spray with a synthetic pyrethrum called resmethrin. Whiteflies are most vulnerable at the nymph stage; repeated spraying may be necessary.

CAUSE	REMEDY
Algae are microscopic organisms that grow from airborne spores. The spores favor moist surfaces containing nutrients like those present in fertilizers. The porous surface of clay pots is an ideal location for them.	Scrub the outside of the pot with a solution of 1 part household bleach to 9 parts of water and rinse off.
Botrytis blight is caused by a fungus that penetrates the plant, robbing it of nutrients. The disease usually starts in cloudy weather and thrives in a cool, poorly ventilated, humid greenhouse and spreads through microscopic spores that are transmitted by insects, water or by human hands.	Remove infected parts of plants. Thin out the plants for better air circulation and keep water off their leaves. For severe infections, spray with the fungicides zineb, maneb, benomyl or captan.
This fungus disease is caused by organisms present in almost all unsterilized soils. It is most likely to occur when plants are overcrowded or overwatered and when the seedbed is cold and damp.	Plant fungicide-treated seeds in a sterile medium. Water early in the day. Keep seedlings in a well-ventilated light area. Damping-off can sometimes be checked by drenching the soil with a fungicide.
Most leaf spot is caused by fungus spores, and high humidity in the greenhouse aggravates it. Another form, bacterial leaf spot, is relatively uncommon.	Provide good air circulation and keep foliage dry. Destroy infected plants and refuse. Treat fungus-caused leaf spot with zineb, maneb or benomyl, bacterial leaf spot with streptomycin.
Powdery mildew is caused by a fungus but unlike most fungi, which burrow into plant tissue, the mildew fungus stays on the surface and seldom kills the plant. It is associated primarily with plants growing in damp shade. It is spread by water and air currents and sustained by high humidity.	Provide air space and ventilation between plants, and avoid watering them late in the day. Spray with karathane, benomyl, folpet or wettable sulfur.
Tobacco mosaic is caused by a virus and is highly infectious. It spreads systemically through the plant's vascular system, so picking off infected fruit or foliage does not check the disease. It is transmitted by handling diseased plants, by insects or by the smoke of infected tobacco products.	There is no real cure. Burn the diseased plants and exterminate greenhouse insects. Destroy weeds, and discard contaminated pots or seed flats. Do not smoke in the greenhouse.
Rot is caused by bacteria and fungi that flourish in poorly drained soils, and it is transmitted to healthy plants by infected soils.	Destroy diseased plants. To prevent bulb rot, dry bulbs or corms as rapidly as possible and dust with arasan. To control stem rot, drench the soil with terraclor, ferbam, dexon or banrot.
Rust is a parasitic fungus whose spores are borne inside the pustules and germinate on moist leaves. When the pustules burst, the spores are spread by moving air or by splashing water.	Buy rust-resistant plant strains. Provide air space between plants and avoid wetting foliage. Destroy infected parts and spray the rest of the plant with zineb, maneb or ferbam.

Characteristics of 102 greenhouse plants

Listed below for quick reference are the varieties illustrated in Chapter 5.

Plant	FLOWER COLOR					TRAITS					HEIGHT			USE		LIGHT		NIGHT TEMP.			NORMAL BLOOMING SEASON			
	White	Yellow to orange	Pink to red	Blue to purple	Multicolor	Fragrant	Trailing	Climbing	Distinctive bloom	Distinctive foliage	Under 1 foot	1 to 2 feet	Over 2 feet	Cut flowers	Pot plants	Bright direct	Partial shade	Cool (45° to 50°)	Intermediate (50° to 60°)	Warm (60° to 70°)	Spring	Summer	Fall	Winter
ABUTILON HYBRIDUM 'GOLDEN FLEECE' (flowering maple)		●						●				●		●	●		●			●	●	●	●	●
ACACIA DRUMMONDII (Drummond acacia)		●						●					●		●	●	●			●	●			
ACHIMENES 'SASSY PINK' (magic flower)			●						●						●		●		●	●	●	●	●	
AESCHYNANTHUS PULCHER (lipstick plant)			●				●		●						●	●	●			●				●
ALLAMANDA CATHARTICA 'HENDERSONII' (Henderson allamanda)		●					●	●					●		●	●	●			●	●	●	●	
ANEMONE CORONARIA 'ST. BRIGID' (poppy-flowered anemone)			●						●		●		●	●	●		●		●		●			
ANTHURIUM ANDREANUM (tailflower)			●						●		●			●	●		●			●				●
ANTIRRHINUM MAJUS 'BRIGHT BUTTERFLIES' (snapdragon)		●	●		●				●			●		●	●		●		●					●
BEGONIA ELATIOR 'APHRODITE PINK' (Rieger begonia)			●		●					●				●	●	●		●			●	●	●	●
BELOPERONE GUTTATA (shrimp plant)				●					●			●			●	●		●			●	●	●	●
BRASSAVOLA NODOSA (lady-of-the-night orchid)	●				●	●			●	●					●		●			●	●	●	●	
CALANTHE VESTITA (calanthe orchid)	●								●				●	●	●		●			●				●
CALCEOLARIA HERBEOHYBRIDA 'MULTIFLORA MIXED' (pocketbook flower)		●	●		●				●		●				●		●	●	●		●			
CALENDULA OFFICINALIS 'PACIFIC BEAUTY' (calendula)		●							●			●		●			●		●					●
CAMELLIA RETICULATA 'BUDDHA' (netvein camellia)			●							●			●		●		●	●					●	●
CAMPANULA ISOPHYLLA 'MAYI' (May's Italian bellflower)				●			●			●				●	●	●		●				●	●	
CATTLEYA BOW BELLS 'CHRISTMAS CHIMES' (cattleya hybrid orchid)	●				●				●		●				●	●		●	●	●			●	●
CENTAUREA CYANEA (cornflower)			●							●		●				●								●
CHRYSANTHEMUM MORIFOLIUM (florists' chrysanthemum)		●	●						●			●	●	●	●		●		●				●	●
CHRYSANTHEMUM PARTHENIUM (feverfew)	●	●			●				●		●	●	●		●		●					●		
CITRUS MITIS (calamondin orange)	●				●				●	●		●			●	●		●						●
CLERODENDRUM THOMSONAE (glory bower)		●				●	●	●				●			●	●			●	●		●	●	
COELOGYNE CRISTATA 'ORCHID HILL' (coelogyne orchid)	●								●	●					●		●						●	●
COLUMNEA 'BANKSII' (Banks's columnea)			●				●		●			●			●	●	●		●	●			●	●
CONSOLIDA AMBIGUA (larkspur)			●	●						●		●	●		●		●				●	●		
CROCUS HYBRID 'VANGUARD' (Dutch crocus)			●							●	●			●	●	●								●
CRYPTANTHUS BIVITTATUS 'TI' (earth star)	●						●	●				●			●		●		●		●			
CYCLAMEN PERSICUM (cyclamen)			●						●		●				●		●		●				●	
CYCNOCHES CHLOROCHILON 'TINNIE' (swan orchid)		●			●				●			●			●		●			●			●	
CYMBIDIUM 'IVY FUNG' (cymbidium orchid)		●							●			●		●	●		●	●						●
CYTISUS CANARIENSIS (florists' genista)		●			●	●			●			●			●	●		●			●			
DELPHINIUM ELATUM 'PACIFIC HYBRIDS' (candle delphinium)	●		●						●			●	●	●		●		●				●		
DENDROBIUM NOBILE 'OROVILLE' (dendrobium orchid)				●						●			●		●	●	●			●	●			
DIANTHUS CARYOPHYLLUS (carnation)	●		●			●						●	●	●		●		●		●			●	●
DIPLADENIA HYBRID ROSACEA (dipladenia)			●					●	●			●		●	●			●	●	●	●	●		
EPIDENDRUM MARIAE (epidendrum orchid)	●								●	●		●			●		●		●			●	●	
EPIPHYLLUM HYBRID (orchid cactus)			●						●				●		●		●	●	●		●	●	●	
EPISCIA CUPREATA 'CHOCOLATE SOLDIER' (flame violet)		●					●		●	●	●				●		●			●	●	●	●	●
ERICA CANALICULATA (Christmas heath)			●						●	●	●				●	●		●					●	●
EUPHORBIA FULGENS (scarlet plume)		●							●			●	●	●		●		●						●
EUPHORBIA PULCHERRIMA (poinsettia)			●						●			●	●		●	●		●	●					●
FREESIA HYBRID 'SUPER GIANT' (freesia)		●	●		●				●			●	●	●		●		●			●			●
FUCHSIA HYBRID 'SPRINGTIME' (fuchsia)	●			●	●		●		●			●	●	●	●	●		●		●	●	●		
GARDENIA JASMINOIDES VEITCHII (gardenia)	●					●			●			●			●		●			●	●	●	●	
GERBERA JAMESONII (gerbera daisy)		●	●							●		●		●		●		●						●
GLADIOLUS HORTULANUS MINIATURE (gladiolus)		●	●						●			●		●		●		●				●		
GLOXINERA HYBRID 'MELINDA' (gloxinera)			●						●					●		●			●	●	●	●	●	
GODETIA HYBRID (satinflower)			●							●		●		●		●		●		●				
GYPSOPHILA ELEGANS 'COVENT GARDEN' (annual babies'-breath)	●									●		●		●		●		●						●
HIBISCUS ROSA-SINENSIS 'TOREADOR' (Chinese hibiscus)		●							●			●			●	●			●	●	●	●	●	
HIPPEASTRUM HYBRID 'LUDWIG'S GOLIATH' (amaryllis)			●						●			●			●		●		●	●				●

	FLOWER COLOR					TRAITS					HEIGHT			USE		LIGHT		NIGHT TEMP.			NORMAL BLOOMING SEASON			
	White	Yellow to orange	Pink to red	Blue to purple	Multicolor	Fragrant	Trailing	Climbing	Distinctive bloom	Distinctive foliage	Under 1 foot	1 to 2 feet	Over 2 feet	Cut flowers	Pot plants	Bright direct	Partial shade	Cool (45° to 50°)	Intermediate (50° to 60°)	Warm (60° to 70°)	Spring	Summer	Fall	Winter
HOYA CARNOSA 'EXOTICA' (wax plant)		•				•	•		•	•			•		•	•	•			•	•	•	•	
HYACINTHUS ORIENTALIS 'PRINCESS MARGARET' (large-flowered hyacinth)		•			•				•		•			•	•		•			•				•
HYDRANGEA MACROPHYLLA 'STRAFFORD' (common bigleaf hydrangea)		•							•			•			•		•	•			•			
HYPOCYRTA WETTSTEINII (goldfish plant)	•						•		•	•	•				•	•			•			•	•	
IBERIS AMARA CORONARIA 'ICEBERG' (hyacinth-flowered candytuft)	•								•			•		•		•		•						•
IMPATIENS WALLERANA 'ZIG ZAG SCARLET' (patient Lucy)			•						•		•				•		•			•	•	•	•	•
IRIS HYBRID 'IMPERATOR' (Dutch iris)			•						•			•		•		•			•					•
JASMINUM OFFICINALE GRANDIFLORUM (poet's jasmine)	•					•	•	•					•		•		•			•				•
KALANCHOE BLOSSFELDIANA 'TOM THUMB' (kalanchoe)		•							•		•				•	•		•					•
KOHLERIA HYBRID 'RONGO' (kohleria)		•							•		•	•	•		•			•	•	•	•	•	•	
LACHENALIA AUREA (Cape cowslip)	•								•	•	•			•	•	•				•				•
LAELIA FLAVA (laelia orchid)	•								•			•		•	•			•				•	•	•
LATHYRUS ODORATUS 'MULTIFLORAS' (sweet pea)	•	•	•			•			•			•	•	•		•		•						•
LILIUM HYBRID 'CINNABAR' (Asiatic hybrid lily)		•			•				•			•		•	•	•	•		•					•
LIMONIUM SINUATUM (notchleaf statice)	•		•						•			•	•	•		•			•					•
LUPINUS RUSSELL HYBRID (lupine)		•	•	•				•			•	•	•	•		•			•					•
LYCASTE AROMATICA 'JOE' (Lycaste orchid)	•								•			•		•	•	•		•						•
MATHIOLA INCANA ANNUA 'BALL COLUMN' (common stock)	•	•	•	•		•			•		•	•		•		•				•		•	•	
MILTONIA HYBRID (pansy orchid)		•							•			•		•		•		•		•	•	•		•
MUSA ACUMINATA 'DWARF CAVENDISH' (banana plant)		•								•		•	•	•	•		•		•	•	•	•		
MYOSOTIS SYLVATICA (forget-me-not)			•					•		•	•			•	•	•	•			•	•	•		
NARCISSUS TAZETTA 'CRAGFORD' (tazetta daffodil)			•	•		•				•		•		•	•	•		•			•			•
NARCISSUS 'UNSURPASSABLE' (trumpet daffodil)		•			•					•		•		•	•	•		•			•			•
NERIUM OLEANDER (oleander)		•			•							•	•		•	•		•				•	•	•
ODONTOGLOSSUM GRANDE (odontoglossum orchid)			•						•	•		•		•	•		•	•				•	•	
ONCIDIUM VARICOSUM ROGERSII (dancing lady orchid)	•								•			•		•		•	•				•			•
PAPHIOPEDILUM MAUDIAE (lady's-slipper orchid)			•						•	•	•	•		•		•		•	•		•			•
PASSIFLORA CAERULEA (passionflower)			•	•		•	•	•					•		•	•			•			•		
PELARGONIUM HORTORUM (common geranium)		•			•				•		•	•		•		•			•			•		
PHALAENOPSIS DIANE RIGG 'PINK MIST' (moth orchid)		•							•			•		•		•		•	•		•		•	•
PLUMBAGO CAPENSIS (Cape plumbago)			•						•			•		•	•	•	•	•				•	•	
PRIMULA OBCONICA (obconica primrose)		•							•	•	•				•		•			•				•
RANUNCULUS ASIATICUS HYBRID (double-flowered Persian buttercup)		•	•						•		•	•		•		•		•			•			•
RECHSTEINERIA LEUCOTRICHA (Brazilian edelweiss)		•							•			•			•		•			•	•	•		
RHODODENDRON 'CORAL BELLS' (Kurume azalea)		•							•			•			•		•			•				•
ROSA HYBRID 'YELLOW DOLL' (miniature rose)	•				•				•			•		•	•	•			•		•	•	•	
SAINTPAULIA IONANTHA 'BALLET SERIES' (African violet)		•		•					•		•				•	•	•			•	•	•	•	•
SALPIGLOSSIS SINUATA (painted tongue)	•	•		•					•			•	•	•		•			•					•
SCHIZANTHUS WISETONENSIS HYBRID (butterfly flower)		•							•			•		•		•	•		•					•
SINNINGIA SPECIOSA HYBRID (gloxinia)			•						•	•	•				•		•			•	•	•		•
SMITHIANTHA 'ORANGE KING' (temple bells)		•							•	•	•			•	•		•		•			•		
SOPHRONITIS GRANDIFLORA (sophronitis orchid)		•								•	•				•		•							•
STRELITZIA REGINAE (strelitzia)			•						•	•			•		•	•				•		•	•	
SWAINSONA GALEGIFOLIA (Darling River pea)		•					•	•			•	•		•		•	•			•				•
TAGETES ERECTA 'ORANGE JUBILEE' (African marigold)		•								•		•		•		•			•		•	•	•	•
TIBOUCHINA SEMIDECANDRA (glory bush)			•			•	•	•				•		•		•		•	•		•	•	•	•
TRACHYMENE CAERULEA (blue lace flower)			•	•			•	•				•	•	•		•			•		•	•	•	•
TROPAEOLUM MAJUS (common nasturtium)		•					•			•	•				•	•				•	•	•	•	
TULIPA HYBRID 'BELLONA' (tulip)		•								•		•		•	•	•		•			•			•
VANDA ROTHSCHILDIANA (vanda orchid)			•	•					•			•		•	•	•			•		•			•
VIOLA WITTROCKIANA (winter-flowering pansy)			•	•					•		•			•		•		•			•			•

Picture credits

The sources for the illustrations in this book are shown below. Credits from left to right are separated by semicolons. Cover—Phillip M. James, courtesy of Mr. and Mrs. Harvey B. Mackay. 4—Courtesy of WGBH Educational Foundation. 6—Lucien B. Taylor, 9—Herb Orth, courtesy of Lord & Burnham. 10—Map by Great, Inc. 13 through 16—Lee Lockwood, courtesy of Russell Morash. 19 through 21—Drawings by Kathy Rebeiz. 22—Peter B. Kaplan. 27 through 32—Drawings by Kathy Rebeiz. 35—Robert Townsend, courtesy of Bill Hazelett. 36, 37—Robert Townsend, courtesy of Bill Hazelett except drawing bottom left by Great, Inc. 38, 39—Drawings by Great, Inc. except top left Dr. Ted H. Short, Ohio Agricultural Research and Development Center. 40, 41—Drawings by Great, Inc.; Robert Townsend, courtesy of Environmental Research Laboratory, University of Arizona. 42—Peter B. Kaplan. 47 through 53—Drawings by Kathy Rebeiz. 57 through 59—Bernard Askienazy, courtesy of Mr. and Mrs. Henry Rothman. 60 through 63—Peter B. Kaplan, courtesy of Mr. and Mrs. H. Phillips Jesup. 64—Robert J. Witkowski, courtesy of Agricultural Research Service, Beltsville, Maryland. 69, 71—Drawings by Kathy Rebeiz. 75—Bernard Askienazy, courtesy of Dr. and Mrs. Martin Sherer. 76, 77—Peter B. Kaplan, courtesy of Mr. and Mrs. Winthrop A. Baker. 78, 79—Phillip M. James, courtesy of Mr. and Mrs. Harvey B. Mackay, 80, 81—Marina Schinz, courtesy of Roger Wohrle. 82—Illustration by Eduardo Salgado. 84 through 147—Illustrations by artists listed in alphabetical order: Adolph E. Brotman, Mary Kellner, Rebecca Merrilees, John Murphy, Trudy Nicholson, Eduardo Salgado. 148, 150—Drawings by Paul Breeden.

Acknowledgments

The index for this book was prepared by Anita R. Beckerman. For their help in the preparation of this book, the editors wish to thank the following: R. A. Aldrich, Pennsylvania State University, University Park, Pa.; Atmospheric Environment Service, Department of Fisheries and the Environment, Downsview, Ontario, Canada; Laurence J. Aurbach, Washington, D.C.; Mr. and Mrs. Winthrop Baker, Duxbury, Mass.; John W. Bartok Jr., Extension Agricultural Engineer, University of Connecticut, Storrs, Conn.; Els Benjamin, Horticulturist, Brookside Gardens, Wheaton, Md.; Claire Blake, Lord and Burnham, Irvington, N.Y.; Dr. Henry M. Cathey, Chief, Florist and Nursery Crop Laboratory, Agricultural Research Service, U.S. Department of Agriculture, Beltsville, Md.; Howard Cross, Lord and Burnham, Irvington, N.Y.; Harry Dewey, Beltsville, Md.; Derek Fell, Gardenville, Pa.; Dr. Harold E. Gray, Lord and Burnham, Irvington, N.Y.; Elizabeth C. Hall, Senior Librarian, Horticultural Society of New York, New York City; William Hazelett, Phoenix, Ariz.; Dr. Ronald Hodges, Adelphi, Md.; Tom Horrocks, Arlington, Va.; Fred and Gloria Huckaby, Tulsa, Okla.; Merritt W. Huntington, Vice President and General Manager, Kensington Orchids, Kensington, Md.; Dr. Merle H. Jensen, Environmental Research Laboratory, University of Arizona, Tucson, Ariz.; Michael Kartuz, Kartuz Greenhouses, Wilmington, Mass.; Mrs. Joan Kasprzak, Rockville, Md.; Bill Longenecker, Reference Division, National Agricultural Library, Beltsville, Md.; John O. McCormick, Opelika, Ala.; Paul McCormick, Solar Energy Research Office, Lockheed-Huntsville Research and Engineering Center, Huntsville, Ala.; Mr. and Mrs. Harvey Mackay, Excelsior, Minn.; Dr. David Mears, Associate Professor, Cook College, Rutgers University, New Brunswick, N.J.; Martha Meehan, Meehan's Miniatures, Wheaton, Md.; National Climatic Center, Environmental Data Service, National Oceanic and Atmospheric Administration, U.S. Department of Commerce, Asheville, N.C.; Ryan Page, Silver Spring, Md.; Dr. John F. Peck, Environmental Research Laboratory, University of Arizona, Tucson, Ariz.; Richard Peterson, American Orchid Society, Botanical Museum, Harvard University, Cambridge, Mass.; Terry Pogue, Rockville, Md.; Ruth M. Pyne, Reference Division, National Agricultural Library, Beltsville, Md.; Professor William Roberts, Cook College, Rutgers University, New Brunswick, N.J.; Dr. David S. Ross, Extension Agricultural Engineer, University of Maryland, College Park, Md.; Henry Rothman, Larchmont, N.Y.; Mary Sanderson, Treasurer, Hobby Greenhouse Association, Wallingford, Conn.; Dr. Ted H. Short, Associate Professor, Department of Agricultural Engineering, Ohio Agricultural Research and Development Center, Wooster, Ohio; Dr. Russell L. Steere, Hyattsville, Md.; Dr. Allen L. Steinhauer, University of Maryland, College Park, Md.; The Vegetable Factory, Inc., Copiague, N.Y.; Dr. Leslie O. Weaver, Extension Plant Pathologist, University of Maryland, College Park, Md.; Marshall Westover, Director, Hobby Greenhouse Association, Vienna, Va.; Roger Wohrle, Wohrle and Waite, Upper Saddle River, N.J.

Bibliography

Aldrich, R. A., and others, *Hobby Greenhouses and Other Gardening Structures*. Northeast Regional Agricultural Engineering Service, Cornell University, 1976.

Allen, T., and others, *Easter Lilies*. The New York and Ohio Lily Schools, 1967.

American Orchid Society, *Handbook on Orchid Culture*. AOS, 1976.

Bahr, Fritz, *Commercial Floriculture*. The A. T. De La Mare Co., Inc., 1922.

Bailey, L. H., *The Standard Cyclopedia of Horticulture* (3 vols.). The Macmillan Co., 1900.

Bailey, William A., and others, *Building Hobby Greenhouses*. USDA Agriculture Information Bulletin No. 357. U.S. Government Printing Office, 1975.

The Ball Red Book, 13th ed. George J. Ball, Inc., 1975.

Bauerle, W. L., and Short, T. H., *Conserving Heat in Glass Greenhouses with Surface-Mounted Air-Inflated Plastic*. Ohio Agricultural Research and Development Center, 1977.

Blake, Claire L., *Greenhouse Gardening for Fun*. William Morrow and Co., Inc., 1972.

Bridwell, Raymond, *Hydroponic Gardening*. Woodbridge Press Publishing Co., 1972.

Brooklyn Botanic Garden, *Greenhouse Handbook for the Amateur*. BBG, 1976.

Chabot, Ernest, *How to Grow Rare Greenhouse Plants*. M. Barrows and Co., Inc., 1952.

Chabot, Ernest, *The New Greenhouse Gardening for Everyone*. M. Barrows and Co., Inc., 1955.

Cherry, Elaine C., *Fluorescent Light Gardening*. Van Nostrand Reinhold Co., 1965.

Crockett, James Underwood, *Greenhouse Gardening as a Hobby*. Doubleday and Co., Inc., 1961.

De Graaff, Jan, and Hyams, Edward, *Lilies*. Funk & Wagnalls, 1968.

Eaton, Jerome A., *Gardening Under Glass*. Macmillan Publishing Co., Inc., 1973.

Flawn, L. N. and V. L., *The Cool Greenhouse All The Year Round*. John Gifford Ltd., 1966.

Free, Montague, *Plant Propagation in Pictures*. Doubleday and Co., Inc., 1957.

Gardiner, G. F., *Greenhouse Gardening*. Chemical Publishing Co., 1967.

Graf, Alfred Byrd, *Exotica*, Series 3, 8th ed. Roehrs Co., Inc., 1976.

Hartmann, Hudson T., and Kester, Dale E., *Plant Propagation*, 3rd ed. Prentice-Hall, Inc., 1959.

James, John, *Create New Flowers and Plants*. Macmillan Publishing Co., Inc., 1964.

Jensen, Merle H., ed., *Proceedings of the "Solar Energy—Fuel and Food" Workshop*. Environmental Research Laboratory, University of Arizona; Energy Research and Development Administration; and U.S. Department of Agriculture, Agricultural Research Service, 1976.

Kraft, Ken, *Garden to Order*. Doubleday and Co., Inc., 1963.

Laurie, Alex, and others, *Commercial Flower Forcing*, 7th ed. McGraw-Hill Book Co., 1968.

Macself, A. J., *The Amateur's Greenhouse*, 6th ed. Collingridge Books, 1974.

McCormick, Paul O., *Solar Heating of Greenhouses*. Lockheed-Huntsville Research and Engineering Center, 1976.

McDonald, Elvin, *The Flowering Greenhouse Day by Day*. D. Van Nostrand Co., Inc., 1966.

Northern, Henry T. and Rebecca Tyson, *Greenhouse Gardening*, 2nd ed. The Ronald Press Co., 1973.

Northern, Rebecca Tyson, *Home Orchid Growing*, 3rd ed. Van Nostrand Reinhold Co., 1970.

Peck, John F., *Insulation, Solar Heating and Improved Evaporative Cooling*. Environmental Research Laboratory, University of Arizona, 1976.

Post, Kenneth, *Florist Crop Production and Marketing*. Orange Judd Publishing Co., Inc., 1949.

Potter, Charles H., *Beneath the Greenhouse Roof*. Criterion Books, 1957.

Potter, Charles H., *Greenhouse—Place of Magic*. E. P. Dutton & Co., 1967.

Roberts, William J., and others, *Heating Plastic Greenhouses with Solar Energy*. American Society of Agricultural Engineers, 1976.

Rutgers Hobby Greenhouses. Leaflet 528, Cooperative Extension Service, Cook College, Rutgers—The State University of New Jersey.

Seymour, Edward L., ed., *The Wise Garden Encyclopedia*. Grosset & Dunlap, Inc., 1965.

Short, Ted H., and others, *A Solar Pond for Heating Greenhouses and Rural Residences—A Preliminary Report*. American Society of Agricultural Engineers, 1976.

Slate, George L., ed., *The Lily Yearbook of the North American Lily Society, Inc.* NALS, 1970.

Staff of the L. H. Bailey Hortorium, Cornell University, *Hortus Third: A Dictionary of Plants Cultivated in the United States and Canada*. Macmillan Publishing Co., Inc., 1976.

Sunset Books, *Greenhouse Gardening*. Lane Publishing Co., 1976.

Taylor, Kathryn S., and Gregg, Edith W., *Winter Flowers in Greenhouse and Sun-Heated Pit*. Charles Scribner's Sons, 1969.

Taylor, Norman, ed., *Taylor's Encyclopedia of Gardening*, 4th ed. Houghton Mifflin Co., 1961.

Walls, Ian G., *The Complete Book of Greenhouse Gardening*. Quadrangle/The New York Times Book Co., 1973.

Wright, C. M., and Hort, N. D., *The Complete Handbook of Plant Propagation*. Macmillan Publishing Co., Inc., 1975.

Index

Numerals in italics indicate an illustration of the subject mentioned.

PRINTED IN U.S.A.